D1645412

Pick of PUNCH

1991

5

Pick of
PUNCH

1991

edited by

David Thomas

A PUNCH BOOK
Published in Association with
HarperCollins*Publishers*

'I said, "I think this caption's a bit of a let-down!"'

HarperCollins*Publishers*
77–85 Fulham Palace Road
Hammersmith, London W6 8JB

Published by HarperCollins*Publishers* 1991

1 3 5 7 9 10 8 6 4 2

Copyright © Punch Publications Limited 1991

A catalogue record for this book
is available from the British Library

ISBN 0–246–13921–8

Designed by Peregrine Haydn-Taylor
& Matthew Le Maistre Smith
of The Groovy Love Foundation

Printed in Great Britain by
Butler & Tanner Ltd, Frome and London

All rights reserved. No part of this publication may be
reproduced, stored in a retrieval system, or transmitted,
in any form or by any means, electronic,
mechanical, photocopying, recording or otherwise,
without the prior permission of the publishers.

contents

DROPPING THE PILOT (BY FORCE IF NECESSARY)

The World According To MR PUNCH

A Right for sore eyes

Has it really come to this? After hundreds of years of painful struggle; after the Civil War, the Glorious Revolution, universal suffrage and two World Wars; after Gladstone and Churchill and Lloyd George, we are now six to 12 months away from a general election in which the two main protagonists will be a featureless nonentity and a ginger tom with as little control of his tongue as he has of his fists.

These two political deadbeats, united only by the poverty of their intellectual achievements, stand opposite one another twice a week, slinging schoolboy insults at one another. 'Opting out, opting out, nahnah, na-nah-nah!' 'Liar, liar, pants on fire!' One of them is bullying and bombastic, the other dull and uninspiring.

Not that we won't all have to get used to seeing even more of Mr Kinnock than ever before. The prospect of a Labour victory now seems a foregone conclusion in the dining rooms of the chattering classes – or at least the ones I've been sitting in recently. Normally one would take this as a sure sign of a Tory landslide – the chattering classes being to political judgment what Paul Gascoigne is to self-control – but in this case they show worrying signs of being right.

The fact is that the expectation of victory is an absolute prerequisite of victory itself. For ten years the Tories have had the massive advantage of the public's conviction (whether happy or not is immaterial) that they were going to win elections whatever the polls might say.

On the other hand, the Liberals are crippled by the belief that they cannot win, no matter what: if everybody who would vote Liberal if they thought they had a chance actually voted Liberal, they would, indeed, have a very good chance indeed.

Now people expect the next election, whenever it comes, to end with Neil and Glenys smirking from the windows of Number 10. Even *Spitting Image* ended its last series with the Labour Party gathered around the cabinet table.

The fact that they had not actually bothered to win an election before marching in only amplified the point. John Major may be the Prime Minister, but no one actually believes it, including, one suspects, John Major. Why, after all, is he so desperate for a public mandate if not to convince himself that he really deserves to be sitting in the PM's chair?

Tory MPs, even those who supported his leadership bid, seem perfectly happy to follow the public's lead. The last member of the Government to whom I spoke referred, without thinking, to 'when we lose the next election', rather than 'if'. And his view of Major's powers of leadership (or lack of) effectively echoed *Spitting Image*'s analysis, which was, 'He's a nice man. But he's a crap Prime Minister.' Not very elegant, perhaps, but accurate enough.

This perception has had an effect on middle-class conversation. People who once turned dinner-parties into orgies of competitive boasting – 'I bought my house for 47 pence six months ago and it's already worth half a mill – by the way, have you seen my latest turbo-powered penis substitute? It cost the bank 80K and it goes like a bloody rocket' – now do their best to trump each other's tales of misfortune. ☞

'It's David Owen – he wants informal talks'

Mad Dogs

As the blood-crazed legions of pit bul
'Killer' Baker, Mr Punch and his loyal do

It is, I grant you, pretty hard to remain sympathetic as yet another downcast City boy tells a tale of sackings and repossession. But nothing wipes the smile off one's face faster than a quick game of, 'And how much is the Labour government going to cost you?'

I did a quick calculation on the back of a credit-card bill, added a bit and doubled the number I first thought of. It transpired that the imposition of Labour's proposed tax scale will mean that in order to keep my take-home pay the same as it is now, the gross amount will have to rise by £1,500 a month. Now, my employers are, as you can imagine, a credit to the accountancy trade and as enlightened and generous a group of gentlemen as ever trod this earth. But an £18,000 pay rise? I think not.

Clearly I am going to have to raise a lot of cash, fast. I can't sell my house, because who can sell a house these days? And anyway, it's so far in hock that it wouldn't do me any good. So, instead, I am going to take a leaf out of football's book and give my vast army of travelling fans a chance to participate in the Mr Punch experience.

Arsenal, for example, is offering its supporters the chance to buy debentures in its new stand at £1,500 a pop. These do not actually entitle purchasers to watch a single game. But they do enable them to snap up season tickets at very competitive prices. In other words, you pay Arsenal a grand-and-a-half in return for which they give you the right to spend another couple of hundred every single year. Brilliant.

So, in my new debenture scheme, you, the readers, send me a personal cheque for, let's say, a tenner. I will then guarantee to send you a hand-tooled letter, written in red biro on the finest copy paper, entitling you to fill in your very own personalised subscription form for *Punch* (£49 for 51 issues, and you can't say fairer than that), thereby assuring your supply of the world's most *Punch*-like weekly magazine.

That's the soft-sell option. There is, however, a much tougher fall-back position that I am contemplating if all else fails. To wit: I will hold the entire readership of *Punch* (which is, according to NRS figures, roughly 287,000 people a week) to ransom, as follows...unless I receive a quid from each and every one of you, I will devote all my forthcoming columns to the tooth-rottingly sweet adventures of my grotesquely cute blonde daughter Prince Pilip and her charmingly be-dimpled one year-old sibling Oohy.

It is, I know, a terrifying threat. You have been warned. 🎭

LIEDER OF THE PACK - A DOGGY TOP 20

Sitting on the Dog of the Bay	The Poop-Scoop Song (It's In His Kiss)
Pit Bull Get Ready	The Theme from Hawaii Fid-O
I Canine Get No Satisfaction	The Hounds of Silence
I'm A Retriever	Bark Side of the Moon
I Love You Just the Way Chihuahua	Hello, Hello, I'm Bark Again
Space Doggity (Hound Control to Major Tom)	Spaniel (Is leaving tonight on a plane...)
A Whiter Shade of Pal	Bark in the USSR
The Winalot Takes It All	Get Bark
Dachshund The Way (Uh-huh, Uh-huh) I Like It	Alsatian to Station
Fifty Ways To Leave Your Rover	Dalmation Under a Groove

---

20 Wild and cur-razy facts

1 Su Pollard was beaten by a singing dog on *Opportunity Knocks*.

2 Princess Anne owns a bull terrier called Eglantyne. Her daughter Zara has a clumber spaniel called Splodges.

3 Most tinned dog food is 70 per cent water.

4 The British spend some £520m every year on feeding their dogs.

5 Pit bull terriers are the only breed that the RSPCA believes to be totally unsuitable as family pets.

6 Statistically, every pit bull in the world will be involved in an attack at some point in its life.

7 There are now more than 100,000 Rottweilers in this country.

8 Mild-mannered snooker star Steve Davis owns one of them.

9 The only dogs allowed into Parliament are police sniffer dogs and David Blunkett MP's guide dog, Offa.

10 In November 1989 *Punch* exclusively revealed that President Bush's spaniel Millie had killed five squirrels in the White House garden.

11 Boy George has trained his dogs to use a special downstairs bathroom.

12 Former Home Secretary David Waddington owns a Norfolk terrier called Basil, who bit a boy's nose the day Waddington was steering a Commons' Dangerous Dogs Bill.

13 Britain's stray dog problem costs at least £76m a year.

14 The film director Franco Zeffirelli has a Jack Russell called Bambina. She howls and barks whenever she hears the voice of Placido Domingo.

15 Postmen's union boss Alan Tuffin claimed that dog attacks were giving his members 'a daily trauma'.

16 The Kennel Club's most popular pedigree dog is the Yorkshire terrier.

17 Animal psychologist Roger Mugford says of Yorkies (and their owners) 'They are very aggressive, trumped-up and pushy.'

18 Famous Yorkie-owners include Elizabeth Taylor and Bob Hope.

19 Actress Nanette Newman was so infatuated with her Yorkie, Fred, that she wrote *The Dog Lover's Coffee-Table Book*.

20 Tory Vice-Chairman Sir Geoffrey Pattie has two Scotties, called Pickles and Corky.

erriers prepare to meet their doom, courtesy of Kenneth
oby unleash a finely-crufted probe into all things canine

AN ANATOMY OF DOGGY SLANG

A body-part-by-body-part guide to the doggy doggerel that litters our language. Compiled with the aid of the Bloomsbury Dictionary of Contemporary Slang, by Tony Thorne

● A dog (n) can be...

● An ugly woman or girl
● Something worthless, eg: 'This car's a dog!'
● A poorly performing share
● A likeable rogue, eg: 'You old dog!'

● To dog (vb) can mean...

● To pester, eg: dog someone's footsteps
● To behave badly
● To mess up or flunk
● To abandon, get rid of; eg: 'Dog the dorm rules now'

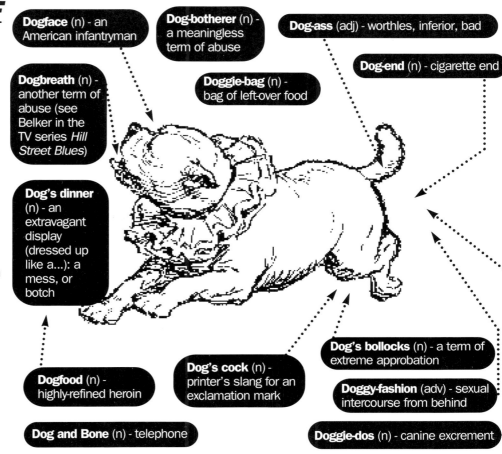

Dogface (n) - an American infantryman

Dog-botherer (n) - a meaningless term of abuse

Dog-ass (adj) - worthles, inferior, bad

Dog-end (n) - cigarette end

Dogbreath (n) - another term of abuse (see Belker in the TV series *Hill Street Blues*)

Doggie-bag (n) - bag of left-over food

Dog's dinner (n) - an extravagant display (dressed up like a...): a mess, or botch

Dogfood (n) - highly-refined heroin

Dog's cock (n) - printer's slang for an exclamation mark

Dog's bollocks (n) - a term of extreme approbation

Doggy-fashion (adv) - sexual intercourse from behind

Dog and Bone (n) - telephone

Doggie-dos (n) - canine excrement

Is your loveable pooch turning into a blood-crazed hell-hound ?

1. *Here's Fifi, your faithful friendly doggy-woggy who wouldn't hurt a fly*

2. *Alarm bells ring with her first frothy mouth attack and terrible howling fits*

3. *Canine catastrophe! She's gone barking! A bone-crunching beast, a real man-eater*

McLACHLAN

Heads down, girls, we'll soon be safe back in dear old England again amongst our loved ones....

If only the others had (sob) made it. Burnt & shot by those madmen (sob) & yet we escaped (sob, sob) If only our transport hadn't been destroyed....

'Stop bleating, Maude! We're just helpless victims caught in a power struggle involving national pride & self interest. Let's hope our beloved Prime Minister can put a stop to it....

Stop! Wait! Quiet! I hear voices! They're not Engl....They're coming this way! Oh my God! They've seen us!

'Ah zo! ze little Anglais sheeps! Zey sought zey could escape ze wrath of ze French farmers, ha....

Pro-Celebrity

Saddam Hussein & Nick Faldo
v
George Bush & Severiano Ballesteros

James Baker & Tom Watson
v
Douglas Hurd & Ian Woosnam

Above: Ballesteros, Faldo, Hussein and Bush prepare to tee off near the notorious 'Bunker of Baghdad'

Right: Grey Men of the green, Baker and Hurd

Gulf Special

Bruce Forsyth & Peres de Cuellar	**US Eighth Army & Reigate & Redhill Golf Club**
v	v
Tony Benn & Jose Olazabal	**Iraqui Light Infantry & Arnold Palmer**

This world tournament now enters its final phase, climaxing on January 15th. The pairs through to the quarter finals are as above. Our expert looks at the course.

Besides being almost totally devoid of grass, the terrain is presenting many formidable obstacles. **'This course is one big sand trap,' said Tom Watson.**

No 4. A tricky hole for Bush and Ballesteros. A narrow fairway, with several tall trees to the left and a small minefield running across the fairway. Once past the dog-leg, the main problem will be the heavy artillery and Saddam's squadron of Soviet-built MIG-27's. Sevvy could try a lofted 8-iron and use the slope to the right.

No 12. The famous 12th hole, much-feared by generations of players for its deep rough, fiendish bunkers, and the fact that the green is Moslem holy territory. Once there, players can only putt facing Mecca, which makes sighting difficult, and puts extra pressure on the approach shot. In addition, caddies are required to cover all exposed flesh, and wear veils.

No 14. The 14th is a deceptively simple hole, but beneath the fairway are four million barrels of crude reserves, making this the most oil-rich hole in the world (after the sixth at St. Andrews). A straight drive with a 1 wood will take the player half-way, but he is then confronted with the Kharg-El-Bayat refinery, where he can drop-out, or try to chip over with a wedge. In the 1977 Open, Lee Trevino took his third from 200 feet up a derrick.

ILLUSTRATION: DAVID HENSLEY

TORIES
TRY OUR MP'S QUIZ

Could you be deselected?

Yes! Yes! Yes! Conservative MPs everywhere will want to take part in our fun-to-follow quiz. Just answer the questions below, then simply add up your total. Mostly a's, you'll survive. Mostly b's, don't panic but make discreet inquiries about other jobs. Mostly c's and you can wave goodbye to Westminster. Before you go, though, have a quick word with Norman Lamont. Wasn't the poll tax in your area far too low?

1 You told your constituents you were voting for Major, but one of them produces a copy of the *Sunday Times* in which you say that Heseltine's your fella! Do you –
a) Panic and blame media lefties?
b) Promise him 1000 extra electricity shares to keep his trap shut?
c) Call his bluff by telling him your replacement would be black?

2 Which description most accurately matches your constituency party?
a) A supportive and dedicated group of patriotic men and women?
b) A bunch of gin-swilling Austin Montego drivers who think she did a marvellous job for the country but isn't it awful about mortgage rates?
c) A cretinous collection of crypto-fascists with a combined IQ of 3?

3 How many times had you visited your constituency recently?
a) Twice a week?
b) Once a month?
c) Can't remember?

4 What is your constituency?
a) Aldershot?
b) Some godawful bit of Home Counties suburbia with a leisure centre and an M&S
c) A large chunk of rural England peopled with retired Rear Admirals.

5 If you were fired, would you –
a) Write a Sunday newspaper column slagging off the government
b) Be able to molest farm animals without worrying about the publicity
c) Tell the constituency chairman you've been having an affair with his wife for the past 15 years.

Iraq Around The Clock

10 *Hits now playing on Baghdad Radio*

1. Loves Me Like Iraq
2. Saudi Seems To Be The Hardest Word
3. Oil Be There
4. Heard It Through The Pipeline
5. Papa's Got A Brand-New Baghdad
6. Sheik Rattle And Roll
7. Kuwaiting On A Friend
8. Ma, He's Making Sheep's Eyes At Me
9. Gasoline Allah
10. Alad Hussein

10 *Films now showing at the Baghdad Multiplex*

1. The Exocet
2. The Eagle Has Sanded
3. A Bridge Too Fahd
4. Call Me Saddam
5. Nomad Max
6. Blame It On Riyadh
7. The Not-So Great Dictator
8. M. Hussein's Holiday
9. A Shah Is Born
10. The Saddam Busters

Now On the Menu at the Baghdad Café

Mustard Gaspacho

Iraq of Lamb

Shat al Kebab

Quiche Bahrain

Nuke Potatoes

Rocket Salad with

Crude Oil and

Vinegar Dressing

(and for Desert)

Devil's Fahd Cake

Bombe Surprise

Zabaghdadlioni

Emir Trifle

GUN & INK

'He's not THAT devout. He's just been run over'

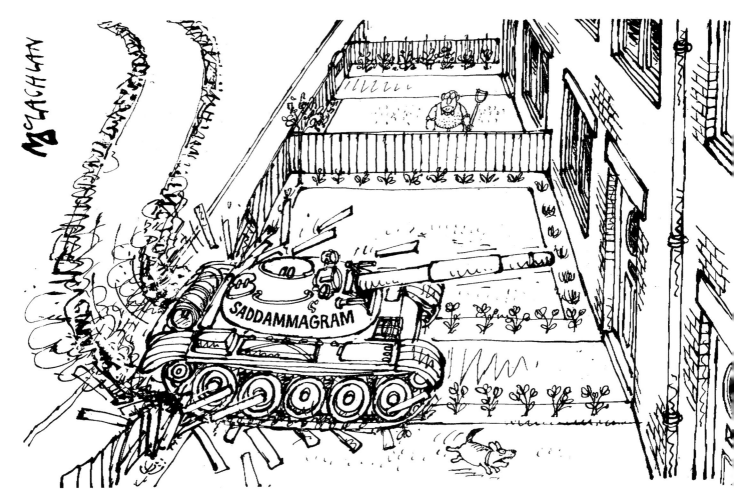

GUN & INK 2

'By Jove, Willie, those SAS Johnnies *are* going in'

'Blimey – even Luxembourg are here'

'And God bless the Iraqis'

'I have to say, I'm beginning to wonder about the British commitment'

101 USES FOR A DEAD TURTLE

by Ken Allen after Simon Bond

(Numbers 1 – 13)

FERGIE

A special Punch holiday update

Exhausted by the stress of moving into her £5m Pizza Hut; shattered by the strain of shaking her bootie at her housewarming party just hours after her step-father's memorial service; utterly shagged out by the effort of teasing her hair into an Ivana Trump quiff-alike, and prostrate from posing for *Hello*, the Duchess of York is doing the only
sensible thing...

SHE'S TAKING A HOLIDAY

Regular readers will know that we take a close interest in Flyin' Fergie, holder of our Vasco da Gama Award for Round-the-World Exploration. Last January we related her holidays since 1986, to wit...

FIVE Swiss skiing expeditions
FOUR French ski'n'shop stops
THREE American sashays
TWO trips to Canada and Oz
ONE wee sesh in Barbados, Mauritius and the Azores

Now we can add this year's travel calendar, viz...

JANUARY: skiing à la Suisse
MAY: Rocking the Casbah in Morocco
JUNE: Mercy dashing USA
JULY: Consoling the family in Argentina and relaxing on the Côte d'Azur
AUGUST: Meeting the mum-in-law at Balmoral
ANY DAY NOW: Heading back Down Under

A friend of Fergie told the ever-vigilant *Daily Mirror*, 'The Duchess works hard and is entitled to have breaks.' Mr Punch agrees without reservation. After all, just doing all that packing would be enough to knacker anyone.

Mag about the house

It is a typical day's retirement in Dulwich. Denis is having his breakfast, Margaret is shouting at the neighbours. She slams the window shut and sits down.

Denis: So, old girl – what are you up to today?

Maggie: *(Sulking)* Ask me properly.

Denis: Oh, not again!

Maggie: I won't answer if you do not table your question through the proper channels.

Denis: *(With a sigh)* Oh, very well. *(Clears throat)* Will the ex-Prime Minister list her engagements for today?

Maggie: *(Briskly)* After breakfasting with my husband I will visit a post office to accept some stamps. I will then visit the Asda mini-mart, where I will meet some employees and moan about the price of things these days. I will be back at Dulwich for *Neighbours*. After tea I will watch *Inspector Morse* before snuggling upwith the latest Jackie Collins.

Denis: If you're popping in to Asda you might as well...

Maggie: Denis!

Denis: Sorry my little angel delight... Is the Right Honourable Lady aware that we are getting a bit low on washing powder? Is she also aware that we have a voucher from the last packet which will give us £1 off the marked price?

Maggie: *(Picks up prepared statement from under toast-rack)* Mr Speaker, may I remind the house that under the Honourable Gentleman's government, our washing powder reserves sank to a record low and we were forced to borrow from the Bennetts next door. The current low stocks are due to a combination of world economic factors, a depressed market, and the fact that the Honourable Gentleman poured the packet over the utility room floor while trying to read the instructions.

Denis: Yes dear. Er – on a point of order, is the ex-Prime Minister further aware that there are only two Weetabix left?

Maggie: *(Bellowing)* Which is twice as many as was the case under a Labour administration!

There is a knock at the door.

Maggie: Ah – that'll be Black Rod.

Denis: No, my little treasury, it'll be Dyno-Rod, about the drains.*It is neither. It is MICHAEL HESELTINE, arriving unexpectedly from the guest wing*

Heseltine: Is the Right Honourable Lady aware that while I fully support her plans to watch *Inspector Morse* tonight, there is a growing band of opinion in the party which would like to watch Jasper Carrott on the other side.

Maggie: My government has been firm in its commitment to law and order. Inspector Morse deserves our full support and we will not be deflected from that policy.

Enter JOHN MAJOR

Major: I am fully behind the Prime Minister in her determination to watch *Inspector Morse*, and can also reassure her that Government forecasts show that more Weetabix will be available next year and that washing powder stocks will be running at record levels. But would she perhaps like to make a nice cup of coffee and put her feet up for a bit?

Denis: Does this mean you won't be getting the Weetabix, cherub?

Enter DOUGLAS HURD

Hurd: If the Prime Minister wants to watch *Inspector Morse*, I want to watch it too. However, if the Prime Minister should be popping out at all, a growing number of my colleagues have persuaded me that I am the person most likely to be allowed to change channels.

Denis: I was looking forward to watching my golf video.

Maggie: *(Rising to shrill pitch)* There is no alternative. My programme is set out fully and clearly in the *TV Times*. The lady's not for turning over!

Denis: Oh, all right. I'll feed the cat.

Maggie: And it's no good nannying that cat, Denis! You cannot allow it to become dependent on handouts of Kattomeat. Let it stand on its own four feet.

Denis: Oh dear...

(He looks at Yellow Pages on the table. Opening it at Merchant Banks, he begins phoning round to find any with vacant directorhips involving long hours.)

Sunday
CORRESPONDENT

You didn't read the broadsheet, you didn't read the tabloid, so THIS WEEK the Sunday Correspondent relaunches in an exciting NEW single column format.

Every week, **FREE** with Punch, we will bring you the **BIG** stories of the week (or the big story of the week, depending on the space available).

Just imagine! No more back-breaking special supplements, no more irritating magazines dropping out of the newspaper. Just SNIP out our radical new single column newspaper with a pair of scissors, pop it into your pocket, and read the nation's top stories at your leisure.

But that's not all!
A brand new editor has been appointed to carry the Corrie into the Nineties. Chirpy Cockney Johnny Jameson, an old Fleet Street hand, started life on the streets of Brixton's notorious East End. But he has worked his way to the top, and was handpicked to  oversee the massive changes at Correspondent House. 'We will be taking a firmly non-political line,' he promised. 'We'll back the Conservatives all the way.'

But that's not all! We've signed up some of the biggest names in journalism, who will be giving their comments on the week's news, every Sunday. Gloria Hunniford will be bringing the latest gossip from the City, and don't miss the trenchant political comment from Roy Hudd.

But that's not all! The Correspondent's star line-up also includes Paul Gascoigne's fashion week, Paul Johnson on rock, and Sir Nicholas Fairbairn's Sex Talk.

THE CORRESPONDENT. BUY IT – PLEASE!

The Jaggers'

21st November 1990
Solemnization of Marriage between Mr Michael Jagger and Miss Jerald Ornery Crittur Hall at St Mandy's, Bali, and afterwards at the Wyman Suite, Hotel Miramar

ORDER OF SERVICE
(The roadies arrive and set up lighting rig, 25,000 watt sound system, erect scaffolding stage and backdrop)

THE MINISTER: Will the Congregation please rise for the Soundcheck.

(Enter the Band from the vestry. They tune guitars and shout 'Two, Two' into microphones.)

THE MINISTER: Dearly beloved, we are gathered here today in the sight of the everlasting, Keith Richard, to join this chick, N——, and this guy, N——, in holy matrimony. For truly is it written, I've been holding out so long, I've been sleeping all alone, Lord I miss you, child.
The congregation now will rise for the Hymn.

HYMN NO.1 'I met a Gin-Soaked Bar-Room Queen in Memphis'

THE MINISTER SHALL SAY: Has any person cause or just impediment why these two should not be joined in matrimony?

MAN FROM BOVRIL'S ADVERTISING AGENCY SHALL STAND: Yes, mate, she's under contract to us.

THE BOUNCERS SHALL STAND. MAN FROM BOVRIL SHALL SIT.

THE MINISTER: Do you, Michael Charles Peregrine Dibdin Jagger, take this woman to be thy lawful wedded wife?

20

match report

THE BRIDEGROOM SHALL SAY: Yeh.

THE MINISTER: Do you, Jerry, take rock's rubber-lipped front-man to be thy lawful wedded husband, after 13 years on and off, for as long as you both shall live, till tax exile do you part?

THE BRIDE SHALL SAY: Yeeeeeeeeeeeah.

MINISTER: Who giveth this woman to be married?

(Mr Bill Wyman shall step forward to give away bride, and also get his divorce done as a job-lot.)

MINISTER: The Congregation shall Stand.

(The Congregation rise, and hold lighted cigarette-lighters over their heads.)

HYMN NO.2 'My Sweet Lady Jane, When Will I See You Again?'

THE MINISTER: Dearly beloved, do not forget thou canst buy souvenir T-shirts and posters outside.

THE BRIDEGROOM SHALL SAY: Do not be tempted by those who would offer you false wares. Official merchandising is clearly marked.

(The Organist shall play a selection from Jagger, Solo Album in A major flop.)

ILLUSTRATION: DAVID HENSLEY

MAGGIE
Telling it to you straight!

We've signed her up! The woman all Fleet Street was after. The woman who gives it to you like a man!

Yes, Punch has a new columnist – MAGGIE. And she's all ours! The Daily Mail offered her even more money than Julie Burchill. The Sunday Times offered her the name of Andrew Neil's hairdresser. The Sunday Correspondent offered a P45. But when we offered Bargepole's home phone number, she came to Punch with a swoon!

Now MAGGIE can comment on vital issues of the day:

*Why are the Happy Mondays so grumpy?

*Is Fergie dieting too much?

*Who's the coolest: Raphael, or Donatello?

READ HER NEXT WEEK, AND EVERY WEEK!

sideswipes

'And I thought David Attenborough was an invasion of privacy'

A film about John Major's leadership is to be made. It will be called *The Greyest Tory Ever Sold*

Mrs Thatcher faces deselection after a member of her Finchley party complained about being represented by 'a bloody nagger'

'Let's hope we sold them old technology'

HIT AND MISSILE

'…and then left at the next traffic lights…can't miss it'

'And this decoy's made entirely from egg boxes and washing-up liquid containers'

'Are we all agreed on "Big Bastard" then?'

Beyond the veil

Direct from Dhahran, a report on Arab women and army rations

The soldier wheezed appreciatively as he passed a gaggle of Saudi women in Dhahran's Al Shula market. 'Sheerit,' he cried, 'look at the eyebrows on that, man!'

Admittedly, they do a stupendous line in arched eyebrows here, but are they attached to some luscious bedouin houri eager to finger feed you with sweetmeats, or Adnan Khashoggi's maiden aunt? You'll never know.

When every woman is a cross between Darth Vader and a bottle of Mackeson even Kate Adie starts to look good.

Little more than baby factories, women here are tied to the home. They are forbidden to talk to strange men, work, drive cars, dye their hair and must wear the all-enveloping black abaya in public. Stealth women, the forces call them.

Saudi men will tell you that these strictures are to uphold female sanctity. It seems a piece of arch hypocrisy when every Thursday their Cadillacs are nose-to-tail on the causeway to liberal Bahrain and more blonde Gulf Air hostesses than you can shake a petro-dollar at.

Just to cast an admiring look over a pretty girl is a long-forgotten thrill. Instead, desperate journalists have a 1-10 grading system based on a girl's shoes. If she clumps in wearing black, orthopaedic court shoes she's probably the boss-eyed virgin daughter of the local Muttawain (religious policeman). But if she tippytoes in wearing pink satin high heels...

Of course you can never quite tell what a woman is thinking behind that chador veil. She is probably concentrating on not walking into a brick wall, but many men would like to have it otherwise. Wild stories abound of Arab girls' sexual insatiability. They're desperate for sex with westerners, it is said, to experience foreplay and other illicit joys.

The pick-up technique is to get in a hotel elevator with a woman then drop a piece of paper with your room number on it. Later, there will be a knock – if she's fought her way through the waist-high piles of notepaper blocking the lift that is.

He rejoices in the name Honas P Dicklicker III but answers to plain old Dick. And he's the only member of the American 82nd Airborne Division who actually likes MREs. Meals Ready to Eat, aka Meal Rejected by Ethiopians, are the US forces staple diet in field and universally loathed by all except the likes of Dick, who you will guess is a dog.

American forces are better equipped than our Desert Rats except in two vital departments – chemical protection and food. The MREs are ready-cooked, vacuum-packed stodge, which they recommend can be heated on an engine block. The beef stews, meatballs and rice, ham and crackers, and dried fruit go down like lead when the Yanks eye our boys with their compo beans and bacon.

The Brit boil-in-the-bag menus are more varied and come in 24-hour packs which include fruit, biscuits, gum, fruit juice and non-melting chocolate. The currency rate is now three compo rations to one US folding campbed.

Naturally the French are dining à la carte with sumptuous sauces, fresh meat, fresh baked baguettes, cheese and REAL fruit. Everyone is convinced they have a secret supply of Chablis.

The Arab forces have a curious concoction – a sort of Halal-killed MRE with lots of vacuum packed mezzah. One characteristic is its remarkable laxative effect, much to the delight of the ubiquitous desert dung beetle who is enjoying a rich harvest this year.

War's an alphabet soup when it comes to jargon and acronyms. Missiles, or 'mistles' as the Yanks insist, get macho names like HARM (high radiation anti-radar missiles) and SLAM (stand-off land attack). Unless they are British, of course, in which case they get called JP233 – comfortingly, it means absolutely nothing.

POWS are now EPWs (enemy prisoners of war), and the old Jeep (general purpose vehicle) has been scrapped for the HUMVEE (high mobility, multiwheeled vehicle).

You wear your IPE (individual protection equipment) in an NBC (nuclear, biological, chemical) attack and pray to God you have been taking your NAPS (nerve agent protection system) tablets.

In Riyadh the multinational forces are run by bewildering bodies such as MARCENT, NAVCENT, CENTCOM and others. I rang the JIB (joint information bureau) to ask who dreamt up these linguistic 'frangs'. They didn't know. It's probably OPSEC (operation security), which is restricted anyway.

For journalists the English language has been the first casualty of this war. To learn all this gobbledygook is to invite a spell in DEPMED (deployable medical services). Assuming all 26 coalition nations have their own jargon, I can see us reviving that old World War II favourite – SNAFU (situation normal, all fouled up).

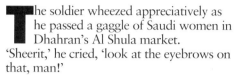

'If you were the only girl in the world and I was the only boy...'

Gerard Evans is a reporter for Today.

Saddam Hussein
My Part in His Downfall

Part one
August 1990

'What do you call a comedian who steals second-rate material?'

'The Thief of Badgags.'

Driver El-Kidgell and I are sitting in a jeep waiting to depart on our summer holiday. Baghdad shimmers in the August haze. Beneath a tree, John Simpson slumbers peacefully, wishing he had more to do.

Little does he know! For this year I have planned the holy-day of a lifetime!

'A jihad!' I cry.

'You've jihad that idea before,' ripostes El-Kidgell, idly swatting at the mother of mosquitos, which is buzzing round him like a malfunctioning Silkworm.

'Let us rise up and smite the serpent of western imperialism,' I suggest.

'OK, O smitey one,' replies my friend. 'When?'

'Where is my army?'

'Up your sleevy, O excellency.' They do not call it Badgags for nothing. I summon my Chiefs of Staff.

'We're going to invade!'

'Where?'

'Just Kuwait and see.' I assemble the glorious sons of Iraq and point them south.

'Off you go, O seeds of the mighty tree that will surely choke the Bush,' I say.

'If you want me, I'll be back here in a very deep and safe bunker.'

by Saddam Hussein

Part two
A few days later

Now truly is the glorious Iraqi cat among the decadent western pigeons! Kuwait is mine(d)! The evil Bush can do nothing about this. He is trying to persuade the United Nations to let him use Force. But we are not afraid of any breakfast cereal!

O, a thousand curses on the pernicious United Nations! All of them are ganging up on me. The only one on my side is King Hussein of Jordan, and that is only because I lent him my name.

Part three
November 1990

The economic blockade is puny and ineffectual. The British are unable to control their own economy, let alone ours! Their exports have fallen dramatically! Especially since they stopped sending us our supergun! Also, Thatcher has gone! The curse of Saddam is upon her! The mother of resignations!

Part four
January 1991

The mother of battles has begun! The perfidious aggressors are ruthlessly attacking innocent civilian targets. The Acme Chemical Warhead Co was hit only yesterday. This attack is entirely unprovoked – at least, that's what I was saying last night on Baghdad Radio. Then I played a few requests, ran a phone-in competition (for which there were no entries, the evil imperialists having bombed the mother of telephone exchanges) and put on Iraq's No. 1 single 'Do the Bartman' by John Simpson.

The sons of Iraq continue to resist! Our glorious Air Force has heroically buggered off to Iran.

'Hence the expression – I-ran away,' smirks El-Kidgell.

Part five
February 1991

We have won a glorious victory! After our six-month trial period, we have decided to return Kuwait and get our money back. We were not satisfied. It was nothing but trouble, and the oil wells kept catching fire.

Tonight El-Kidgell and I were watching *Whose Line Is It Anyway?* Clive of Anderson told his two decadent contestants to perform a scene 'in the style of Iraqi soldiers'. Immediately they put their hands in the air and walked out of the studio. I do not find this funny and shall be writing to the Broadcasting Complaints Commission.

STEVE PUNT
(with apologies to Spike Milligan, the mother of all humorists)

ILLUSTRATION: DAVID HENSLEY

'My God! The Iraqis have got Trabants!'

Let no one, however, least of all Saddam Hussein, think that the Benns, Kents and Thompsons represent anyone in Britain except the hardcore rent-a-mob who would be out in protest if we tried to resist an invasion from Mars.

Daily Mail, Monday, January 21

Would you fight

What would be the peaceniks' response to an alien invasion? A good place to start was at the daily press conference held by the Committee to Stop War in the Gulf at the House of Commons. **Marjorie Thompson**, chairperson of the Campaign for Nuclear Disarmament, was happy to answer the question. 'If an alien force invaded the earth – and I would stress that they couldn't be considered alien just from the colour of their skin *(green – Ed)* – of course we would protest,' she said. 'CND is not a pacifist organisation. A lot of our people are trained in non-violent resistance.' As in, presumably, *Star Wars IV – Gandhi Strikes Back*.

A rather different answer was given by **Sarah Hipperson**, a member of the Women's Peace Camp which has been holding a vigil outside the Foreign Office since the conflict began. Was it true that she and her comrades would set up a Peace Camp even if the earth was invaded by Mars? 'That's quite correct,' she said. 'People on Mars are not my enemy. I refuse

Peace campaigners offer to shut up for half an hour in return for complete and utter withdrawal of alien forces. Martian troops beat a grateful retreat

Ken Livingstone takes sensible precautions against direct hits from a hostile spaceship

to have enemies. All life is entitled to a space on this earth.' The notion that they've already got a perfectly good planet of their own did not, it seem, cut much ice with this devotee of multicultural society.

Bruce Kent, described by Paul Johnson as a 'professional peace agitator', was more ambivalent. 'I would have to consider the situation,' he said. 'If an alien force arrived I would want to talk to them and find out what they wanted. They could be much more sane and rational than us. We might be able to learn a great deal from them.' True, but only if they spoke English. Few of us can yet manage Martian, although *The Late Show*'s Michael Ignatieff has occasionally come pretty close.

Another of the peace campaigners singled out by Johnson was **Emma Thompson**, the well-known actress and wife of Kenneth Branagh. How would she respond to a Martian invasion? 'I said everything I want to say at the demonstration last Saturday,' she said. 'I really have nothing more to add.' However, a careful reading of her speech revealed no mention of any form of extra-terrestrial life, Mr Branagh included.

One of the most vociferous opponents of the war has been **Tam Dalyell**, the Labour MP for Linlithgow. He campaigned for sanctions to be given more time before hostilities broke out and was one of 34 MPs to demand a ceasefire in a Commons debate last week. Would he feel the same way if we were fighting Mars instead of Iraq? 'I don't think it's a very meaningful question,' he said. 'I'm from a tank crew and I'm not a pacifist.'

There has also been some opposition to the conflict in the House of Lords. **Lord Hatch**, one of three peers to speak out against the war, considered the question very carefully. 'What kind of military weapons are going to be used against Mars?' he asked. 'It seems to me it's an extension of the question of whether you should use nuclear weapons against nuclear weapons. It's mutual suicide.'

One must, of course, bear in mind the natural sympathy felt by parliamentarians for slimy creatures with more than one head. After a long and refreshing lunch, many of their own colleagues look like that too.

Bernie Grant, the Labour MP for

Peace protesters would not even fight an invasion from Mars, claimed Paul Johnson in the Daily Mail. Could this possibly be true? TOBY YOUNG investigates

the Martians?

Tony Benn offers Martian leaders a copy of his book in exchange for hostages

Tottenham, was one top legislator who was not prepared to commit himself on the war of the worlds issue. 'I don't know whether I'm prepared to make a statement on this,' he said.'It's quite clear that you're trying to turn this matter into a joke and it's not a joke.'

The Socialist Workers Party, on the other hand, took the matter extremely seriously. **Pat Stack**, a member of the SWP's Central Committee, said, 'Given that there's no life on Mars I would think it was the biggest con yet offered by the military for justifying war.'

So far, the responses to the question had been somewhat ambiguous. It was clear that for a really definitive reply I'd have to approach **Noam Chomsky**, Ferrari P Ward Professor of Modern Languages and Linguistics at the Massachusetts Institute of Technology and the 'brains' behind the peace movement. What would he do if the earth was invaded by Mars? 'I would oppose it but only on the condition that all diplomatic efforts, including sanctions, had been exhausted,' he said. 'The right way to respond to aggression is the peaceful way set down in the Charter of the United

Nations.' What the 'brains' may not have noticed, however, is that the Martians have not, as yet, signed the UN charter. From their point of view, death-ray lasers may be a perfectly justifiable substitute for negotiation.

Not everyone was prepared to cooperate with our public spirited, freedom of information-inspired survey. Among those who declined to answer the question were Tony Benn, Ken Livingstone, Tony Banks, Margot Kidder and Arthur Scargill. One respondent was even downright hostile. **Mary Ellen Brill**, co-ordinator of the Gulf Peace Team which has set up a Peace Camp a few miles from the Saudi border, answered as follows: 'I don't respond to those questions. I think they're ridiculous. I really disapprove of people who ask those kind of questions. I really don't want to be quoted on this and if you quote me and I find out about it I'll sue you. If you'll excuse me, I have work to do. Good day.'

But what of the man who had started this whole controversy in the first place?

Emma Thompson demonstrates the CND intergalactic combat suit

What would **Paul Johnson** do in the event of an inter-planetary conflict situation? His answer was a credit to any hard-working hack; 'I don't think I'd fight, because I'm 62. But I'd write a quickie book about the war.'

'I think we're in trouble. It's eaten Jennifer'

Welcome to Kuwait, sir, dinner is served

Seven months of occupation, but the chandeliers were still intact

I drove into Kuwait City to be treated, rather undeservedly, as a conquering hero. But glorious liberator or no glorious liberator, I still faced the prospect of another uncomfortable night sleeping in the car. As darkness fell, though, a soft voice in my ear invited me to share his humble abode – and would my colleague (*Today* photographer Colin Davey) like to kip down for the night, too?

Our host, Nasr, was a shy young man who drove us home in his ancient Toyota. We were looking forward to a night on the sofa with Primus brew-up coffee, so it was a bit of a shock to pull up outside a 40ft high floodlit arch, built of marble and leading to a gilded cathedral of a house, littered with Louis XV furniture. As servants took our bags and prepared beds, we were shown the dining room with seating for 200 (lit by eight chandeliers) and a drawing room with 22 sofas. There were chandeliers in the bathroom, too, but I was more interested in what was then a very welcome luxury, sit-down lavatories. Dinner would be served within the hour, we were told. What time would we like breakfast? This was Dahai suburb, the Beverly Hills of Kuwait.

Nasr apologised for the car ride. The family had hidden the Mercs in the basement, he said, after the Iraqis had stolen 750 of his uncle's BMWs. We were picking our jaws from the floor as Nasr explained that his uncle owned the BMW franchise for Kuwait. Other uncles owned the concessions for every make of American car, also Toyota. And the uncle who owned our house provided every spare part for Japanese marques.

We were anxious to meet this gentleman, just in case he wanted to add his personal thanks for the heroic liberation of his country. Alas, he was not only in bed by this time, but he lived next door. This multi-chandeliered marble mansion was just the guest wing.

Such wealth defeated even the Iraqi looters, who had called round five times with their removal vans. But they took one look at the size of the job and beat their customary retreat.

'Uncomfortable? Of course it's uncomfortable – I've got a red nose on underneath!'

Life before the occupation was rather kind to the average, pampered Kuwaiti. On their 21st birthday, each gets around £40,000, with another £250,000 when they marry (£260,000 if they marry another Kuwaiti). There is an old joke in the city about an American who asked a Kuwaiti whether making love to his wife was pleasure or a chore. It must be pleasure, the Kuwaiti replied, or he would surely get a Filipino to do it.

On our way to Kuwait City, we met two Iraqi soldiers – members of the 'elite' Republican Guard – who promptly surrendered to us. Mindful of the Geneva Convention, we bunged them half a piece of melted Galaxy and a bottle of Volvic, while we decided what to do with them. We frisked Talal and Abdullah, as they were called, and set off in our Landcruiser in search of someone to hand them over to. This was a tense time, so Colin Davey decided he should try to convince the prisoners of our close contacts with Allied Forces. Picking up my mini-tape recorder, he let out a shriek of radio crackle and babbled into the machine – 'Oscar, Bravo, Seven-Up to Tango, Zulu Ford Sierra. Bringing In Prisoners. Over.'

Colin then rattled off a couple more messages to the tune that should Talal and Abdullah try any funny business, they'd be in big trouble. With the ice broken, I asked in pidgin English what our captives did in Saddam's army. Abdullah replied in perfect English: 'We are radio operators.'

His colleague nodded wearily towards us: 'You...Sahafi, yes?' This is Arabic for journalist. The game was up, and the two soldiers harumphed loudly and tutted their disgust. They allowed us our moment of glory, though, so we handed them over to some Egyptians, who were friendly, rather than to some Syrians, who weren't.

Every war has its hotel (the press corps hotel, I mean) and the Gulf was no exception. But even in a country as dreary and neanderthal as Saudi Arabia, the Al-Fao was an outstanding hellhole. Our host, the unctuous Mr Saleh, tripled room rates on our arrival (to cover overheads, he explained, as plaster fell from the ceiling).

He provided rooms as damp as the Kew Gardens hot house, and sheets which bore more blood stains than the average field hospital. His restaurant offered chicken and rice fried in Duckhams Hypergrade, or cold pizza. The man from the *Daily Mirror* had the only sit-down loo but he jealously guarded this after it was blocked up accidentally. By the man from the *Sun*. 🔊

Gerard Evans reported the Gulf war for **Today.** *He has now come home for a bath.*

Consul of war

As war-war is swapped for jaw-jaw, ANTHONY LEE recalls the Al-Hashemi School of Diplomacy (Principal: Iraq's former ambassador to Paris)

Mr Abdul Razzak Al-Hashemi, former Iraqi Ambassador to Paris: the father of all envoys

It was Karl von Clausewitz, the military strategist and non-peacenik, who said that war is merely the continuation of political relations by other means. And Iraqi political relations certainly entered a new and thrilling era of international repute with the occupation of Kuwait.

'Cometh the hour, cometh the man,' as mystic sages are prone, equally mystically, to incant. Well, the hour did indeed produce the man, Mr Abdul Razzak Al-Hashemi, the then Iraqi ambassador to Paris and his country's most senior ranking diplomat in Europe. Trained (appropriately enough in view of the spoils) as a geochemist specialising in oil production, Mr Al-Hashemi is also a former Minister for Higher Education. This enabled him to instruct us students from his unassailed position of graduate *magna cum laude* in the school of Iraqi Diplomacy.

As the crisis 'progressed', it fell to Mr Al-Hashemi's lot to educate us in the complexities of the Iraqi position. Plump and circumlocutory, he was a jovial television raconteur – one who brought to the appearance of a superior ice-cream salesman the vivacity of a horse meat trader and the sincerity of a used car salesman whose only merchandise is a Skoda with no engine. Through the miracle of media teaching technology, students learned the following ground rules of Iraqi diplomacy...

1. Deny everything

On 17 September 1990, seven weeks after the invasion of Kuwait, Ambassador Al-Hashemi appeared on BBC1's *Breakfast News*. He was asked by anchorman Nicholas Witchell to comment upon accusations of murder, arson and looting by Iraq's army of occupation. The ambassador maintained a stoic dignity. They were 'all one-sided stories...all of it is not true.' Pressed to explain why identity documents had been seized from emigrating Kuwaitis, the ambassador brought his mastery of Iraqi foreign policy to bear upon the matter. 'I don't have any information about that.' This confirms the next rule:

2. If denial fails, plead ignorance

Meticulous in his insight, the ambassador again added to the store of world knowledge on 27 September. Here he answered a *Breakfast News* report that embassies in Iraq had been told it was a crime punishable by death to shelter their own citizens.

'I don't have any information about this...' he said. Nor did he have too much information about the identity of his interrogator, greeting Nicholas Witchell as Mr Winchell, under the impression perhaps that Walter, the late king of US gossipmongers had spawned British issue.

3. Use logic

Having pleaded an understandable ignorance on the diplomatic policy of his own government regarding fellow diplomats, the ambassador opined that 'this definitely is an internal security matter, so not that important really.' Mr Witchell did not take kindly to this: 'So you are saying a threat to execute diplomats is not a threat of any importance are you?'

The ambassador's tailored hackles rose at this gross assertion of Iraqi indifference to the sanctity of human life. He explained quite rightly that they were not executing diplomats, 'foreigners are not diplomats, so let's differentiate between the two.'

4. Appeal to higher ideals

Iraqi diplomats must never forget that they serve a higher ideal of undoubted probity and grace. Faced, on the 29 November 1990, with a cruelly unconvinced Jeremy Paxman on BBC2's *Newsnight*, Mr Al-Hashemi postulated the world's alternative to threatening war against Iraq: 'A very simple alternative is to sit and negotiate like a civilised people, because any problem cannot be solved without negotiation.'

Mr Paxman, obviously as ignorant of the mores of Iraqi policy as the ambassador was of their consequences, seemed stupefied: 'You invade a foreign country, you hold innocent people hostage and you expect us to negotiate with you?'

The ambassador was pleased to expound: 'The problem is not Kuwait now.' Unsurprisingly, the ambassador had said 12 days earlier, 'there is no more government of Kuwait.' Yet still,

'Iraq is offering to negotiate peacefully and as President Saddam Hussein has said, he is willing to give sacrifices for the sake of peace through serious dialogue and negotiations.'

5. Treat prisoners of war correctly

One of the sacrifices Ambassador Al-Hashemi's master was willing to make, was the safety of the prisoners of war. To Western eyes such callous indifference to human life seemed barbarous, but students of Iraqi diplomacy were taught the truth on 20 January. 'We will obey the Geneva Convention, but as far as the prisoners of war are concerned, we will be obeyed by the numbers that the US and British Allies are announcing their losses; everything they don't announce we are not going to recognise.'

6. Persuasive argument is best

'The United States and whoever is with her are heading to a big, big disaster and big, big surprises that they never think of.' 20 January, *Newsnight*.

As von Clausewitz also said, 'War has its own grammar, but not its own logic,' and one must assume that the Iraqis prefer von Clausewitz on diplomacy too.

7. If all else fails, blame the Israelis

This reliable old ploy looked like failing the master diplomat since the Chosen People had unsportingly chosen not to land a pre-emptive zinger on their Iraqi adversaries. So, on 18 January, to ensure Israeli enthusiasm for the venture, seven Iraqi Scud missiles landed in Israel. The master diplomat explained to Walter Winchell Junior (the genuine article) the reason for this unprovoked assault. 'The whole conflict all along is an Arab-

Israeli conflict.' Student swots may recall that Iraq invaded Kuwait after the latter refused to forego $35bn of loans and to reduce its oil production in Iraq's economic favour. No matter, for the ambassador was able to amplify the depth of the conspiracy. 'Israel is in the war all along. If it is not carrying any military operation directly that does not mean that it is not involved indirectly so far.' Mr Winchell seemed not overly impressed with the ambassador's reasoning.

Alas, for students of tele-diplomacy, on 6 February, Iraq terminated diplomatic relations with members of the international alliance, and Abdul's diplomatic number was up. Even Mr Winchell seemed a little lachrymose as he terminated their last illuminating exchange, referring to Mr Al-Hashemi's recall. Taking his leave of France, Mr Al-Hashemi rebuked his host country (whose language he apparently refused to speak) as being the loser with Iraq and the whole Arab world because of its policy. He then flew off to Amman and as we all supposed, to undiplomatic, and uncharacteristic, silence.

Imagine the delight we students experienced when the following Sunday, up he popped, the genial genie of the cathode ray, beaming bonhomie to a David Frost switched to severe George Smiley mode. The master diplomat did not baulk, even in the face of Agent Frost's helpful, if Smileyesque suggestion that Abdul might apply for political asylum so that he could tell us what he really thought about Saddam Hussein. The ambassador drew a veil, if not several veils across such thoughts and thereafter danced into diplomatic oblivion. Who knows if we shall see his like again, flogging the philosophy of Saddam Hussein? It was a rotten job, but somebody had to do it. On the other hand, perhaps not. 🖋

Here's how the ex-Iraqi ambassador fended off TV's grandees

Jeremy Paxman BBC Newsnight:

● Mr Paxman asked: 'Can you give an assurance that those pilots you currently hold will be treated in accordance with the Geneva Convention?'

Mr Al-Hashemi was unperturbed at Paxo's ignorance of Iraqi sophistication. 'If they admitted in two to three weeks time that they lost a pilot two to three weeks ago, it might be too late.' Simple. You *can* kill people who don't exist.

Nicholas Witchell BBC Breakfast News:

● Mr Witchell said of foreigners in embassies being sheltered by diplomats: 'That's plain common sense, isn't it?'

Mr Al-Hashemi looked distinctly dubious at this. He brightened up to explain Iraqi-style diplomatic immunity.

'Kuwait is no longer a state, so the embassies in Kuwait, the ex-embassies in Kuwait, are no longer under the Vienna Convention, that's for sure.' Easy really.

Dan Rather CBS Evening News:

● Answering why Israel's involvement had been magically transformed by unprovoked Scud attacks, Mr Al-Hashemi said: 'Israeli planes took part on the raids in Iraq today.'

'Is that a fact?' asked Mr Rather, ever the newshound.

'Yes, it is and we have documents we are going to release later.' Surprisingly, the documents never materialised.

My Poll Tax Plan

by Michael Heseltine

I was delighted to place my talents at the disposal of the Prime Minister when he took office, and I was further delighted when he presented me with the challenge of finding a replacement for the Community Charge. I have been applying myself rigorously to the alternatives for some considerable time now, and last week I was able to announce detailed plans to enter a full period of consultation about the best timing for further consultation.

If anything, the Conservative Party is about choice. And it has always seemed to me an injustice that local chargepayers should have only one tax to choose from. With this in mind, I intend to introduce these following new charges:

● **Local Income Tax** Calculated according to the portion of one's income earned locally. Long-distance commuters would benefit enormously, since they would therefore pay none at all, while people working at home would pay 100 per cent. My colleagues have described this plan as 'utterly unworkable and a potential catastrophe' so it is the ideal successor to the Community Charge.

● **Roof Tax** Adapted from the Labour Party plan, but calculated according to the slope of the roof, flat-rate or steep. Ministers are already worried about leaks, although some householders may be insulated against the worst effects. 'What is absolutely clear,' I have told the Prime Minister, 'is that roof tax provides unlimited scope for terrible puns.'

● **Taste Added Tax (TAT)** Would depend on the look of your property from the outside. Owners of pink stone-clad semis with satellite dish, false leaded windows, mooning garden gnomes, 'Beware! I live here' Alsatian stickers, false carriage lamps and ruched nylon curtains could see sharp increases. The Duke and Duchess of York have already applied for a rebate from this tax.

● **Nuisance to the Community Charge**
Owners of loud dogs, people who set their car alarms to go off if a mouse moves within 100 yards of the car, possessors of stereo systems that register more than ten on the Richter scale, and people who wait for fine sunny Sundays before lighting bonfires, will all be paying more. The working party also recommends additional penalty fines for people who make telephone calls during the last ten minutes of *Inspector Morse*.

● **Fitted Kitchen Unit Tax** I have discovered that kitchen units are broadly indicative of the size of a household and its income. Thus a large number of solid-wood units (including plate-racks and those glass-fronted ones that go in the corner) would indicate a middle-to-high income family, while one self-assembly cupboard would indicate a single, lower-income householder. (Or a middle-to-high income family with a stingy, DIY-incompetent husband.) But do sink units count double and could payers apply for a rebate if a door comes off?

● **Miserable Bastard Tax** Assessed according to how much of a miserable bastard the householder is. The register will be compiled by throwing a shuttlecock into his/her garden and seeing if they throw it back.

● **The Poll Tax** A suggestion that everyone should pay an identical amount, regardless of income or ability to pay has been dismissed out of hand as patently absurd. 🐍

'Not yet, Mr President, we think they've started copulating again'

'I think I've just spotted the Prime Minister'

The Conservative Party: Major's manifesto in full

THIS GENERAL ELECTION IS VITAL FOR THE future of all of us. All of us, that is, in the Parliamentary Conservative party. Let us reflect on some achievements of the last four years.

1. Mrs Thatcher introduced the Poll Tax.

2. We have got rid of Mrs Thatcher.

3. We have got rid of the Poll Tax.

4. England nearly got to the World Cup Final.

Here are the main issues and policies which we'll be putting before the voters.

Poll Tax
'Let's do something about it'

In our last manifesto, we pledged to do something about the rates. After an exhaustive and lengthy five minute chat, Mrs Thatcher and Kenneth Baker decided to replace it with the Poll Tax. Some faint-hearts said it would be an electoral liability, but today we can all see the Poll Tax for what it is – an electoral disaster. Michael Heseltine and I said all along it wouldn't work. I remember going home one weekend and finding Norma stomping round Huntingdon shouting 'Can't pay, won't pay.' So we're jolly well getting rid of it.

Defence
'We'll hope for the best'

The Gulf conflict has proved what we all know so well – America is bigger than us. It also proved that Britain produces the best high-tech, state-of-the-art weapons in the world; and will sell them to anyone.

Health
'It's a very important issue'

Since I became Prime Minister, I have had a few aches and pains and felt jolly tired. I am a man of the people so I headed straight for my local NHS clinic and was impressed by what they told me – 'We're only open Tuesdays and Thursdays.' As Norma always says, 'If you've got your health, what else matters?' – and I think this could apply at national level too. I fully support the NHS – they've supplied me with spectacles since I was a boy.

Transport
'Do something about traffic'

You know, I haven't always had a chauffeur-driven limousine to take me where I want to go. I used to have to use trains and buses like everyone else, and that experience taught me that it's much nicer to have a chauffeur-driven limousine. If only there weren't so many traffic jams. We presently have a working party looking at options for public transport – these include laser-guided monorails, hover-trams, personal ionic-drive bubble-pods, and most outlandish of all, building some railways.

Europe
'Time to make up our minds'

As I said to Chancellor Kohl, I want Britain to be at the very heart of Europe. The reason is simple. If, come 1992 we're not there, alongside the Germans, the French, the Spanish and Italians, we will get dumped on from a great height. As for the single currency – well, I can't see what all the fuss is about. After all, we joined the European currency system the moment we went decimal, really. I like the idea of knowing that one franc fifty centimes is the same as one pound fifty pence. It would save some right old ding-dongs with Norma in the Boulogne hypermarket.

Broadcasting
'Is really quite good'

Mrs Thatcher didn't like TV much and never watched it but Norma and I enjoy a good evening in front of the box. So I don't agree with handing television over to the money-men. I think I'd like to see something other than soaps and gameshows. Namely, I'd like to see me. I've got this great idea for a mini-series about the humble son of a circus acrobat who rises to high office. If any ITV company will make it (and put Jane Seymour in it) I'll let them keep their franchise.

Education
'School is very important'

You know, our children are our future, and it's vital that we invest in their education. I could never get this across to Mrs Thatcher, who used to say 'But what use are GCSEs? They're not economically productive.' I used to say that we were producing the most stupid and uneducated population in Europe, but this didn't worry her. 'If they can't read newspapers or speak foreign languages, John,' she'd say, 'then they'll never find out, will they?'

The Economy
'We're in a bit of a pickle'

Oh crikey! I knew you'd want to know about that one eventually. Look, let me be quite honest – it's all a bit of a mess. But then, everybody's in debt. Even the Germans and Japanese are having trouble. So comfort yourself with the thought that once again, the British were there first.

Employment
'We're right behind it'

Labour really can't have it both ways. They go on and on about how we ought to spend less on defence, and then when we do, they moan about job losses. Believe you me, if Lamont doesn't sort out interest rates and Michael doesn't knock this local government finance thing on the head, then unemployment is going to be increasingly on my mind.

Vote Conservative – The party that sort of believes in Britain, in Europe, but retaining sovereignty, you know, sort of

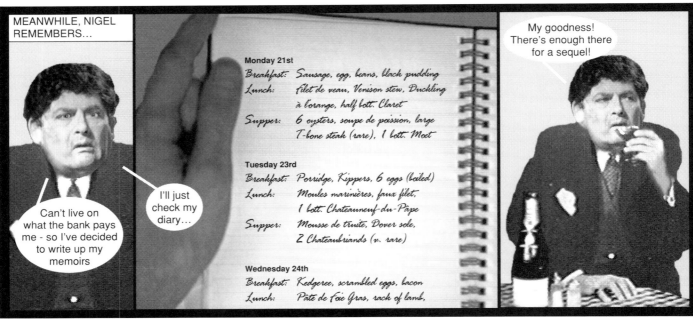

OLLIE...

It's a right rivetting Reed!

Some wag once dubbed me and my actor acquaintances, the Last of the Hell Raisers. What utter rubbish. We were the first of the Hell Raisers. And I was the firstiest of the lot.

Who remembers that time at the White Horse Hotel when I twisted someone called Vince Bullock's neck and heckled some Dutchmen? I certainly don't. Apparently they were Danish. Well, I gave 'em a real Viking warrior welcome!

Sinking pints

But if you didn't drink in the Sixties, you weren't a real actor. Ricky Harris, Ricky Burton, Ricky Chamberlain... er, Pete O'Toole – we all knew how to sink a pint and raise a laugh.

The fighting was the best

Pints, curries, in the nude!

bit by far. I just love a bit of rough and tumble. It's harmless, character building and helps you make new friends like Peter Stringfellow.

Togs off

Nothing wrong with a bundle is there? A few pints, a swift curry and then it's togs off for a quick grapple with your chums in front of a roaring fire.

It's a manly thing to do. S'not suspicious, is it? Nothing *dirty* about it. Nothing *shameful* . Look, I'll show you how. Here...give me...put your...get 'em up, you little man. Yeah? Yeah? Come on, tough guy. Hard, are you? Come on, *outside!*

Maggie's special message for Ollie

★ **THREE CHEERS FOR Mr Oliver Reed. Despite all his troubles and setbacks, he's making a fine comeback. I too have had my trouble and setbacks. But no one has asked me to make a comeback. It's a funny old world, isn't it?**

COME ON, OUTSIDE!

★ I'm a softy really. I love dogs. I once rescued a stray dog in Italy. I called him the General. Me and my lovely wife, Josephine sent him flowers when he was in the kennels. Guess what I say to him now before walkies? That's right – come on, *outside!*

Tarby's 'bum' slur shame

ONE STEAM JOB I do remember – fondly as I recall – was at a *This Is Your Life* shindig. I wound up next to old flat nose Patrick Mower. And then I lobbed some Parma ham on to another flatnose, Alan Minter. And what gratitude do I get? Just that so-called golfer Jimmy Tarbuck calling me a 'bum'.

Guzzling

I've hit some irons in my time too, you know. I got so mad. Maybe I'd been guzzling some champagne. What of it? No harm in that. Is there? S'not anti-social behaviour is it? Wanna start? Wanna barney? Come on, you little weasel. *Outside!*

Exclusive!

Alistair Beaton reveals the secret text of an imminent speech to the House of Commons by John Major, the most popular Prime Minister since Churchill

ONLY COMPARATIVELY rarely in the field of human conflict has such a considerable amount been owed by quite a lot of people to a fairly insignificant number of persons. I refer, of course, to the seven and a half million people who have not yet paid their community charge. I should like to point out that in **fighting** to complete our wide-ranging review of alternatives to the community charge, we shall struggle as best we can on the beaches, we shall make our **position** as clear as possible in the fields and in the streets, we shall endeavour to sort things out in the hills, we shall, if at all possible, seek to avoid what might conceivably be thought of as **surrender**.

When I warned the House that the Cabinet would fight on alone, the Honourable Members opposite took it upon themselves to suggest that in three weeks the Government will have its neck wrung like a **chicken**. To them I say today, some like **chicken**, others like a full English breakfast in a Happy Eater. Despite the temporary setback suffered by our troops at Ribble Valley, I say to the House today: 'Give us the **implements**, and we will attempt to complete the job within the fastest possible time scale.' This is not the concluding phase. It is not even the commencement of the concluding phase. But it is, perhaps, the concluding phase of the initial stages of the commencement.

Let us therefore **brace** ourselves to do what may be advisable in terms of the opinion polls, and so bear ourselves that if the classless society lasts quite a long time, men will still say, 'This was their finest change of emphasis.' ✎

sideswipes

IRAQI P.R.

TRYING TO MAKE A MOLEHILL OUT OF A MOUNTAIN OF PEOPLE

Tory public relations is to try to make John Major more interesting before the next election. It's asked Kitty Kelley to write his biography

Gerald Ratner is to be sued for claiming he made a fortune selling 'total crap'. Jeffrey Archer had the idea first

TODAYS SERMON, SUNDAY OPENING

'Jesus was a carpenter: he didn't buy self-assembly furniture'

A bard act to follow

Franco Zeffirelli's film of *Hamlet*, with Mel 'Is this a Lethal Weapon I see before me?' Gibson in the title role, will have its first British screening this week.

The film, which also features Glenn Close, Alan Bates, Paul Scofield, Ian Holm, and Helena Bonham-Carter, will go on general release in April.

This is just one of a series of unlikely-sounding Shakespeare film and TV adaptions. Here are some that have yet to be released:

Jeremy Beadle's *Romeo and Juliet*

The scene: a chapel outside Verona. Juliet is lying on the floor, apparently dead.

(Enter Jeremy Beadle, disguised as 'Friar Lawrence')

BEADLE :(*Speaking in a stage whisper*)
Romeo Montague from Mantua doth return,
His deceas-ed tottie to espy.
And yet, what he doth not know,
Is that she hath to Beadle written,
This scam to set up and to film.
But hark! Our patsy approaches and I must be gone.
(Hides behind altar)

(Enter Romeo. He sees Juliet and looks distraught. Audience titters expectantly)

ROMEO: Beauty's ensign yet
Is crimson in thy lips and in thy cheeks,
And death's pale flag is not advanced there.

(Beadle makes extravagant gestures behind Romeo's back. Audience splutters and chortles)

ROMEO: I will stay with thee
And never from this palace of dim night

Depart again...
Eyes look your last,
Arms, take your last embrace! and lips, O you
The doors of breath, seal with a righteous kiss
A dateless bargain to engrossing death!

(Romeo prepares to kill himself. But before he can do so, he sees Beadle emerging from behind the altar, holding a microphone. Audience guffaws)

ROMEO: Oh what? It can't be...
Thou (*Bleep*)I cannot credit this!
Thou hast taken the (*Bleep Bleep*)

(Juliet rises from the floor, grinning. Romeo playfully swipes at Beadle. Audience wets itself. Beadle walks to front of stage)

BEADLE: Well, that's all we've got time for this week. But don't forget to join me a week from now, when I'll be dressing up as an old witch and telling Mr Angus Macbeth of Glamis that he's going to be King of Scotland!

Woody Allen's *Hamlet*

The film opens with Hamlet (Woody Allen) waiting outside Elsinorn, a house in a smart Danish suburb of New York. The house is named after Hamlet's grandparents, Elsie and Norman. Norman was a cab driver whose son studied hard, went to college, and got a good job as King of Denmark. Business was good, but then Old King Hamlet was brutally murdered. Young Hamlet is awaiting the ghost of his father.

(Enter ghost of Old Hamlet)

HAMLET: Is that you father?

GHOST: Who do you think? Joe DiMaggio?

HAMLET: Are you really dead? What do you want with me?

GHOST: Look at you. When you gonna get yourself a proper job? Thirty already, and still only a prince. What sort of profession is that for a good Danish boy? Do you want to disgrace your momma, or what? You could have been a doctor or lawyer by now. Take my example, Hamlet. Study. Go to night school.

HAMLET: All right, all right. Just tell me two things. How did you die, and are there girls after death?

The scene switches. Hamlet is lying on a couch. Beside him, a middle-aged woman is taking notes.

HAMLET: For years I lived with the knowledge that my father had been brutally muurdered. OK, so he lived in a rough neighbourhood. But now he tells me that my uncle did it. Now my uncle wants to marry my mother, so my father's murderer will be my father. Compared with me, Oedipus had a good deal. At least he got to sleep with somebody. All I get is Ophelia.

The scene changes. Hamlet has changed into doublet and hose and is wondering whether the question is to be or not to be, and whether he can fit the answer on one side of the paper only.

(Enter Ophelia)

HAMLET: Nymph, in thy orisons be all my sins remember'd. And let's face it, with sins like mine you'd better broaden your orisons.

The films ends as Claudius is confined to a hospital bed by the stress of running the Kingdom of Denmark and coping with Gertrude's rapacious sexual appetite. Hamlet is offered a writing job in Los Angeles. Ophelia follows him to California, where she gets a job as a cinema usherette.

A Midsummer Night's Nightmare on Elm Street VI

The most lamentable comedy, and most cruel fate of Pyramus and Thisby. Also a teenage slasherama. Starring Freddie Krueger as Bottom.

Teenage sweethearts Pyramus and Thisby are looking forward to their first night of love when they are attacked by a manic creature with long fingernails and a donkey's head. After their heads have melted and worms have burst from their eyeballs, they are saved by the Jedi Fairy King, Oberon Ken-Obi, who rescues them despite being in the wrong film. Freddie returns for *A Midsummer Night's Nightmare on Elm Street XX – Driller Killer Love Babes*, in which he terrorises Romeo and Juliet – two cute kids on an Italian vacation – into an early grave.

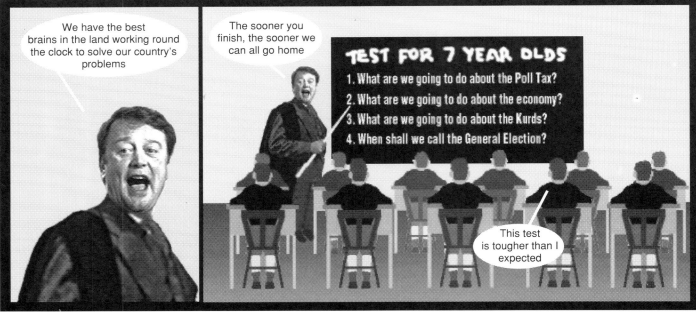

The editor of *That's Life*, Shaun Woodward, is to be the Conservative Party's new director of communications. ROLAND WHITE heralds a new style of party political broadcast.

That's Right!

Fade out 'Theme From The Dambusters'. Viewers see a set of dazzling teeth with three grey men (John Major, Tom King, Douglas Hurd) sitting in the background.

ESTHER RANTZEN: Thank you, and a special thank you to Mr D Quayle of Washington who sent in this mooning Saddam Hussein doll. Isn't he lovely?

But now something more serious. Tonight this country faces perhaps the most difficult political crisis since Suez. So to test public opinion, we took our cameras into the streets to see if anybody can tell us just what *this* is.

Produces picture of the Prime Minister. Scene switches to London shopping mall, where Esther is thrusting picture under the nose of an old lady in a garish headscarf.

OLD LADY: Oo, is it something you eat?

ESTHER: I'm afraid not, madam. Can't you guess?

OLD LADY: No, but I'll dress up as a cabbage and dance the lambada if you like.

Back to the studio.

ESTHER: Mr Bryan Gould, of New Zealand, has contacted the programme to ask...

TOM KING: What are you going to do about the Poll Tax?

ESTHER: And the answer is...

JOHN MAJOR: Nothing.

ESTHER: Our next letter comes from a Mr Emir, of Kuwait. And you've got a familiar problem, haven't you, sir?

TOM KING: Dear Esther...

ESTHER: He writes.

TOM KING: I'm having terrible trouble with my neighbour. I've been complaining about the noise for years, but he just doesn't listen. And, of course, the council just doesn't want to know.

ESTHER: So we telephoned Iraq.

DOUGLAS HURD: Nothing to do with us.

JOHN MAJOR: They said...

DOUGLAS HURD:...This is an aggressive outrage by the friends of Zion upon the mother of Islam. We will drive out the perfidious forces of the infidel in a bloody jihad!

ESTHER: That wasn't very good news for Mr Emir.

TOM KING: So we contacted Mr George Bush, who works for Mr Emir's local Security Council. He's had a lot of experience dealing with noisy neighbours.

JOHN MAJOR: What happens next?

ESTHER: We asked.

TOM KING: *(Putting on a terrible American accent)*. President Hussein has only one choice. He must leave Kuwait, and he will leave Kuwait. I am comfortable with that decision.

ESTHER: On Mr Bush's advice, Mr Emir asked all his neighbours to gang up on Iraq. And Mr Bush has offered to lend the Emirs the 1st and 2nd Marine Expeditionary Force, the 1st UK Armoured Division, the 82nd Airborne and Armoured Division, 113,000 Islamic troops and a self-erecting step-ladder. So, sir, let us know how you get on. Now over to 'Doc' Schwarzkopf, who will be dressing up as a guava and asking passers-by to join him in a chorus of 'The Desert Song'...

That Was A Party Political Broadcast On Behalf Of A Carrot That Looks Like A Willy

Exclusive satellite listings

As a supplement to the new all-channel Radio and TV Times, we present the listings of the future – satellite TV. Luckily the satellite programmes never change. So you just cut out this page and re-use it again and again. Happy viewing!

SKY ONE

Transmitted via the Astra (Sky) and Marcopolo (BSB) satellites. We apologise to regular Sky viewers for the intrusion of quality programmes, but unfortunately the situation is beyond our control.

8.00 Teenage Mutant Opera Singers

9.00 Pages From Skytext
Written by Christopher Biggins

10.00 Here's The Young Doctors
A movie-length special from the hospital sitcom soap, starring Dr Lucille 'Lucy' Ball.

Top interviews with Angela Rippon

12.00 True Confessions
The Dish. Should an aspiring intellectual risk the ridicule of his friends by installing a satellite dish?

12.30 Sale Of The Century
With your host, Peter Marshall, and the lovely Maria Rice-Pudding. Special guests are popsters the Bay City Rollers.

1.00 Another World
It's those cute college kids having a wonderful time. Featuring a special guest appearance-fee for Bill Cosby.

2.00 Sale Of The Century
It's that Marshall man again.

2.30 The Bionic Witch
Lindsay Wagner and Elizabeth Montgomery star in this action-packed comedy thriller drama about an indestructible half-witch, half-machine.

3.00 Sale Of The Century
Another chance to catch edited highlights of the show, complete with a bonus re-run of the 2.00 *Sale of the Century* special special...

4.00 Operatic Endurance
Highlights of the Japanese game show in which the contestants are forced to sit through intense quantities of televised opera and sumo wrestling. Who will last the longest before getting up and switching off the TV?

5.00 Sale of the Century

SKY NEWS

Featuring Sky News bulletins repeated repeatedly throughout the day, alternating with repeats of repeated repeats on the hour. Also featuring updated repeats, and repeated updates, 24 hours a day.

5.30 Business Merger Report
An in-depth look at the financial side of satellite TV. Anthony Simonds-Gooding on life at the wrong end of a takeover bid.

9.00 Operatic Business News
Up-to-the-minute reports on the City's reaction to the Tosca flotation.

10.00 Beyond 2000
The latest developments in programmes about technology. Today: innovations in digital operatic recordings for satellite TV.

10.30 International Business Merger Report Week

11.30 Those Were The Archive Clips
Angela Rippon looks back through whole reels from days gone by.

12.00 It's Your Gulf Crisis
Sky's Middle East news report with a difference – catch up on the latest developments and join in with our Gulf Crisis Quiz.

2.00 Business Merger Report

3.00 Target
Norman Tebbit and Chris Tarrant host another edition of the hilarious political chat-show quiz for all the family.

5.00 Beyond 2000

What a carry on with bouncy Barbara

6.00 Business Merger Report

7.00 Repeat Of The Week
A look back at your most requested repeat news item.

9.00 Those Were The Archive Clips

11.00 Those Were the Ballets
Ballet clips with Angela Rippon.

SKY MOVIES

Transmitted via the Astra (Sky) satellite.

10.00 – 11.00 Foetal Attraction
Babies, fatherhood, revenge and violence are the themes of this laugh-a-minute study of schizophrenia. Starring Michael Clueless and Glenn Dose.

12.00 – 2.30 The Slob
When the inhabitants of a small English town subscribe to satellite TV, a strange new breed of creature appears – 'satellite slobs'. Who can save the world from these terrifying zombies? With Ken Roast.

4.00 – 5.30 Three Men And A Police Academy

Bernie talks turkey on Eurosport

Tom Smelleck, Ted Damson and Steve Gottanerve star in this hilarious tale of three bachelors whose lives are turned upside down by an offbeat baby cop.

6.00 – 8.00 Mad Maxwell
A futuristic publicity-crazed media tycoon who fights a constant battle with the Murdoch Riders, a dangerous gang of press barons. Starring Melvyn Mackenzie.

8.30 – 10.00 Raiders Of The Chitty-Chitty Rambo Ninja Trek Terminator 3
Sylvester Gibsonegger in the all-violence action movie. When crazed, ex-Nam psycho Al Bullet jets into Cambodia on the trail of Nazi gold, there's only one thing on his mind – brutal, bloody revenge!

10.15 - 12.15 Sky Wars
Anthony Simonds-Gooding is the tragic satellite commander in this brutal hi-tech space adventure. Thrills and chills aplenty as the Skylings of Planet Mur war with the Squarions from solar-system BSB.

12.30 – 2.00 My Stepmother Is A Squarial
Kim Brasserie and Dan Android star in a chaotic cosmic comedy. When little Vicky Titch comes home from school to find her wacky father has married a filmnet decoder, the fun begins!

EUROSPORT

Transmitted via the Astra (Sky) satellite.

7.00 Pro-Celebrity Chicken Strangling From Redcar
The best of today's action from the Entrail League. Jack Butcher commentates.

9.00 Venezuelan Tenpin Darts Championship
Live action from the Joquee Weesione Latin American league.

11.00 Classic Cock-Fighting From Behind The Loughton Country Club
A 'behind the scenes' look at this controversial, dangerous and violently blood-thirsty sport. Gary Smeg hosts.

12.00 International Professional Turkey Sexing From Norfolk
Highlights from the Bernard Matthews Mini Kievs Tournament.

1.00 American Power Tiddleywinks
Exciting, action packed footage from the semi-finals of the All-American world of winking. Your host is Vince Syrup.

3.00 The UK Pro-Am Open Knee-Capping Tournament
Live from the Bobby Sands Tea Rooms, Hunstanton. Join in the fun as the contestants 'whack 'em & crack 'em!'

6.00 The Benson & Hedges Trans-Europe Wheelchair Rally
Direct from our heli-camera, we're on the the trail of heavy smokers in wheelchairs. Serge Forward commentates.

8.00 The Big Opera Match
In this first ever SKY/BSB co-production, Nobby Stiles, Keith Chegwin, Trevor Nunn and Gazza star in this fourth round replay of Puccini's *Madam Butterfly*, live from White Hart Lane. The winners of this game will go on to meet Manchester Utd in the final at Glyndebourne next year. Your commentator is Ian St. Greavesie.

Shining star Cheggers lets rip at 8pm

Fun, games and some great pop tunes with those madcap minstrels, the Bay City Rollers. They're special guests on Sale Of The Century: Sky One at 12pm

LIFESTYLE

10.00 Everyday Workout
Get ready for a hard day in front of the box, with your remote-control hand with Cynthia Schtup and Bruno Brooks.

Sex in frecks with hunky Bruno Brooks

10.30 Search For A Bargain
Can't afford it? Don't worry, our credit-card telly-shopping scheme lets you spend in the privacy of your home.

11.00 Shopping Lifestyle
For those of you who just 'can't say no', another chance to flex your plastic.

12.30 It's Your Credit Card
The game show in which contestants guess their opponents' financial secrets.

1.30 Murder On The American Express
The home-shopping thriller series, starring Jessica Flex-Account and Tom Argos.

2.30 The Great American Shopping Show
An array of goods – yours for a credit card.

4.00 The Sell-A-Vision Shopping Channel
From now till midnight, eight hours of non-stop shopping for all the family (provided they're credit-worthy). Sell-a-Vision Shopping Channel will not be held responsible for promoting bankruptcy.

CNN

6.00 Napalm In The Morning
Shape up, boys and beat battle fatigue with Bobbie Batista's breakfast workout!

6.30 News Of The War
The world's press reviewed by British editor Andrew Neil. Sponsored by Nabisco.

8.00 War Update
The big Baghdad ball game live as it happens. Or if it hasn't happened, exclusive coverage of what might be happening, or what would happen if that didn't happen. It's a wild, happening show!

9.00 It's A Mad, Mad, Mad, Mad War
Zany comedy live from the combat theatre.

10.00 Oh, What A Lovely War!
Three housewives guess how high the Gulf War has pushed our advertising rates.

11.30 Crisis In The Gulf
Lots of people shouting, lots of guys in combat fatigues, lots of blurry videos, and a terrific light show.

12.30 Watch Out, Bilko's About!
Live from Baghdad, a CNN crew follows Ernie and the motor-pool as they hunt for spare parts in the bomb-shattered city. All goes well until Dobermann finds an unexploded Tomahawk missile.

1.00 News Update
The rest of the world's news.

1.01 Back To The Gulf
Yo, we're back on the road to Baghdad and are we gonna kick ass! We gonna boot butt, then we gonna boot more butt because that's what made Uncle Sam great. Yessir!

This has been a Steven Mosco production

Simon Bates

He writes with wit and clarity, he does a lot for charity

ISN'T IT FUNNY that, however strong you are, there comes a time when life seems to, I don't know, just seems to get on top of you, I suppose?

I guess that what I'm trying to say is that just because somebody doesn't seem to feel the pain on the outside, it doesn't mean they're not hurting on the inside.

And that's just how it feels for a lady who's written to me. I'm not giving her full name, let's just keep it at Her Royal Highness Diana, Princess of Wales, Countess of Chester, Duchess of Cornwall and Countess of Carrick.

❋ ❋ ❋ ❋ ❋

Well, to look at her, you would think she had everything. A handsome husband, two wonderful children, a house in London and spacious country retreats in Gloucestershire and Scotland.

For years she and – no, let's just call him Charles – were blissfully happy. Then, and like so many family tragedies this just came out of the blue, Charles had a tragic accident. Diana just thanked her lucky stars that Charles was still alive, she just wanted to give him all the love that a wife can give, she just wanted his arm to heal again. But I guess

that's just not the way life turns out. After the accident, Charles had some time to think. And perhaps because of that – who knows? – he and his wife just seemed to drift apart.

Diana spends a lot of time on her own now. And you know how it is, when you're thinking about your hopes, your fears, your dreams and all that kind of stuff, you get to wondering about what might have been. And that's how it was with Diana.

In her lonely bedroom, she says her mind keeps going back to one tune, a tune with all sorts of happy memories, a tune which always seemed to be playing when she and Charles were together...

(Insert National Anthem here please)

BATES

I've done a lot of work for charity, but I don't talk about it. Jimmy Savile has also done a lot of work for charity, and he, too, doesn't talk about it. Yet he is now Sir James Savile, OBE, and I am plain Simon Bates. I guess it's a funny old world, isn't it?

BOX

i

I'M A TERRIFIC BLOKE

I'm, I don't know, really one of the most popular guys around. Now, that sort of stuff could go to a bloke's head, but not me. I'm still 'one of the boys' and that's something I'm very proud of. Only last week I was joking with the guys on the door as I went into Broadcasting House. 'Hi guys, it's your golden hour because here comes Batesy,' I said. They were really bowled over, but came straight back quick as a flash. 'Excuse me, sir, have you got a pass?' they said. Now isn't that terrific?

ii

John Major, what a nice guy

There aren't many people who can say with hand on heart that they are, if you like, 'close' to John Major. But he and I have always shared an interest in social justice, in the fight against tyranny, and in supporting Our Boys in the Gulf.

So it will come as no surprise to learn about the long evenings we spend together in the flat above Number 10

Downing Street talking about how we can put this country back on its feet. And let's face it, that's what's important to us right now.

Only the other night, I asked the Prime Minister if he enjoyed my show. 'Oh yes,' he replied. 'Especially the recipes with little Raymondo and Arnold, your talking dog.' Wow, I guess that's just the kind of guy he is.

iii

iv

HE'S MATEY, HE'S BATEY, HE'S IN YOUR NO 1 PUNCH

'How was I supposed to know
Beatrix Potter suffers from
pre-menstrual tension?'

Getting into a State

Dillie finds it won't be over 'till it's over over there

There is little enthusiasm here in the US for the Gulf War. Even the gung-ho have their reservations. The money would be better spent ending the war on the streets of Washington DC; Washington Square even. Unlike Vietnam, however, they're not blaming the troops this time. On the radio, a woman was explaining her presence at a peace rally.

'I've got no argument with the soldiers,' she said. 'They're just doing their job. It's the Government I blame. And I want the world to know that President Bush is acting without my say-so.'

If the *Weekly World News* is anything to go by, President Bush is acting on the say-so of Mr Ric Flair, Wild Man of Wrestling. According to the paper, high-ranking government sources have confirmed that the President launched Operation Desert Shield only '…after the snarling ring villain urged him to knock Saddam Hussein on his butt…When Nature Boy talks, the White House listens.'

There is a picture of Ric. At a glance, he's a cross between Jocky Wilson and Diana Dors. Shoulder-length coiffed blonde hair, and a torso the size of Arizona, he certainly looks the man to do some serious butt-kicking. And since the launching of Desert Shield, George has been in constant contact with Ric, seeking his advice. It's reassuring to know that at least Mr Bush doesn't look to astrologers for guidance on world affairs.

Travelling up to New Hampshire, my connecting flight between Manchester and Lebanon was cancelled, so the airline provided me with a taxi instead.

'Hi! I'm Jerry!' said my driver, six-foot-three of affable New England Man. We talked, naturally, of the war.

'My cousin's out there with the military. He's in the front line,' said Jerry. 'I sure hope he gets back home safe. I sure hope he kicks Saddam's butt.'

Jerry expanded on his theme as we drove through the night. 'Yeah, we should kick ass,' he said, sounding strangely Presidential. 'We should kick ass, 'cause that's what we do. We are ass kickers, man. We are THE ass kickers.'

He laughed: one of those unnerving laughs that makes you wonder where he's hidden the cleaver.

'Tell you what we gotta do,' he went on, warming up. 'We should just go in there with the bi-i-ig bombs, man, none of this surgical shit, and we should just bomb everything, women and children most of all, and show them we're serious. Yeah. That'd end the war pretty damn quick.'

We drove on, the snow swirling in the light of the headlamps. 'It's real pretty countryside up here,' he said. 'You could see it, if it weren't dark.' He laughed again, and I felt underneath the seat to see if the cleaver was there.

'You hear that Mrs Hussein got out of Iraq? Bet you those Israeli guys are lookin' for her. Man, there ain't nothin' they can't do, those Israeli dudes. Tell you what they should do if they find her?'

'What?' I asked, more to show that I was listening than because I wanted to know the answer.

'They should bolt her to the side of a building in Tel Aviv, man, and say, OK Saddam, now send those Scud missiles over. Hit us, baby, hit us. Yeah. Anyways, those Scuds ain't worth a damn. We got Patriots. Yo! What a name, Patriots!'

The journey was endless, and Jerry unstoppable. 'What they should do, see, they should just bomb the shit out of Iraq, just total the whole thing and all the people, and then say to the Palestinians, hey, here's a big empty country, you can have it. Then rename Iraq Palestine.'

We arrived, at last, in Lebanon, New Hampshire. I'd have settled for Beirut, but at least the cleaver hadn't manifested itself. Jerry bade me a fond farewell. 'Still don't know what we're doin' fightin' a war all those miles away, man. Seems real crazy to me. Anyways, hey, nice talkin' to ya.' And he drove off into the night.

My friend Fern says it's all testosterone: 'Listen, they should put President Bush and Saddam Hussein in the same room, make them drop their trousers, and hand them a slide rule. End of War.'

It's not a bad idea. Perhaps Ric Flair and Jerry could be on hand to ensure fair play. And perhaps a little bit of all-round butt-kicking too. 🐟

'Yes, I lived the American dream – in my sleep!'

Simon Fanshawe

Curl up and diet

Which is worse, fitness or fatness? It's a gruel, gruel world

When Oliver Twist asked for more he was either courageously defying authority or being a right little porker. Because I like to eat, to me he's a role model. I've been known to ask for more of things I didn't even like just so I could eat. So a chap who wants seconds of gruel is my kind of guy. I don't want to give the impression that I'll eat absolutely anything, though. I won't touch blancmange or broad beans, but I suppose that's the price of a public school education. I can remember nothing of Latin or Greek but the taste of old school food will go with me to the grave.

This love of eating has two main disadvantages. The first is that despite what I have said, I actually like good food better than bad food. And liking good food in Britain is the most serious sin on the list after adultery and disliking Gazza. This is a bad attitude. While I admit that committing adultery with Gazza after a good meal would be both an insult to the cook and a venal sin, the love of good food on its own is, in my book, close to holiness. But in our sceptred, now semi-detached-to-France, isle it is regarded as something only indulged in by homosexuals (of whom I approve), the upper classes (for whom I have a worrying affection) and

frequently in connection with sex (of which I have a distant memory).

In Britain, to eat is a necessity but to enjoy it is a weakness of the flesh. Most people would rather smoke and drink themselves senseless and throw cash at the essentials of life (doing the pools, polishing the Vauxhall Astra, marrying off their children, buying more Dire Straits albums and washing in Radion) than spend an appreciable sum of money on a good, not even great, meal. Good food in this country is still limited to the idea of a decent steak (well cooked), Black Forest Gateau (not cooked) and Liebfraumilch (should be cooked). As a result, the main problem with dining out in this country is that it's practically impossible to eat good food without corporate finance. This means that not only am I getting very portly, but very poor as well.

The second disadvantage is fatness, or more correctly, fear of fatness. Like so many people, I'm not fat, I just think I need to diet. There's a difference. Being fat means that you can't get through doors, that if you sit on people they suffocate, and that if you lose three stone you're still fat. Wanting to diet is not about being fat, it's about being guilty. Sometimes I wish I could just eat and get fat and be done with

it. But if, over a sustained period, I eat lots, I develop tremendous feelings of guilt and an involuntary, irresistible need to go to the gym. This is a hideous experience. I'd rather listen to the Liberace CD collection. My trainer puts me through so much pain that by the end I feel that if she's so keen on 'feeling the burn' she should just go straight to Hell. What is worse, the exercise doesn't do all it's supposed to because afterwards I feel I deserve something nice. So off I go to eat the weight of a Sumo wrestler in doughnuts and ice cream. I feel I've earned it.

At this point, I'm back to square one, so I start a diet. The best ones are 'calorie controlled'. It took me a while to understand that it's supposed to be me who controls the calories and that they don't do it themselves. But now I've got that under my belt, I'm doing well. All you need for a calorie controlled diet is good maths. What you need to know is how much you are allowed each day. One thousand calories a day is 7,000 a week, 30,333 a month and 364,000 a year. Equipped with this information you are ready to start your diet.

On day one, stick to the one thousand. Even on day two just restrict yourself to a lettuce leaf, a low fat yoghurt and a violently sexual fantasy about a chocolate eclair and you'll be fine. On day three get out the calculator. If you want a nice Devonshire cream tea with fruit scones and extra jam at about 3,000 calories, go for it. Just borrow from next week. It works every time. You bought the house and the car with money you didn't have, so what's the harm in opening an obesity overdraft, borrowing the odd calorie from tomorrow, and the day after and the day after that...the trouble is that in the end, a combination of a diet and a calculator means that while trying to lose weight you put on a stone and a half now and you can't eat at all in 1993.

So my resolution this year is simply to drop dieting and exercise and just not to eat so much. But I worked out that if I live till I'm 70, I've got 36 New Year's resolutions left. I reckon that if I don't stick to it this year, I can make two next year and it'll be fine. Gruel anyone? 🦔

'It doesn't seem fair. I've lost 110 pounds but I'm still ugly, boring and stupid'

'You ask me to liven up your sushi diet then you complain'

'God! I hate a health-conscious parrot'

'It's simple. I buy all the diet plans then I can't afford any food'

'Actually, Doris is on the Viz diet plan!'

eally really good..!
We can't afford to monkey around no more...
The lads gave me 110 per cent!
I blame the Media myself!
YER! I hurt him wiv my left-jab in the Second round, but then he...
Let's give credit where credit is due.
Well–you can't win 'em all!
Nil desperand
I played well yesterday but this morning I was all tense..!
First hole I hit two-wood, then pretty good five-iron..
Really really bad..!
ZZZZZZZ
The lads are keen as Mustard...
The other side was t better Tea that's a

When the quote comes in

A sportsman's words can leave the press gang all at sea

Eddie Edwards glanced around the Press Room and saw 73 journalists waiting to take down his every word. There were Canadians, Americans, Japanese, Scandinavians and a group of proud, proprietary Brits, and they were there to listen to the most incompetent ski-jumper in the history of snow. So he thanked them for coming, puffed out his pigeon chest and proceeded to fill their note-books.

He told of his early, struggling days when he worked in a Scout camp and lived off their rejected food. He recalled how he had broken his jaw on a hill at St Moritz and tied it up with a pillow case to save on medical bills. He spoke of the difficulties of flinging himself from a 90-metre hill, with his spectacles steaming up on take-off and his helmet falling off in flight and overtaking him on landing. Finally, he confided his ski-jumper's prayer: 'Lord, may I get through this day with everything intact.'

I have long since forgotten Calgary and its Winter Olympics. But every time I am required to endure a rendition of 'The lads gave me 110 per cent', I remember Eddie with grateful affection.

Popular fallacy insists that only football produces such wearisome clichés. Not so, although it is probably true that only a Fourth Division football manager could have ascribed his team's success to 'the harmonium in the dressing room', and only Sir Alf Ramsey could have speculated upon England's chances of success against 'them Moroccyans'.

But rugby men are equally culpable, usually in accents mildly more refined. Some of my sensitive colleagues felt personally slighted by the England team's decision to boycott the press conference after their recent success in Cardiff. Victory wasn't really victory, they suggested, without the captain Will Carling announcing how pleased he was for the lads while cautioning us that these were early days and they were taking each match as it came.

England have now relented and normal service will be resumed with Carling reading from his familiar script after the forthcoming game with Scotland. I am reminded of the desperate plea which one rugby writer made to an earlier England captain: 'I've got to get ten paragraphs out of this. So say something, even if it's "No Comment".'

Rugby Union, of course, exists in that twilight world where money dares not speak its name. In the overtly professional sports, the players give press conferences at the drop of a hack.

The golfers, by and large, perform with all the passion of the speaking clock: 'First hole I hit two-wood, then pretty good five-iron to 12 feet, left the putt short, holed for par. Second hole...', and so on; 70 shots committed to mechanical memory. Occasionally, they surprise you with a small quip, like Tom Kite last year at St Andrews: 'The 13th is a great golf hole. It gives you a million options, not one of them worth a damn.'

Tennis players are blessed with similarly improbable memories, effortlessly summoning every plink and plunk of a frantic five-setter. Their narrow-eyed intensity is matched by the American press, who file into that charmless cavern beneath Wimbledon's Court One to inquire: 'Tell me, Bahris/Jahn/Ivahn, how did you feel at 15-30, third game, second set. Like, what was going through your mind?'

Their British counterparts tend to yawn through these exchanges, biding their time before slipping in an innocent query about the sex life of the star.

Such a question was asked at the most memorable conference Wimbledon ever staged, and it resulted in a chair-scattering brawl between a London tabloid and an Oregon broadsheet. McEnroe stormed out of that one in a four-letter fury, pursued by an earnest young lady from Georgia who was yelling: 'One more question, Jahn. How tall are you?'

The boxers are most co-operative by far, cheerfully answering the most outrageous questions while the doctor threads stitches through their eyebrow. And their one-liners are usually worth recording. The awesome Sonny Liston once beat up a gentleman named Chuck Wepner, popularly known as the Bayonne Bleeder.

'Is he the bravest man you've ever seen?' they asked Liston later. 'No,' said Sonny, 'his manager is.'

If all sportsmen were like Liston, or even Eddie Edwards, how easy would be the job of the quote-gatherer. Alas, most of them tend to react like the great Grover Collins from Tennessee. You will remember how Grover soured his moment of glory with an unforgivable cliché.'When you're the champion', he said, 'there's always some upstart out there, waiting to shoot you down.'

From a man who had just become the undisputed butterbean-eating champion of the world, we expected something rather better. 🖋

Patrick Collins is chief sportswriter of the Mail on Sunday.

A NEW WORLD RECORD! SEVENTY-FIVE CLICHÉS WITHOUT REPETITION IN A THREE MINUTE INTERVIEW.

Well, David...

For a while I lost the run of the balls...

...and Wayne drew clear at 8—6...

But I took advantage of a fluke shot in the fourteenth frame...

...then forced a break of 118 to level...

...and finally inched to a 50-2 lead.

I knew the title was mine when Wayne missed a simple black shot!

At which point, David, for the first time in my professional career, I felt in danger of losing control of my facial expression.

My oh my!

I WON! I WON! I WON! I WON! I WON!

Cue barging

To succeed in snooker a man has to have balls

For vitally important medical reasons this column has been written well before the beginning of the 487th World Snooker Championship, live from the Crucible Theatre in Sheffield. Snooker-related catatonia is not a widely-acknowledged psychological condition, but it certainly affects me every year at around this time. Eyes glazed, mouth agape, nostrils flared, all brain activity put on hold – yes, Eddie Charlton's just played another safety shot.

Of course, there's so much snooker on TV now that many people don't take any notice of it at all any more, other than to check up that Stephen Hendry has won as usual and that Steve Davis, though beaten 5-0 in the fourth round by a table lamp, is still saying that he's 'never felt better'. There are millions of ranking tournaments now, most of them played in places like Greenland and Liberia in pathetic attempts to widen the appeal of the sport. And with sponsors changing annually – so that you never know whether the Walker's Crisps Classic is really the Peppermint Aero Classic, the Vauxhall Astra Classic or the Heinz Alphabetti Spaghetti Classic – none of the tournaments really mean very much. But the World Championship is different. For one thing it lasts two weeks – and that's just Cliff Thorburn's annual match against Terry Griffiths. For another, it's sponsored by a really unglamorous brand of cigarette. And for a third, it has David Vine.

For these are the two weeks in which this most enigmatic, indeed mythopoeic of sports commentators devotes his body, soul and remarkable sweater collection to snooker. For 21 hours a day, we see Vine smiling cheerfully, interviewing defeated players ('I lost the run of the balls, David') and then introducing one of those ghastly hotchpotches of flukes and trick shots edited to the tune of Scott Joplin's 'The Entertainer'. It's a virtuoso performance – even the occasional snatches of Steve James or whoever is on the neighbouring practice table, are brought off with rare skill, so that the viewer is never left to suspect the real truth – that there's nothing more interesting to show. It's only

a shame that Vine's erstwhile deputy, the Son of God, won't be there to fill in when the going gets that little bit too tough.

And tough it will get. Snooker is no longer, sadly, an old man's game. All the characters of recent years are either, like Ray Reardon, completely past it, or, like most of the rest, so comfortable in beneficent middle-age that the fire seems to have gone out of their play. As a long-standing fan of both Dennis Taylor and Cliff Thorburn, I have been saddened to watch both men's gradual decline, to the point where Thorburn is not even in the top 16 any more, replaced by another zit-encrusted 12-year-old who can clear the

CHAMP

EX-CHAMP

table in a femtosecond. The relentless young Garys and Waynes of today somehow lack a certain charisma.

Of course, we still have Jimmy White. Is he, as they say, the best player never to have won the World Championship? Will he do it this year? Probably not, but everybody loves sport's great underachievers and White is adored in a way that poor old Steve Davis (career winnings £3m) could never be. Only last week, the Legendary Gnarled Rocker, Rod Stewart, told a new story about him in *Q* magazine. Recently arrived in England, Stewart found himself phoned up at six in the morning by fellow LGR, Rolling Stone Ronnie Wood, who was in some distress as at that precise moment, the aforementioned J White (for it was he) was assaulting his television set with a poker. It had clearly been a long night.

It's hard to imagine Steve Davis doing anything with a poker, unless of course he didn't have his cue handy. The problem with Davis is that there isn't even any pleasure in him losing any more, as he does it with such tedious frequency. Indeed, now I find I almost want him to win – and positively root for him when he plays one of the Garys and Waynes with wispy bits at the back of their skilfully sculpted barnets.

During the World Championship, though, all this is incidental. During snooker-related catatonia, the sufferer is not aware of such interesting things as results. All he can recognise are the clack of balls, the neutral tones of the referees, the unbelievably dreary tones of the players-turned-commentators, the embarrassed coughing of the audience (most of whom are desperately hoping that their bosses won't spot them when the match is repeated in the evening's highlights), the tumultuous applause given to flashy but routine shots, the strange silence that greets genuinely good shots, and, of course, Ted Lowe. The rest of the world doesn't exist. See you in a fortnight. 🐦

The pluck

Your man PETER TINNISWOOD

A pigeon clattered into the very centre of my chest. A brilliant feat of navigation, considering my slight, nay emaciated, build. It was as if a Sunderland flying boat were about to make a perfect landing in the middle of a senior citizen's paddling pool.

I was in the 1991 European City of Culture and desperately trying to find some. I was walking down a small, slinking side street off Grafton Street in search of a gents' lavatory.

It was ten o'clock of a fine, soft morning in early May, and the bird hit me with a startled thwack just above my building society paying-in book. The bird fell to the ground. It lay there motionless. I looked down on it, mortified and riddled with guilt. Good God, only three days earlier I had purchased an ashtray the size of a grouse moor from the Royal Society for the Protection of Birds.

As I stood there helplessly, feeling my shins turn pink with embarrassment, I was approached by an elderly gent elegantly dressed in bowler hat, bottle green spats and Barbour coat.

He examined the bird carefully for a moment, clucked his tongue three times and then with fastidious delicacy booted it hard in the rib cage. The pigeon opened its eyes, blinked gravely, shook its head, staggered to its pink, spindly legs and then launched itself into the air.

'That, my dear sir, is what we should do to all the bloody poets and painters in this God-forsaken city,' said the elderly cove.

And that, sez I, is what I call a city of culture.

I neither saw nor heard anything finer the whole of my stay in that beguiling and bewitching, infuriating and enchanting city where cart horses still clop down O'Connell Street, beggar women still accost you with their snot-festooned babies outside churches and pubs and the news vendor says to you after you've bought a paper: 'God bless you, sir. God bless you.'

If you know the brooding violence of Stockholm, the shyness of Oslo and the frenetic gaiety of Copenhagen, you'll feel at home in Dublin. It is the world's greatest Viking City. It has the presence of the misty Norselands. Its heart and soul are steeped in Scandinavian melancholy and guilt. Its charm, its excitement and its uniqueness is that it has transposed on this rich loam the full bloom of Irish fecklessness and gaiety, its excesses and prejudices, its wit and unrestrained, joyous friendliness.

It's summed up to me perfectly by the statue of James Joyce in Earl Street North. In the afternoon I paused there for a while to polish the silver band of the new bent-stem pipe I had bought shortly before my encounter with the kamikaze pigeon.

I looked at the statue of this great writer, revered and reviled in his own city, scorned and spurned in his own country, but never ignored – and round his jaunty walking stick someone had padlocked a rusting, sit-up-and-beg bicycle with a snuff-stained saddlebag the size of a small airship.

That's real culture for you. And so is buying a pipe.

Many years previously on my first visit to this lovely, porter-throbbing city I had bought a pipe for a friend. I presented it to the assistant, a cavernous-chested ancient with eyelashes the colour and texture of thick twist navy cut tobacco, who congratulated me on my choice and wished me many long and happy years of hacking and spitting with it.

I told him it was not for me. It was for a chum. The assistant frowned deeply.

'And what is the stature, colouring and temper of your friend, may I ask?' he said.

I described him fully, falling a morsel short of the slander I felt in my heart. The assistant whisked the pipe away, rummaged for several minutes in a rickety black oak cabinet and then returned with a pipe that looked like a sizeable fragment of the central heating system of the RMS Mauritania.

'Now this, sir, is the feller you're after,' he said. 'And if you're thinking of buying a box of matches for him, my consultative services are at your disposal.'

The sights and sounds of Dublin: the grey, milky light clinging and coiling round College Green.

The great, noble ceiling of Madigan's bar.

'Do you sell wine?' said a man.

'Yes,' said the barman.

'What colour?'

'White.'

'In that case I'll have two glasses of red.'

of the Irish

discovers some Dublin entendre

The chatter and clatter of Drumcondra, great hunks of bruised and purple meat in the windows of its butchers shops, the smell of strong tea and sizzling white pudding, dogs running loose and snapping, a lone black man mysteriously carrying a pair of roller skates under his arm.

All good crack. All good culture.

The great ebb and flow of Phoenix Park and the sweep of the Bay. The wind clackering the rigging of the fishing boats in the harbour at Howth and herring gulls mewing on the green and my taxi driver, the splendid Johnny Freeman, offering me advice on the arts and guiles of living the gracious life – everything from the emergency extraction of a wisdom tooth to the finest way of de-scaling a copper electric kettle.

The wondrous speech patterns. I arrived early at my hotel and the receptionist said: 'Now your room's not quite ready yet. Tell you what I'll do, sez you, I'll have a pint in the bar while I'm waiting. You will, of course.'

Drinking that sublime pint in the bar and reading the *Irish Times*, the finest morning newspaper in the whole of Europe, literate, pungent and a typographical wonderland.

So what's on this year in the European City of Culture?

What's on is Dublin itself. There's nothing more to be said. The galleries, the theatres, the concerts – fine. But the city and its people put on the best show by far. Listen to the people for just a second or so and you have a stage play of wit and drama, you have a symphony of lilting melodies and an opera to thrill the cockles of the tiredest old heart. Wander round and look and you have canvases fit to grace the finest galleries in the world.

The money clinks in your pockets – it's real money, too. Pound coins that look as though they mean business and mock the pathetic fly buttons that masquerade as coins across the puking, mewling Irish Sea.

The pavements sidle and whisper under your feet and you realise suddenly the greatest joy of all in Dublin. It is the only city in the whole of the world where you can potter around talking to yourself and no one takes a blind bit of notice.

That really is the mark of culture. That really is the sign of gracious and civilised living.

When they pick a location for the World's First Congress of Congenital Self-Talkers, Dublin is the natural.

As official delegate from East Molesey I shall take my place proudly in the conference hall and I shall chatter away the hours happily talking to myself. And I shall listen to the others talking and in the evening I shall trudge slowly back to my hotel and I shall say to the receptionist: 'My brain's not quite ready for bed yet. Sure and neither is any other sinner's in Dublin, sez you.'

But he won't hear – he'll be too busy talking to himself.

ILLUSTRATION: PETER SCHRANK

HONEYSETT

The Evil Lead

'Norman's got a wonderful boss, he often drops in on employees in his helicopter'

'Quick, get the car, there's a hedgehog
in the back garden'

'No, he doesn't worry me, I'm usually in bed by the
time he starts flying about'

CHECK YOUR
BOTTLES ARE
EMPTY
SERVICE

BOTTLE
BANK

'We all have parasites, Mr Jones. Yours just happen to be a bit on the large side'

'I'm sure we'd like to give Group Captain Peabody a big hand for his talk and demonstration on the Red Arrows'

'Can't stand dirty feet on seats'

How to be a has-been...
SOCIAL CLIMBER

The hey day

You've checked into the Waldorf and checked out with Beatty. You've dined with 'Heini' and tea'd with 'Taki'. But it's all downhill from here.

The slippery slope

1. *Hello!* invite themselves to your country home. But you haven't got a country home. 'I've got a timeshare in the Algarve,' you plead.
2. Mollie Sugden is 'invited' instead. You go to Ascot in a feather covered beret. But it's the year of the pill-box. You go to the Royal Enclosure and make friends with...
3. The royal bouncer. At a West End first night you arrive with Patrick Mower. You leave with an ex-Prime Minister. You ditch him when you discover he went to a state school. The *Tatler* condemns it.
4. 'Foul snobbery,' they say. 'I'm an egalitarian,' you squirm. You go to Gstaad. But Everyone's at Klosters.

The futile gesture

5. You call the *Sunday Times* style section to tell them about your invitation to the forthcoming royal wedding.
6. But *Private Eye* reveals how much you paid for it. You go out with Donald Trump...
7. But he returns to his wife. You become a model...
8. 'An Airfix model,' sneers Nigel Dempster. Debs' godfather Peter Townend puts you on his famous 'party list'.
9. 'Not to be invited,' it says. You ask the royals and half the House of Lords to a 'fab party'. Your aristocratic mother turns up. So does your father...

The killer blow

10. In his dustcart. You declare society junkets immoral and retire to his council flat in Plaistow.

The cruel twist

After your death, from excessive birching for a parking offence, the combined Inns repent. They hold a special dinner in your honour. 'It's very special,' says the Chief Commoner, 'we only hold 35 a year.'

MIKE CONWAY

ILLUSTRATION: GRAHAM HIGGINS

The Grand

Who is Britain's Number One
passion burns brightest for
Punch **set the course for**
picked a field of runners and
watch the action. DUNCAN
best Tattersall check

The Runners

Name: Yasmin le Bon
Form Guide: Beautiful supermodel, seen on all the best catwalks. But suffers from a husband who may be giving away several pounds to all the other runners.
Odds: 10-1

Name: Naomi Campbell
Form Guide: South Londoner-turned-supermodel. Dazzling looks, dangerous boyfriend (Mike Tyson). But is she any more than a clothes-horse?
Odds: 25-1

Name: Jerry Hall
Form Guide: Y'all know Jerry. Tall Texan with huge feet who may, or may not be married to Mick Jagger. Designs exotic swimwear. Advertises Bovril. Crashes parties.
Odds: 7-2

Name: Jasper Conran
Form Guide: Frock-designing son of Terence and Shirley. Has style in the blood. Too, too divine for words, my dear.
Odds: 15-8, second favourite

Name: Hamish Bowles
Form Guide: Outrageous, cross-dressing Style Director of *Harpers & Queen* magazine. Writes about new clothes, collects old ones.
Odds: 5-1

Name: Katherine Hamnett
Form Guide: Designer of red-hot gear for modern sex-kittens (and their cats). Famous for her political t-shirts. Serious and principled.
Odds: 10-1

Name: Bruce Oldfield
Form Guide: Barnado-boy designer whose clothes are worn by London's ladies-that-lunch and who is adored by all all of them.
Odds: 12-1

Name: Selina Scott
Form Guide: Newsreader-turned-*Clothes Show* presenter. Looks like Princess Di. But is that enough?
Odds: 20-1

Fashional

Fashion Victim? Whose frocks and furbelows? a style steeplechase, riders, then sat back to TERRACE put on his and made the book

Name: The Princess of Wales
Form Guide: Quite simply, the world's most famous clothes-horse. Her wardrobe has been one of the world's biggest news items for a decade and shows no sign of flagging.
Odds: Evens, favourite

Name: Marie Helvin
Form Guide: Ex-mega-model, ex-wife of David Bailey, ex-TV presenter, now designing a line of body-fitting clothes. A game filly, but are her best days behind her?
Odds: 8-1

Name: Denice Lewis
Form Guide: Famous-for-being-famous model and stars' escort. Seen everywhere. Looks stunning.
Odds: 25-1

Name: Lucy Ferry
Form Guide: The wife of Bryan. Always dressed in impeccable couture clothes by Chanel or Christian Lacroix. As thin as she is rich.
Odds: 7-2

The Course

As with all such *Punch* exercises, the atmosphere was one of ruthless scientific inquiry mixed with rigorous journalistic objectivity. A hand-picked team of high-style observers (a team that must remain anonymous for fear of retaliation from frenzied fashion folk) determined a set of questions that would have to be answered by any prospective Fashion Victim.

These questions did not cover the basic facts and figures of fashion – we assumed that any top-class performer would already be fully-informed – but concentrated instead on the principal qualities required by anyone willing to devote themselves to a life of style.

So, we wanted to know, did they really, really care about clothes – ie more than any reasonable human being would deem necessary, appropriate or morally justifiable? Did they seek out every possible opportunity upon which to display them? Would they go to any length to acquire the perfect figure or face – and then would they change them again when the Gods of fashion dictated? And finally, how well did they know Karl? Karl who? Karl Lagerfeld, dummy. We're talking about the reigning King of Couture. (Yves Saint Laurent is Monsieur le President.)

The course was arranged on a fence-by-fence basis. Fall at a fence and you were out. It was tough, even cruel. But, hey, that's what fashion's all about.

The Paddock

Runners in the race were whittled down from a long list of possible contestants. Piles of newspaper cuttings were consulted. Mounds of magazines were torn apart as we rooted out our chosen tribe. The judges were looking for a representative cross-section, covering all that glitters most brightly – and least profoundly – in our society.

Our final shortlist therefore contained 12 contestants (see left). There were three designers, one journalist, three models, three rock stars' wives and one TV personality. There was also the Princess of Wales. One of the world's most famous women, gorgeously dressed, famously beautiful – and the strong ante-post favourite.

And now, with no more ado, it's time to go down to the start. They're under starter's orders. And they're off! ☞

Fence one: **The Envelope**

The first fence, an open ditch, posed an apparently simple question: 'Would the runner go to the opening of an envelope?' In other words, just how likely is our would-be Miss or Mr Fabulous to be seen exchanging little jokes with another fashpacker at some ritzy metropolitan soirée? Jerry Hall, Yasmin Le Bon and Marie Helvin all sailed over this one: no A-list event can get beyond Z without one of these three looking sultry in a tiny black number.

The Princess of Wales also handled this fence with ease, but for a different reason: any self-respecting envelope would give its gum to see Diana turn up for its opening. Hamish Bowles – the 'Style Director' of *Harpers and Queen* magazine – also leaped over, his only criterion for a party being 'Fab! But what's the dress code?' (This is, incidentally, an important consideration for Hamish, a broadminded chap who sees no reason why a gentleman shouldn't turn up for a do in a nifty little Chanel skirt-suit.)

Sadly, however, other contestants were less fortunate. Katherine Hamnett (queen of ripped denim and micro-velvet – happy to come to a Punch Lunch, but much too busy saving the planet to go to PR parties) fell at the first. And both Bruce Oldfield and Lucy Ferry (the wife of Bryan) stumbled – nei-

Say cheese! (Main pic) *Boxer's moll Naomi Campbell (left) gets friendly with hot pop tot Sinitta.* (Above) *It's tiny skirts, but big smiles for model girlfriend Denice Lewis (right) and rock wife Julie-Ann Rhodes*

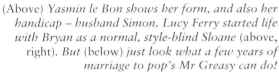

(Above) *Yasmin le Bon shows her form, and also her handicap – husband Simon. Lucy Ferry started life with Bryan as a normal, style-blind Sloane* (above, right). *But* (below) *just look what a few years of marriage to pop's Mr Greasy can do!*

ther are to be seen swilling cheap white wine at average ligathons. But their high society high profile (lots of pix in *Vogue* and *Tatler*) saved them in the end.

Fence two: **Kissy-kissy**

Closely related to the first hurdle, the question here is: 'Just how likely is our candidate to give a hearty "Mwah! Mwah!" when confronted with another contestant?'

The finest jump here came from the mystery model Denice Lewis. This former companion of red-blooded Romeos Jason Donovan and George Hamilton was seen at a January party clasping three different men on three different newspaper pages; to wit: Charles Dance, Robbie Coltrane and a 'mystery admirer' in, respectively, *Today*, *Today*, (they love her down there!) and the *Mirror*. Equally kissable is Streatham Supermodel Naomi Campbell – just make sure that Mike Tyson doesn't see you doing it.

The big faller was Selina Scott. Beloved though Selina is by the media, far though her fame may have spread (remember those American TV contracts?), and gorgeous though she may be as a clotheshorse, her personality is less than entirely welcoming to casual acquaintances. There's a tiny touch of Snow Queen about the red-blooded princess of satellite TV.

Fence three: **Lagerfeld's brook**

This is the first really strenuous challenge – one that may well sort out the nags from the thoroughbreds. Simply: 'Can a quick

phone-call get them lunch with Karl Lagerfeld?'

Once again, the Princess sails over. There's no one in the world who'd say 'No' to a snack with her – Prince Charles excepted, of course – but Karl would have to accept one caveat: Palace protocol prevents her from buying French frocks (though she was photographed arriving in Paris wearing one of Karl's red Chanel numbers – she knows how to get to the Gallic heart).

Equally successful was Hamish Bowles. We actually put in a call to Karl on his behalf and were immediately put through to the maestro. Impressive stuff, and we think we can take the lunch date for granted.

So can Lucy Ferry, but Denice Lewis comes crashing down. Being a pal of Robbie or Jason does not qualify one for friendship with Karl the Gaul. We doubt whether she could get through to him without being put on definite hold ☞

Our two finalists. Jasper Conran (right), short on style? Hamish Bowles (above) dresses sensibly for a day at the office: skirt, Chanel bag and mum's housecoat

– in fact that's just what happened to our determined *Punch* reporter posing as Denice. Marie Helvin was also a goner here. Perhaps Karl was feeling the competition from her new bodywear clothes collection.

Fence four: Pop chair

Fashion and Pop – it's a marriage made in heaven. Everyone knows that a top model comes free with a lad's first platinum disc. And once he's got his tottie, any self-respecting popster nips down to Gianni Versace for a suit like Eric Clapton's (and Phil Collins's, Sting's, Bruce Springsteen's, et al). So how much rock cred can our competitors come up with?

This is a doddle for Jerry Jagger-Hall and Lucy Ferry. But Yasmin le Bon is a surprise faller – she may be married to a singer, but he's ugly, naff and passé (none of which adjectives apply to her, by the way).

The PoW copes well; she may not have married into the trade but she certainly likes to fraternise with its merchants, much to hubby's horror. Bowles just stumbles over this one, as he can adapt to any, even heavy rock, circle, and Naomi, though not married to a star, certainly appears on the right videos. Jasper, despite the intellectual pretentions, has not completely shunned the pop world. Over he goes.

So, having completed the first nail-biting circuit of the course the remaining runners are Jasper Conran, Jerry Hall, Bruce Oldfield, Naomi Campbell, Hamish Bowles and The Princess of Wales. With these half dozen left, pundits believe that the PoW must be a dead cert but read on...

Fence five: Fab speak

Fashion is a world where you talk it like you walk it. So we want to know: 'Parlez-vous frock?'

Jasper Conran springs over this one: he's got the vocab ('So Coco, don't you know', 'Less is more, Muir is less', 'Fab', 'heinous') the gesticulations (pursed lips and hip-check) and the perfect pitch (a slightly nasal, drawling, bored delivery). Hamish's arch delivery, reminiscent of Cecil Beaton, also helped. He describes his entire life in the manner of a fashion caption – air stewardesses, for example, are 'Trolly Dollies'.

The Princess of Wales, despite a milennium of breeding and a top-class education has the innate and enviable ability to speak with the common touch (what other royal would write that she was 'over the moon'?), and has even stretched her retentive powers to recall the latest lingo 'Fab frock, my dear'. All the runners got over this one.

Fence six: Sartorial extremes

The question posed here is: 'What laughable limits and

physical tortures and mutilations are you prepared to got to to to get The Look?'

Way ahead at this fence was Naomi Campbell; a permanent diet, and an endless variety of wigs, false eyelashes and expressions. A close second was Hall; this, after all, is a woman who, for Bovril's sake, dresses like a chicken in public. Hamish – now in drag for a Philip Treacy hat show, now an androgynous plaything on a Gaultier catwalk – sailed over this, as did Jasper in his myriad permutations of navy blue Peter Pan. The PoW has never resorted to surgery, but has managed to keep the whole world in a state of suspense over her latest hairstyle or wardrobe manipulation. But Bruce Oldfield, her pal, was a faller – he remains eternally lean and immutable – does he really only have one dark polo neck?

Fence seven: **Tunnel vision**

'Do they think of nothing else but fashion?'

The true fashion victim automatically answers, 'Is there anything else?' The PoW, however, – what with her sons, her charities, and her mother-in-law's armed forces – has to think of a lot else. She is a sudden and dramatic faller, much to the consternation of the crowd.

Hall also falls – the determination to get that ring has preoccupied her for some years now, and all those houses and babies are another distraction. Hamish really thinks and dreams of nothing else and while Jasper tries to coat this frivolous world with a touch of intellectual varnish, at heart he enjoys little outside the world of design. What would you expect with Conran blood coursing through his veins?

Fence eight: **Own creativity**

It's bye-bye Naomi Campbell. Aside from herself, she has shown little interest in any creative endeavour. So we're left with Bowles and Conran, and its neck and neck as we approach the last hurdle...

Fence nine: **Fashion extremes**

The acid test. 'Do they really believe in it?' With these two fighting it out as we come into the straight it looks like a Stewards' Enquiry. But, at the very last moment, there is one final faller – and it's Jasper.

Of late, a cloud of maturity has cast a menacing shadow over the poor young Conran, and there may even be signs of a frustrated search for the heavier side of life. This will never do. So it all comes down to...

Fence ten: **The finishing post**

It's Hamish Bowles! You've probably never before heard of this floppy-haired fashion freak. He toils in obscurity, known only to those in the know. But, by unanimous acclamation of the *Punch* Probe Team, Hamish is the ultimate man of fashion. A wit, a dandy, he is the very personification of all that is *la mode* – a veritable Beau Brummel, and possibly Belle Brummel too.

We take great pleasure in saluting a famous winner.
MISS FABULOUS. 🐌

But Darling, where did you get it?

A dozen vital wardrobe items for the fashion victim

1. Gucci loafers: simple slip-ons at £175 the pair

2. A black leather Chanel handbag: a wee little baglet for a mere £415

3. Psychedelic lycra leggings: make any woman look like a hippy light show

4. A Day-Glo coloured Parka with fake fur trim on hood: look like a wally and glow in the dark – all in one go!

5. A thick black hairband worn low over the brow: guaranteed to make the brightest babe look like a simpleton

6. Silicone: plastic breasts are a fashion essential

7. A few Eastern crystals slung round the neck: because, like, you're really into, y'know, exploring your soul...man

8. An Armani catalogue tucked under the arm: but, then again, there's no reason why your soul shouldn't be well-dressed

9. Thigh high boots: great on Diana Rigg, stunning on Julia Roberts, totally dubious on anyone else

10. Any animal-print garment: in the immortal words of Lulu, 'I'm a tiger, I'm a tiger'

11. Seven inch high heeled Vivienne Westwood court shoes: aka courting disaster. NB: don't plan to go out – you can't actually walk in them

12. Lycra cycling gear: the cycle itself is a strictly optional extra

Alien journos

Is there a story the tatty tabloid won't swallow?

There would be without the *Sunday Sport*? Without the fearless investigative work of its tenacious reporting team, we would never have found out that Hitler was a woman, or that a World War II bomber had been found on the moon, or later that a World War II bomber had disappeared from the moon, or that a London bus had been discovered in Antarctica, or an extraordinary succession of fat ladies had been discovered almost anywhere the *Sport* looked.

Every week the *Sport* supplies a diet of racy tittle-tattle, of the sort matched only in the Style Section of the *Sunday Times*. Where on earth do they find these stories? We wondered if there was any story which the *Sunday Sport* would reject as untrue, uninteresting, or just plain bad taste. So, putting on our best heavily-disguised voices, we offered them the following bait.

MY MAM'S A SPORT STUNNA!

Our caller spoke in a heavy Mancunian accent, with a determined manner. John Burke-Davies picked up the phone at the Manchester news desk.

'Oh 'ello. My name's Keith Reid mate! I'm phoning about your Big Boobs contest. You see, I know someone who I think would win it, only thing is she's getting on a bit, well actually she's 74. And you see, the thing is it's actually me mam, like.'

'(After uncontrollable laughter) Sorry, I wasn't laughing at your mother. Really. But, exactly how big is she?'

'Well, she's got a 64-inch bust.'

'(Gargantuan laughter) Sorry again. Have you spoken to her about it?'

'Well I haven't, no. The thing is mate, I feel a bit embar-

Spoof my Sport

JOHN HIND and STEVEN MOSCO in fearless probe

rassed, like, to be honest, to ask her to pose what wi' her being me mam, like, and I wondered if you could think of any way of approaching her, like?'

'Can I ask what her full measurements are? I mean – is she 64-64-64 for instance?'

'Er, well, I don't know mate. I mean, I only know she's 64 up-top, like, cos I see her bras lying about the house, you know.'

'How old does she look, Keith?'

'Oh, I don't know, pal. Late fifties or so. She's quite an attractive woman, y'know.'

'I think the best thing you can do is give me her name.'

'It's Mavis, mate – Mavis Reid'

'Leave it to me. I'd like to get someone on to your mum personally, see whether she's interested.'

BALKAN BOMBSHELL'S THREE OLIVES

Our caller, 'Jeremy Cunliffe', had a respectable, but slightly nervous voice. He phoned the *Sunday Sport*'s London news desk. It was answered by Gary 'the Mouth' Thompson.

'(After formalities) I've just come back from a Greek island, where you can't get the *Sport*, actually, but anyway, I don't know whether this sort of thing would be right for your paper but there's a woman there, believe it or not, this is completely straight-up, who's got three breasts.'

'Ohhh yes!?'

'Now I don't know if there's that many women who have that.'

'Got any pictures we could run?'

'Yes, but nothing head and shoulders, that's the problem. I had to do them surreptitiously.'

'So you can't tell she's got three?'

'Oh yes, it's very definite that she's got three from the picture.'

'Is she good-lookin'?'

'Sort of, yes. But she's a bit of a sad character. The way people treat her's a bit, well, upsetting I suppose. But is that the sort of thing you'd be interested in?'

'Yeah, course! If it's a good picture – why not?...I mean, we'd do it as, y'know 'Warning To Holiday Brits – The Three-Breasted Woman Of Greece', or whatever.'

'Would I get paid for it?'

'Oh definitely, yeah. Say, a hundred quid...two hundred quid, maybe. Where are you calling from?...Can we pick it up?'

MY MUM'S TURNING INTO ELVIS

Our caller, the respectably voiced Alan Cunliffe, phoned Gary Thompson at the *Sunday Sport*'s London office, having been passed on by the *Sport* in Manchester who 'thought this kind of story was more for the Sundays.'

'Hello, I'm calling about my mother – I suspect she's been taken over by the spirit of Elvis Presley.'

'Oh yeah? Why's that then?'

'Well, it all started round about 1977 when he died. She started behaving strangely. She'd never been interested in music before then, but all of a sudden she started singing his songs everywhere – I'd come home from work at the shoe shop to find her screaming 'Hound Dog' and 'Jailhouse Rock' while she was doing the dishes.'

'Oh yeah.'

'Then she started to wiggle her hips in a very suggestive manner, making pelvic thrusts all the time, which was quite embarrassing when visitors came round.'

'Will your mum play ball with the story? I mean will she talk to us? This sounds like a good one.'

'I'm not sure. The thing is, she's become a bit of a recluse now, and she's started eating a lot, so she's got quite fat now. She just locks herself away much of the time, dresses in white flares and dark glasses, and sings cabaret songs.'

'Well give us your mum's number and we'll ring her up and see what she's got to say.'

'Is this the sort of story you'd be interested in running then?'

'Oh yeah. We do a lot of reincarnation stories and stuff like that. What's your mum's name? Irene Cunliffe? OK, I'll get one of the lads to give your mum a call and see if we can do a story on her. Thanks for ringing.'

YOU AIN'T NOTHIN' BUT A HOUNDDOG!

I SAW ROBBO'S FACE DOWN MY LAVVY PAN

Our caller rang John Burke-Davies at the *Sport* in Manchester, and spoke in a sharp Mancunian accent.

'Hello mate. Me name's Dave Wedbury. I'm phoning from Manchester. I've gorra story that might interest ya. It's a bit like one you had on't cover on Sunday about Gazza's face on White Cliffs of Dover.'

'Ohh, yes?'

'What it's actually about is that last night I came 'ome from the pub and when I got in there was like this apparition of Bobby Robson floating in the lavatory in me 'ouse. I mean I'm totally sort of mystified about it. And like I had a couple of me mates with me they all saw it. Now, I mean, if we can get a photo of it, if it happens again tonight, would you be interested in seeing it at all?'

'I'd certainly be interested in seeing it, yes.'

'Right, now, would you pay for a photo like this?'

'Err, yeah. But it wouldn't be an arm and a leg. I should tell you that.'

'I mean, wha's sor' of amount, like?'

'Maybe 50 quid, say. I'm not sure what you've got there, but I'd like to see a picture. Have you got the address? (Becoming more serious now) Can you make sure it's to the *Sport* and not the *Sunday Sport*?'

GIRLS GIGGLE AT MY GRAPEFRUITS

Our caller had an East Midlands accent. He spoke to Neil McKay, news editor at the *Sport* in Manchester.

'I wonder whether you'd be interested in this. I have...right,

to get to the bottom of this a...a...a doctor has told me I have extraordinarily large, er, testicles.'

'Ohhh.'

'I know that sounds ridiculous. But apparently it's a glandular something or other, which he says is extremely rare. I went to a local doctor called Singh, who put me onto this specialist just off Harley Street who said it's partly hormonal, apparently.'

'What's your name?'

'Stephen Mainwaring.'

'With a V or a PH?'

'PH.'

'Can you tell me how large they are, Stephen?'

'Oh, well, some bloke I drink with says they are like grapefruit, But that's exaggerating.'

'What problems does it cause you?'

'It's more a sense of embarrassment, at swimming-pools and on holiday.'

'Let me take your number and phone back after lunch.'

'OK, yes. But if you did write about my testicles would there be anything in it for me?'

'A few quid, yes, 50 quid. Or more, maybe, if they're really big. But I don't know whether we could show them. Can you describe them for me?'

MY TOTTIE'S TONTO OVER TINPOT TYRANT

Our caller, 'Jeffrey Frask', spoke to *Sunday Sport* reporter Gareth Woodgates, in a reasonably posh voice.

'I feel a bit stupid calling you, Gareth, but my wife, my wife is well, infatuated is the best word – infatuated with Saddam Hussein, believe it or not.'

'Your wife?'

'My friends say "Dismiss it as a joke", but the way I see it, it's serious. She collects pictures of him. It's partly, I know, because she's always had this thing for dark men with moustaches – David Niven, Clark Gable, the sort of people you might get in Fry's Turkish Delight adverts but now she's been collecting these bloody pictures of Hussein.'

'Are you serious?'

'Oh – absolutely. In a sense, it's just bloody ridiculous, really – what I've had to put up with over the last four or five weeks. Obviously, I can see that there's nothing profoundly wrong in her going on about him.'

'She has fantasies about him, as well, does she?'

'Well, I am certainly given the impression she finds him very appealing. I mean, what do you make of it? If you had a wife who fancied Saddam Hussein and cut out cuttings of him, would you not find it rather bizarre?'

'Well – he's not the most appealing character.'

'Well, that's the point – she thinks he's dashing.'

'And is it really getting to you?'

'Yes, it seems to me to have become an obsession.'

'Does she video him, when he's on the box?'

'She has.'

'Listen, Jeffrey, I think it's entirely possible we might want to come round and meet Mrs. Frask and take some pictures.'

'But I wonder what she'd think of me telling you?'

'Well, she wouldn't have to know, would she?'

With that our telephonic investigation ended. The *Sport* also printed a series of letters sent to them by us under a range of aliases. These presented pert agony aunt and businessman's friend Fiona Wright with a range of bizarre sexual conundra. Sadly, however, considerations of space and good taste prevent their publication here.

'I warned her about eating dead sheep'

The David Icke

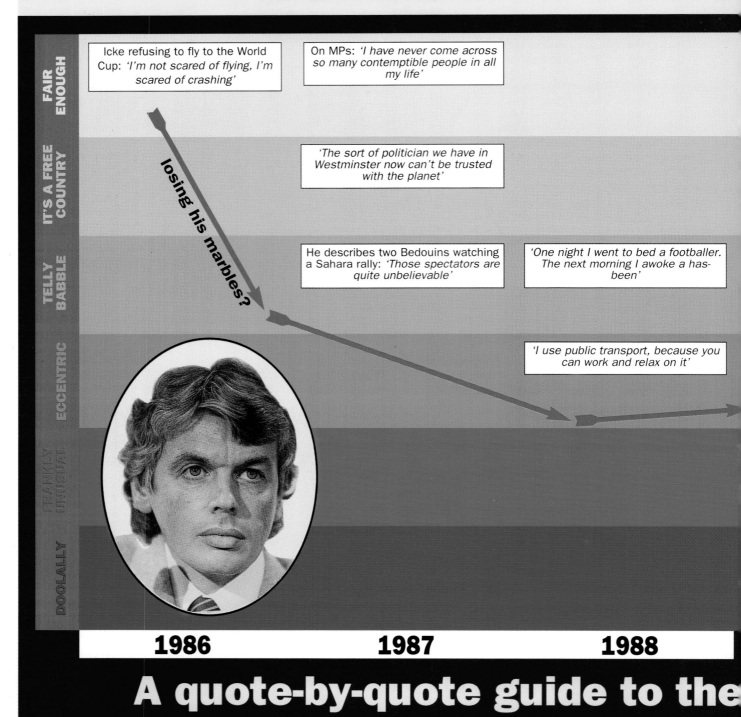

FAIR ENOUGH

IT'S A FREE COUNTRY

TELLY BABBLE

ECCENTRIC

FRANKLY UNUSUAL

DOOLALLY

Icke refusing to fly to the World Cup: *'I'm not scared of flying, I'm scared of crashing'*

On MPs: *'I have never come across so many contemptible people in all my life'*

'The sort of politician we have in Westminster now can't be trusted with the planet'

He describes two Bedouins watching a Sahara rally: *'Those spectators are quite unbelievable'*

'One night I went to bed a footballer. The next morning I awoke a has-been'

'I use public transport, because you can work and relax on it'

losing his marbles?

1986   **1987**   **1988**

A quote-by-quote guide to the

When David Icke decided to change his job description from 'snooker presenter' to 'Son of God', few people were more surprised than his local vicar. He told the *Daily Express* that the Lord's would-be offspring had never been to his church. 'He's never shown any sign of being enthusiastically spiritual in the past,' said the sceptical cleric. 'It's unlikely that he's the Son of God.'

This, it seems, is the general theological consensus. We con-

tacted a number of religious leaders to canvass their opinion. 'You're the experts,' we said. 'Is David Icke the Fourth Man in the Holy Trinity, or what?' Frankly, they were less than enthusiastic about the *Grandstand* man's claims to divinity.

'As far as I'm aware, the Church of England Doctrine Commission doesn't have him on the agenda for its next meeting,' said a spokesperson for Lambeth Palace.

'I think it very unlikely,' said a spokesperson for Cardinal

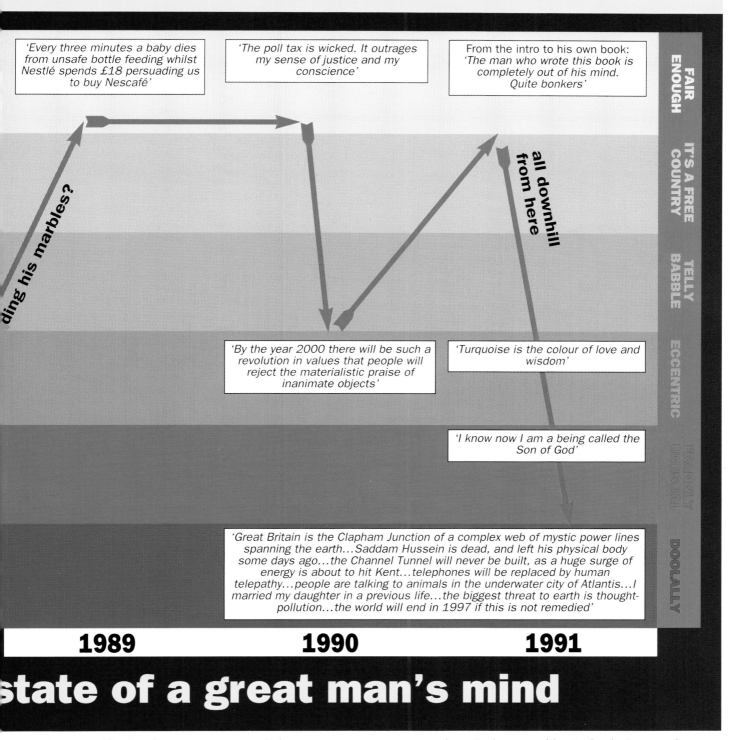

Marbleometer

'Every three minutes a baby dies from unsafe bottle feeding whilst Nestlé spends £18 persuading us to buy Nescafé'

'The poll tax is wicked. It outrages my sense of justice and my conscience'

From the intro to his own book: 'The man who wrote this book is completely out of his mind. Quite bonkers'

FAIR ENOUGH

IT'S A FREE COUNTRY

TELLY BABBLE

ECCENTRIC

FRANKLY UNUSUAL

DOOLALLY

...ding his marbles?

all downhill from here

'By the year 2000 there will be such a revolution in values that people will reject the materialistic praise of inanimate objects'

'Turquoise is the colour of love and wisdom'

'I know now I am a being called the Son of God'

'Great Britain is the Clapham Junction of a complex web of mystic power lines spanning the earth...Saddam Hussein is dead, and left his physical body some days ago...the Channel Tunnel will never be built, as a huge surge of energy is about to hit Kent...telephones will be replaced by human telepathy...people are talking to animals in the underwater city of Atlantis...I married my daughter in a previous life...the biggest threat to earth is thought-pollution...the world will end in 1997 if this is not remedied'

| **1989** | **1990** | **1991** |

...state of a great man's mind

Hume, the spiritual leader of Britain's Roman Catholics.

Wondering if the Jews would be a bit more welcoming of the news that a Messiah had come to usher in the new millennium, we contacted Adler House, seat of the Chief Rabbi, Lord Jakobovits. But alas, no. 'I don't think the Chief Rabbi would comment on such a claim,' said a spokesperson.

Elsewhere, Mr Icke's revelations Jahweh-wise have sadly fuelled cruel speculation that he may have – as the Australians say – a roo loose in the top paddy. Or that he is, to use language with which he is all-too-familiar, one pot short of a frame.

Has he, to put it bluntly, mislaid his marbles? In a search for conclusive evidence, *Punch* researcher Steven Smethurst combed the cuttings to produce this definitive guide to David Icke's psychological state-of-play over the past few years. We believe that it will prove to be an invaluable tool for our readers. As the old saying has it: the public has a right to know. 🐒

Wapping Yarns

Eastern Europe's tyrannies have fallen. But what of East London's? How long can the Murdoch gulag survive? STEPHEN PILE on the *Times'* new leader. RICHARD LITTLEJOHN on life under the *Sun*'s Kel-boy MacKenzie

How do they do it? How does the Henley Centre for Forecasting know? In December 1989 we were all roaring round in Porsches, wearing red braces, firing everybody, snarling at employees and phoning New York from the back seat of the car. Then suddenly several bods in Henley piped up that on 1 January, 1990 we would have a caring decade with more interest in human relations, greening the supermarket and gentle behaviour.

And just look at it. By 4 January Norman Fowler had resigned from the Cabinet to spend more time with his family. (What is this, a hippy commune?) Then Peter Walker follows suit, then the Berlin Wall comes down, then Mandela is released and then every totalitarian state bar Cuba collapses overnight. And it was still only March. I mean, Henley is a quiet place. How do they hear all this?

And then, with Eastern dictators falling by the minute, all eyes turned to Wapping. Until now, the hardline Murdoch states had shown little sign of a thaw. The tyrants seemed secure, the gulag unchanging. High walls still surrounded the Wapping plant and, at Checkpoint Charlie, border guards dressed like absurd South American admirals still strutted beneath the gaze of a security camera.

Serfs at the *Sunday Times* still groaned under the iron rule of the hated hardliner, Andronil, who has just seized a local radio station and is now haranguing the London populace between six and nine every morning with his tough, rasping views on his own breakfast show. But observers now believe that his days in supreme power are numbered and I will tell you why.

For some months there have been small signs of change inside the gulag. Crazed Kelvin MacKenzie, editor of the *Sun*, was forced by outside opinion to appoint an ombudsman to deal with human rights and complaints. He then held a press conference to explain his paper's brutal policies. In the West we assumed this was just window dressing that masked an unacceptable regime.

But then came the news that stunned the Free World. Charlie Wilson had fallen as editor of the *Times*. The suffering masses on the paper, who have been through so much, received the news in silence, their feelings now battered beyond any kind of reaction. The revolution had come quietly. The howling Scots tyrant was gone. Vaclav Jenkins was taking control in the name of civilisation, standards and decency.

Only now are full details beginning to reach the outside world of the horrifying regime that Charlie ran. For years, people escaping from the gulag had spoken of a small, foul-mouthed ex-Marine boxing champion throwing typewriters across the office, bawling out his executives in front of terrified staff and shouting 'I hate poetry' at the literary editor.

But even these eyewitness accounts pale when compared with new evidence coming out. Some shaken survivors even speak of the sheer difficulty of finding printable anecdotes that could be used for a leaving speech in his honour. One reporter offered for inclusion an apocryphal but oft-repeated story about how Charlie had lost his temper with his ex-wife and held the poor woman out of the window by her ankles.

A cartoonist said: 'I've got an anecdote. One day I went into Charlie's office and the conversation went like this:

Cartoonist: 'Please may I have paternity leave?'

Editor of the *Times*: 'Do you know how old I am?'

Cartoonist: 'No, Charles.'

Editor: 'I'm 50 today.'

Cartoonist: 'Congratulations, Charles. Happy birthday.'

Editor: 'Do you know why I won't be having any more paternity leave?'

Cartoonist: 'No Charles, why?'

Editor: 'Because my sperm has gone all yellow and manky.'

Among cartoonists this became a bit of a catchphrase. 'Oh, I'm feeling rather YAM today.'

Other survivors have spoken of terror mingled with affection. Once, in a meeting of senior executives, Charlie took off his jacket, said 'Excuse me' and launched himself flat on his belly across the coffee table. He then invited the most rounded and

🐉 Wapping yarns

Pickwickian of the executives present to follow his example. 'Uh, no, no, not for me, thank you, Minder,' he replied. (The editor of the *Times* was openly called Minder in honour of the semi-criminal TV series. The nickname pleased him.)

Some brave souls tried to wind Charlie up in the hope of getting another foul Charleyism to put in the growing collection. During one tantrum Charlie was throwing a mass of inadequate pictures in the air. 'I'm thinking of leaving this paper,' said a crushed executive. 'Oh yes?' said Charlie nastily. 'And what are you going to do?' 'I'm thinking of writing my autobiography, Charles.' This was too much for the editor of the *Times* who exploded 'Oh yes, and what are you going to call it? I'm a f****** c***?'

Like Mussolini and Stalin, Charlie made the railways run on time. He produced the paper on a moonlight flit to Wapping and he was the right man to edit an old, creaking British institution in the Eighties. But Murdoch is faster than anyone to spot the winds of change.

After only four days in office, Vaclav the Liberator stood on a desk near the art department. 'It is said I am a mild man. Well, I won't be throwing typewriters across the office.' The message was clear: Charlescu is dead. The adoring, grateful masses listened to this literate, thoughtful man as he spoke of a return to the highest journalistic values.

In fact, his appointment seems a typical bit of Murdoch opportunism. He had handed in his notice at the *Sunday Times*, as everyone does when they stop to think about it. He was moving his column to the *Indy*.

This outraged the ageing Australian ideologue who has been traumatised by the success of the *Indy*. After only two weeks of publication he knew that this was serious competition. He has never quite got over the discovery that you could actually make money by going upmarket.

When the *Independent* poached Miles Kington from the *Times* Murdoch went beserk. And when Jenkins started off down the same path, Murdoch offered him the editorship. The fact that he initially turned it down shows how much the currency has been devalued since the days when Harold Evans and Charlie Douglas-Home thought the job worth fighting over.

He was asked to sleep on it and next morning this principled man sacrificed his life and his own proper work writing columns to help this ravaged community find self-respect. In everything he has said, done and written since then he has shown himself to be a man of the Nineties.

First, his editorials have abandoned Charlie's coarse Thatcherite triumphalism (one of them even called for the legalisation of soft drugs). More significantly, a *Times* leader criticised Edwina Currie for the frivolity of her views on Romania. It is the end of the line for that kind of ranting, simplistic story.

Second, he told his broken staff that he would not be bringing in his own people. He has shown genuine enthusiasm for the existing team's skills and for getting the best out of them. Profile writers describe him as liberal, whereas he thinks he is Thatcherite, but it hardly matters because he has that all-important feel for debate and consensus that is the inevitable European and global path before us.

Things are going well and already the paper is ceasing to be a cause for shame. It is all a far cry from the blood-curdling conflicts that Harold Evans describes in *Good Times, Bad Times*, his record of editing this paper. But will it last? What has happened? Is the Wapping revolution like Czechoslovakia or Romania?

The key to this lies in Murdoch's surprise appointment of Andrew Knight as managing director of his entire operation in Britain. There was something odd here, cynics cried. Knight was respectable. There was nothing remotely shady about him. He had just transformed the *Daily Telegraph* from the sort of social embarrassment your great aunt reads into a sharp, elegant, modern and increasingly independent newspaper. Why was Knight invited to Wapping? It was like getting Cardinal Hume to reorganise a brothel.

The only possible explanation is that Murdoch is now facing death as anyone who has seen the seat of his trousers will tell you. If you ever see old men you will know that their bottoms wither away to nothing. It is nature's way of preparing us for the long centuries ahead when it will not be necessary to sit down. Anyone who has seen Murdoch in recent years will know that he is now bottomless and his trousers hang. Put this together with his conversion to Christianity and the fact that he has given his wife a seat on the board of News Corporation and the plan becomes clearer. The day is coming when, Lenin-like, he will be embalmed and stuck in a Portakabin near the main gates at Wapping. And so he is looking for an heir. In Britain he has at last found the elegant, disciplined, Oxbridge, establishment figure of Knight who is the other side of the complex Murdoch character.

So where does this leave Andronil? He is a Maoist who believes in permanent revolution. His appetite for blood on the carpet is undimmed by years of tyranny. And he is still driven by the need to fight some mirage establishment of which Peregrine Worsthorne seems to be the only surviving member. At a leaving dinner for a staff man, Andronil gave a speech raving about his hatred of the Oxbridge élite.

Has he really thought this one through? After all, people who go to Oxbridge quite often do so because they are extremely clever. Margaret Thatcher went and she was the daughter of a grocer. Jenkins, Knight, even the bottomless Murdoch all went. On his morning radio show, we have heard the voice of the dinosaur. In one tirade he dismissed global warming as 'a millennial fad' and said that if London's climate became Mediterranean and Scotland was like Colorado that suited him fine.

Later he tore into Dave Nellist, the Labour MP for Coventry, asking if he would support an anti-poll tax group that was allegedly Militant inspired. 'I have to think,' said Nellist, 'of my old ladies in Coventry who have to put money in the jam jar on the mantelpiece...'

'Yes, yes, I can hear the violins,' snapped the dictator, 'Will you be supporting this group, yes, or no?' Andronil is not given to gentle, persuasive questioning.

A lot of people don't agree with a word Dave Nellist says, but on this occasion he won complete sympathy because Andronil lacks the subtlety required for these more complex, democratic days.

The hooligan right-wing views that seemed refreshing in the Eighties now merely jar. He may not worry about global warming and poll tax objectors but Mrs Thatcher, the Cabinet, every scientist on the planet and all the *Sunday Times* readers do. Simplistic ravings are no longer enough. Get thee to Henley, Andronil.

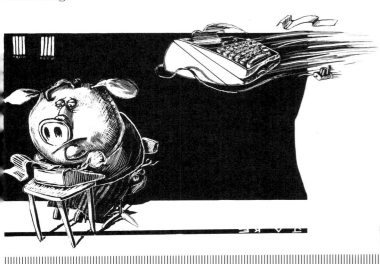

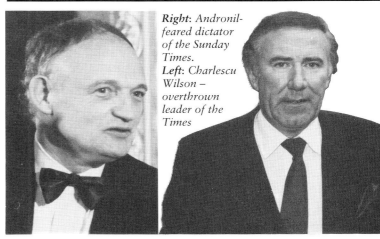

Wapping Heroes ... and Villains

Right: Andronil-feared dictator of the Sunday Times.
Left: Charlescu Wilson – overthrown leader of the Times

Murdoch – the Supreme Being with two former henchmen, now non-persons

Vaclav Jenkins – white hatted hero of the revolution

EXCLUSIVE!

Sizzling *Sun* Man's ordeal. He tells all to your No. 1 *Punch* ☞

CRAZY KELVIN ATE MY BRAIN

Sun man Littlejohn tells his own shock story

IT USUALLY occurs just before dinner in the muesli belt.

'I don't think you've met Richard,' our hostess says to another guest, probably a media analyst or an outreach co-ordinator with the People's Republic of Islington. 'He's a journalist.'

'Oh, how fascinating,' they respond, taking another swig of Bulgarian Chardonnay. 'Which newspaper?'

'*The Sun*,' I inform them.

The news is about as welcome as Marietta Higgs at a playgroup. Embarrassed silence is followed by throat-clearing and subject-changing.

That's me, folks. The man in the Bateman cartoon.

Our hostess comes to the rescue. 'He did used to write for *The Standard*, you know,' she explains. Sighs of relief. At least I'm not going to fart at the table or eat my petits pois off my knife.

Over dinner, once the initial shock has worn off, someone remarks that they quite enjoyed a piece they'd read in the old Currant Bun.

'But you look like a *Guardian* reader to me,' I bait them.

'Actually, I am. But my secretary brings

The Sun to work.'

That's the usual excuse. Or 'I found one on the train.' Or 'I don't buy it myself, but we have to MONITOR the tabloids for our anti-sexism committee.'

Someone must buy it. It sells 4,000,000 a day and has more ABC readers than the broadsheets put together.

Reading *The Sun* is like masturbation. Everyone does it, but very few admit to it.

After 20 plus years, Britain's biggest selling daily newspaper is still an outsider.

It may support the Prime Minister, but it is by and large anti-politician, anti-establishment and libertarian in a way the fascist 'liberals' in the chattering classes are not.

That's why I joined. There's a terrace mentality about the place. No-one likes us, we don't care.

The football analogy is apt. To get into *The Sun* editorial offices at Wapping, you have to walk under a a sign reading: 'You are now entering SUN country.' It is as daunting as the 'This is Anfield' notice greeting visiting teams in the tunnel at Liverpool FC.

What attracted me most ('How are you going to make The Money last for 600 words?' – Kelvin MacKenzie) was the

refreshing lack of pomposity which characterises other popular papers.

If it's funny, it usually gets in the paper, no matter who it upsets. *The Guardian*-reading guardians of our morals admire that philosophy in 'alternative' comedians, but abhor it in *The Sun*.

Some of the best stuff never makes it in to the paper. Like the Lizometer, which was to have swung backwards and forwards as La Taylor see-sawed between life and death.

Or the photograph of David Rappaport's funeral, with one normal-sized man surrounded by dwarfs. 'Caption it Gulliver's Travels,' said MacKenzie, before he thought better of it.

The paper's irreverence and vitality emanate from MacKenzie, who retains a schoolboy's enthusiasm.

In seven months, I've yet to see the ranting demagogue of Fleet Street myth. But then they say Ceaucescu was a shy man with a sense of humour, too.

If you set out to offend people, merely working for *The Sun* puts you ahead on away goals before you start.

While the chattering classes find it so offensive, I'm happy to be in the Bateman Cartoon.

'I've come in period costume'

'I'm sorry, Ma, but how many times have I told you it's not safe down these alleyways?'

'So it's true – lorry drivers do pull out when you least expect it'

Dukes of

As Princess Anne gets nabbed again,

There is a small but happy band of Britons which looks on the motorway system not as an endless parade of queues and contraflows but as a delightful link between one's palace up in town and one's hice down in the country. They know that these hundreds of miles of tarmac are specifically designed for their pleasure, their indulgence and personal performance testing of some of the fastest cars in the land.

'What ho!' they cry as their high-speed Pirelli Cinturatos bite the tarmac of the M4 where it begins its majestic journey west, cresting the Hammersmith flyover just in front of Mr Beecham's Lucozade factory.

'Jolly good!' they cheer while indulgent chief constables line their routes saluting as they pass at velocities which would have frightened Juan Fangio, let alone the horses.

Who are these sultans of speed, these viceroys of velocity, these potentates of power?

Stand up, Windsor Road Warriors. This outlaw road gang is none other than our own Royals, the fastest family in the land. And now, in the week after Princess Anne was twice booked for giving it too much green welly in Gloucestershire, *Punch* is proud to present the complete, unexpurgated, ticket-by-ticket account of their magnificent motorised escapades, starting with...

ⓘ115 HRH PRINCE CHARLES, THE PRINCE OF WALES

CAR: 5.4 Litre V8 Aston Martin Volante
ENDORSEMENTS: None
TOP RECORDED SPEED: 115 mph

Underneath the cultivated, English gentleman exterior beats the heart of an Ayrton Senna. Not only does Charles drive one of the world's fastest cars, but he can really

put the pedal to the Royal metal. Off public roads, he once drove the late Graham Hill's Formula 1 Brabham racing car around Thruxton race circuit at 150 miles an hour – and span off.

Back among the hoi polloi, he was clocked at 115 mph travelling along the M4 between Windsor and Gloucestershire by a woman who later explained: 'I was doing 70 when Charles absolutely rocketed past me. I followed him down the motorway doing between 105 and 115 all the way. His bodyguard was clinging desperately to the dashboard.'

Charles has also had a number of other brushes during his motorist days, including driving along a footpath around Windsor, scattering the strollers before him, and has even had a delightful piece of motoring junk mail from a company eager to get him to enter a competition.

Addressed to Mr HRH Prince, Charles Buckingham Palace, The Mall, it read, 'Dear Mr Prince, what would your neighbours in The Mall think if you pulled up outside Charles Buckingham Palace in a brand new red Ford Fiesta, complete with sun roof and alloy wheels?'

What indeed.

ⓘ110 PRINCE MICHAEL
CAR: Bentley Mulsanne Turbo
ENDORSEMENTS: Four
TOP RECORDED SPEED: 110 mph

For someone who has been the President of the Royal Automobile Club for more than ten years, Prince Michael sets a pretty bad example. He's been fined for speeding and careless driving, and was once presented with a certificate by the British Safety Council for driving in the annual London-Brighton veteran car rally 'like Toad of Toad Hall'.

The citation read: 'Presented to Prince Michael of Kent for the extraordinarily bad example he set other drivers through acts of stupidity on the road.'

The fastest speed he's ever been booked at by the police is 110 mph, five short of the record set by his Royal cousin. But on the other hand, he did manage to do this in a 50 mph speed limit area, making him the most reckless Royal rocketing around the roads of Britain today.

He's also the most recent one to have been banned from driving – although only for a fortnight – for doing 103.7 mph on the M4 in July earlier this year.

'He remembered passing a number of vehicles in the centre lane proceeding not very much slower than himself,' his brief told the Magistrates Court at Chippenham in Wiltshire.

The Prince pleaded guilty to the offence, committed on one of his regular 108-mile commutes between his London and Gloucestershire homes. The trip must usually take him around an hour.

FAR OUT! GROOOVY!
YO! CHUCK

hazard...
Chris Ward reads the royal log-book

'My other car's a Bentley,' toots the heavily be-Toaded Prince Michael as he goes for that royal speed record

⬤110 HRH PRINCE EDWARD
CAR: 3.5 litre V8 Rover Vitesse
ENDORSEMENTS: None
TOP RECORDED SPEED: 110 mph

Rock Steady Eddie isn't known as much of a macho man, but he's gaining something of a reputation – as yet unendorsed by the police – as a real speed merchant on the roads. When it comes to speed, at least, he's Really Useful.

Not only did he once almost beat former Formula One champion Jackie Stewart in, of all things, a Land Rover race, he's also known for terrorising the wildlife of Scotland at speeds of up to 110 mph.

'They shot past me,' said one shell-shocked Scot who had the pleasure of being overtaken by the Prince on the A9 between Perth and Stirling.

'The car kept weaving in and out of the traffic and was twice flashed by oncoming traffic.'

Buckingham Palace, of course, chooses not to confirm Ed's speed. 'As far as I can recall,' recalled one aide vaguely, 'it was more like 70 mph.'

What? Windsor? At this time of night?

⬤110 HRH THE DUCHESS OF YORK
CAR: 5 litre V12 Jaguar XJS
ENDORSEMENTS: None
TOP RECORDED SPEED: 110 mph

Fergie comes in joint second with Edward and Michael in the Royal speed stakes, but is never likely to become a courtroom star following the fitting to her car of a police radar detector.

This attachment – a present from the Duke of York who has one on his Jag – is less-than-popular with the police.

'Such a device is illegal,' intoned a spokesman for the Police Driving School at Hendon where all members of the Royal family are given lessons in driving at speed (ostensibly for the purpose of avoiding terrorists).

The Duchess clearly learned her lessons well. She was spotted travelling at 110 mph by one Brian Davis shortly before her Jaguar was in collision with a Ford Fiesta in a contraflow system on the M4 near Reading.

'She was travelling so fast that my car wobbled,' Mr Davis complained, but Thames Police said it would be 'difficult' to prosecute her 'without more evidence'.

Those wild eyes, that windswept hair, that immense sigh of relief because someone other than Fergie is driving

⬤105 HRH THE PRINCESS ROYAL PRINCESS ANNE
CAR: Bentley Mulsanne Turbo
ENDORSEMENTS: One, plus a warning
TOP RECORDED SPEED: 105 MPH

Anne was for years the queen of the Royal speedsters. She was the first Royal to end up in court for speeding, being fined £40 back in 1977 for driving along the M1 at 96.1 mph, although she'd also received a written warning from the Thames Valley Police five years earlier after being timed travelling at up to 100 mph on the M1 and M4.

Then she fell behind for many years. While her relatives upgraded almost yearly to the latest, fastest models, she was content with her Reliant. Now, one year on from her split with Captain Mark, she's back in the race, clocking up splendid times in her new Bentley Mulsanne Turbo. She can also claim to be the most-spotted speeding Royal, with members of the general public volunteering to have seen her travelling variously at 105, 100, 90, 80 and 60 mph (in a 30 mph zone). ☛

Disaster strikes intrepid prang-meister Mark Phillips as he follows Mark Thatcher's short cut to Gatcombe Park

(104) CAPTAIN MARK PHILLIPS

CARS: Various
ENDORSEMENTS: At least four
TOP RECORDED SPEED: 103.6 mph

Although only a member of the Royal family by marriage, and merely the fourth fastest in a motor, Captain Phillips has gone out of his way to make up for his handicaps by being the most-pranged Royal driver.

No less than six major accidents have blotted his copybook. They range from turning over his Land Rover during a promotional tour of Australia to writing off his Range Rover in a head-on collision with an Aston Villa footballer, to writing off a racing car at Silverstone at 100 mph and totalling his BMW by smashing it head-on into another car during a dangerous overtaking manoeuvre.

But his finest hour came on that familiar M4 motorway when the local Royal-busting boys in blue clocked him at 103.6 in his 3.5 litre V8 Rover Vitesse.

Prince Charles can't stand his wife's driving. He thinks it's a monstrous car bungle

(100) HRH PRINCESS DIANA THE PRINCESS OF WALES

CARS: Jaguar XJS, 2.9 litre V6 4x4 Ford Sierra, 1.6 litre Escort XR3i
ENDORSEMENTS: None
TOP RECORDED SPEED: 100 mph

Diana has worried other motorists on the M4 so much that she's been warned to slow down by Scotland Yard – this after an incident near her Gloucestershire home, Highgrove, when she was clocked at 96.1 mph.

'The way she drives along these roads is very dangerous,' says trembling Muriel Wiggins, aged 60, who lives just down the road from Di.

'Luckily everyone gets out of her way as soon as they see her coming – I have seen her sitting in her driveway revving up her car to roar away.'

Diana has taken recently to pottering around in a Jaguar, having been denied a 155 mph 5 litre V8 Mercedes 500 SL convertible by her patriotic hubby.

Princess Diana's just the ticket when it comes to driving buses. There's always plenty of room up top

(97) VISCOUNT LINLEY

CAR: 5 litre V8 Mercedes 500 SL convertible
ENDORSEMENTS: Three
TOP RECORDED SPEED: 97 mph

Unfortunately for Lord Linley, the cops don't seem to have quite the same degree of reverence for him as they do for the likes of Charles, Anne and Diana, and they happily nick him before he can get wound up to really high speeds.

He's tried a number of ruses to avoid them, including buying a souped-up Morris Minor which, whilst an apparently standard model to the casual observer, is in fact capable of more than 100 mph.

Now he's given up the subterfuge and has picked up the Merc that Diana couldn't have to go with his equally un-English 800cc BMW motorbike.

Ironically, his most recent offence – doing 97 mph on his motorbike – was committed just a day after driving his incredibly valuable Aston Martin DB5 into the back of a Porsche and mere minutes after a little old lady crunched into his bike with her shopping runabout. She made him late for a date, and he was speeding to try to get to it on time when the cops pounced.

He can, however, hold his head high when it comes to bans – four months off the road last year for doing 80 mph in a 40 mph zone, and five months the year before for doing that 97 mph on – yes! – the good old M4.

Look out London, Hell's Viscounts have hit town

Fergie's upset: ' When I asked you to reach for a Yorkie, that wasn't what I had in mind!'

HRH PRINCE ANDREW, THE DUKE OF YORK

70

CAR: Jaguar XJS
ENDORSEMENTS: None
TOP RECORDED SPEED: 70 mph (But he was in a 30 mph zone at the time.)

The Duke has mysteriously managed to escape the attentions of his mother's constabulary during the whole of his motoring career, including the famous incident earlier this year when he drove the wrong way up a one-way street.

Back in June he moved one-way signs in Windsor and forced other motorists to swerve out of his way as he hurtled towards them because he was late for lunch with mum. Even normally-loyal *Sun* readers voted 35,252 to 1,669 to string him up by his driving licence, but those faithful chaps of the Thames Valley Police felt he could not be prosecuted.

'A decision was taken,' said a spokesman, 'at the highest level not to prosecute. Prince Andrew and his private detective have been torn off a strip by a senior policeman who has told them that any repeat will end up in court. Prince Andrew can consider his wrists soundly slapped.' How splendid.

HM THE QUEEN

60

CAR: Anything she pleases
ENDORSEMENTS: None, but does not have to carry a driving licence
TOP RECORDED SPEED: 60 mph (Admittedly, it was in a 30 mph zone.)

Her Majesty really does own all the roads in the country, unlike all those Volvo drivers who only think they do. And she does like to travel at speed, as she demonstrated back in 1976 when, late for church, she put her foot down in her old 3.5 litre V8 Rover and trav-

elled the three miles from Windsor Castle to church at 60 mph.

'The Queen was three minutes beyond British Summer Time for the 11am service at St George's Chapel, Windsor,' explained one Royal spokesman bizarrely.

The Duke passes on some Hellenic driving tips: 'As soon as the donkey gets here, we'll be off.'

HRH PRINCE PHILIP, THE DUKE OF EDINBURGH

50

CAR: Electrically-powered Bedford van
ENDORSEMENTS: None
TOP RECORDED SPEED: 50 mph

Philip qualifies as the most eccentric Royal motorist. No wind-in-the-hair merchant, he prefers to potter around London and down to Windsor in his strange executively-upholstered, electrically-powered van, capable of a top speed of just 50 mph.

He does own a Range Rover, capable of a more Royal 110 mph, but only uses it for pottering in the Highlands.

'I don't like the noise which most vehicles make,' he explains. 'And I can't stand the smell or smoke which designers have decided should belch into my window just as I am overtaking a heavy lorry.'

HM QUEEN ELIZABETH, THE QUEEN MOTHER

?

CAR: See below
ENDORSEMENTS: None
TOP RECORDED SPEED: None

The Queen Mum doesn't actually do a great deal of driving in this, her 10th radiant decade on the planet. But she deserves an honourable mention here for her noted love of fast cars and her keen appreciation of their finer points. 'I have a Jaguar XJ12,' she says, 'and it goes like a bomb.' 🖋

From pillar to post box

Primrose Thornbury's *The Letter Boxes of Worcester* was never meant to be the sort of book to set the pulse racing or the publishing world alight. Never the sort destined to be found blazing, 'Soon To Be a Major Motion Picture Starring Tom Cruise and Meryl Streep' in gold leaf letters on the shelves of airport bookstalls. Indeed, it is not a work that has yet found a publisher at all.

Ms Thornbury's manuscript, however, was attracting significant interest at the latest meeting of the Letter Box Study Group, held the other day in the Welfare Suite of Birmingham District Letters Office. Yes, a few of the several dozen photographs making up the work may have been out of focus. But far more were fine, if not moving portraits, of which the finest of all was Ms Thornbury's study of an aluminium letter flap set into a blue

The Marlon Brando of SAE receptacles

wall beneath the receptionist's desk at the Department of Social Security in Vine House, Farrier Street, Worcester.

Skiing down Everest naked with a carnation between your teeth may be some people's idea of fun but it cannot compare for sustained excitement with trudging the country spotting, photographing and, most of all, measuring letter boxes. Indeed, after parasailing, hang-gliding and bobsleighing down the Cresta Run on a lavatory seat, letter box spotting is one of today's fastest-growing leisure activities and looks set to become The Next Big Thing.

So it was that 70 of Britain's most dedicated letter box spotters descended on Birmingham to meet their peers, trade news of sightings and display their collections of letter boxes and all things related to them. They came from Middlesborough and Bournemouth, Swansea and Worcester itself to set out their treasures on tables abrim with everything from renovated lampboxes to model Post Offices and a complete set of Postman Pat bubble bath and talc.

Dave Carless, PRO for the District Letters Office, opened the proceedings by welcoming delegates and announcing the Post Office's decision to mark the occasion by donating to the raffle 'a unique cover signed by the District Head Post Master'. But apart from a tour of the sorting office after lunch and a brief talk about letter boxes on ocean liners there was little other formal business to get through. Nor was any letter box spotting *per se* planned.

Instead, delegates clustered in twos and threes exchanging news of pillar boxes in Ealing and posting suites in Milton Keynes, photographs of blue pillar boxes at Chester Zoo and opinions on the experimental new pointy-headed letter boxes sighted near Sheffield. 'They're made of polypropylene,' said someone, reflecting the general disgust.

Mary Lillistone from Sheffield was showing a fellow delegate her collection of 500 photographs and postcards of letter boxes, amassed in spite of both her intense dislike of the colour red and the inevitable bemusement of fellow citizens. 'It's funny the way people look at you when you are taking pictures of post boxes,' she reflected. 'I had a security guy pass me at the Post Office the other day. I had to show him my membership card.'

Meanwhile, Harry Mac from Liverpool was displaying a montage of photographs entitled 'Foreign Pillar Boxes Sighted in

---

Tips for would-be Letter Box Spotters

Once you have finished spotting, photographing and, of course, measuring your own nearest letter box, you may want to move on to rarer examples by spotting boxes sporting the ciphers of, for example:

● **Edward VII** – of which there are less than 140.

● **Edward VIII** – even rarer because he, of course, was never crowned. But a dozen or so were still put up.

● **Queen Victoria** – the first monarch to dignify letter boxes with her cipher, 'VR'. Not, in fact, all that rare, compared to Edwardian boxes.

● Penfolds, which are hexagonal in shape and getting on for 200 in number.

● The 20 or so surviving letter boxes which were put up between 1853-59, when each region was able to make its own, until the Post Office came out with a standard one in 1859.

● The pillar box in Union Street, St Peter Port, Guernsey – the only survivor of Britain's original six letter boxes, all put up in the Channel Islands in 1852.

● No one at all. There are a small number of letter boxes which, for one reason or another, were made with absolutely no cypher or letters of any kind on them.

● In the end, however, there are no rules to letter box spotting. 'You just go out and spot what you want,' says Sally Jones, secretary of the Letter Box Study Group.

You thought those little red things in the High Street were just somewhere to park your letters, didn't you. Wrong. For some they are open-mouthed crimson Aphrodites. PETER FREEDMAN enters the strange but true world of letter box fanciers

This cutie can show you Post Offices you've never dreamt of

Bravely shouldering the red box's burden

This Country'. Examples ranged from 'A Norwegian Box at Lark Lane, Liverpool for the Special Use of Visiting Norwegian Seamen' to 'A French Box at Wigan (Note Circular Collection Indicator Tab).' Not that Mac was only interested in UK-based foreign boxes. 'I've been all over the world looking at post boxes,' he said.

He had just informed me that Britain's first post box was put up in Guernsey in the 1850s, and was in the process of informing me that until a couple of years ago no one in this country had to walk more than 440 yards to reach a pillar box, when a fellow delegate interrupted to tell me, 'They call him Mister Letter Box,' prompting Mac to shrug, 'Well, you have to have some interest in life.'

But why do people spot letter boxes? 'Why do people spot trains?' answered Sally Jones, secretary of the Letter Box Study Group, and the woman photographed on the front page of the *Solihull Times* this past 21 September for helping to save a rare Victorian pillar box ('one of only two in the West Midlands') from falling into disrepair. 'People get a heck of a lot of fun out of it. Yes, a lot of people laugh at us – to start with, anyway. But then they get hooked.' Her own parents, for example, were now forever stopping their car to get out and inspect letter boxes. At the very least, people start to look at letter boxes in a whole new light.

Harry Mac's interest grew out of his work with the Post Office, which he joined as a messenger in 1928, rising to become head of his own department. 'I looked after post boxes all my life. I knew them as works of art.' The Post Office itself, he said, now realised that post boxes were a respected part of our her-

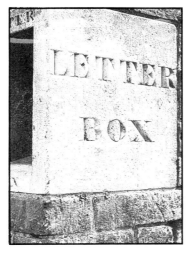

Moses's own box, on the corner of Sinai Road and Red Sea Drive

itage. 'They used to give them away or sell them as scrap. Now, they're looked after very carefully. And it will cost you a thousand pounds to buy one.'

'A letter box is a letter box is a letter box,' said Gertrude Stein, or might have done, if consulted on the matter. In which case Harry Mac would have put her straight. 'I myself have full information on 287 different types of letter boxes in this country,' he said. 'There's probably a lot more.' Quite true, confirmed Sally Jones. People were still finding letter boxes hitherto unknown to the Study Group.

The Letter Box Study Group itself was set up in 1976. Or, as Harry Mac recalled, 'I opened the *Courier* (the Post Office newspaper) and it said, 'Anyone interested in pillar boxes?' And I couldn't believe my eyes because I couldn't believe there was anyone else interested in them.' The Group recently signed up its thousandth ever member and is growing fast. It holds two national meetings a year.

The current membership of 600 divides between those who collect full-size or, more often, miniature letter boxes and those who go out spotting, photographing and measuring the real thing. Thus, Sally Jones has some 500 miniature letter boxes in her house in Birmingham plus a real one in her garden. She also has 30-odd scrapbooks containing postcards, Christmas cards, newspaper cuttings: 'Anything with a post box on it.'

Far more numerous, however, are the spotters and measurers. Among the things they spot and measure are the height of the letter box, the size of its aperture and crown, and the details of its cipher, denoting which monarch reigned when the box went up. 'I can walk through an area, look at a pillar box and tell you when the area was built,' said Harry Mac.

The Group also puts out a quarterly newsletter. 'If a member has been out surveying post boxes in a particular area, they might write an article,' said Sally Jones. If they live in Worcester they might even make it a book.

Another activity is lobbying for the conservation of old letter boxes. 'If you battle hard enough with the Department of the Environment,' explained Sally Jones, 'you can get a post box registered as a listed building and it can then never be removed from the site.'

✍ *To join The Letter Box Study Group, write to Sally Jones, 43 Miall Road, Hall Green, Birmingham B28 9BS.*

McLACHLAN

The beat goes on

The Metropolitan Police campaign to be more polite to the public has had far-reaching results...

'Wayne, I'd like you to meet Dave, Mike, Greg and Bob. This is Wayne – Wayne molests children'

'It's the new policy madam – Blankets in the summer, duvets in the winter'

'Uh oh – looks like the Mr Nice and Mr Nice routine'

'Getting there, sergeant, getting there'

'By the way, how do you think Chelsea will get on **next** week, against Spurs?'

Publish and

Would publishers recognise God-given genius if you sent it to them in a plain brown envelope? PETE SILVERTON finds out

As sorry as they were, Virago Press really did feel they had to turn Adolf Hitler down. 'Being a feminist press our priority is to publish women's writing,' began their reply to his synopsis and sample chapter for a book to be entitled *Nation And Race* – a thinly-disguised retyping of *Mein Kampf*. 'But good luck elsewhere,' they added.

The Adelphi Press, on the other hand, were impressed by Adolf. As a vanity publisher, they knew what they liked and they knew their market – the soft ego of the desperate to publish. *Nation And Race* was their kind of book. Adolf's submission, they told him, 'shows a novel approach to what is basically a philosophical theme. The writing is good and the subject matter interesting.'

(Without getting too sidetracked for the moment, it should be pointed out that the subject matter, philosophy and writing were of this order: 'The European inhabitant of the American continent, who has remained racially pure and unmixed, will remain the master as long as he doesn't fall a victim to the defilement of the blood.')

Samuel Beckett, by contrast, just didn't have what it takes. Even the vanity publishers turned him down. 'Not suitable for inclusion in our scheme,' was the Book Guild's judgement on the Nobel prize-winning writer and his offering of *Stirrings Still*, a story directly copied from his last published book.

Not that Adolf Hitler was exactly the name on the bottom of the letter. No, his name for the campaign was Thomas Jeremy. And nor was Samuel Beckett quite himself. He was R White.

It's an old trick, sending famous manuscripts to publishers under false names. Back in 1975, American journalist Chuck Ross sent the first 21 pages of Jerzy Kosinski's *Steps* – a winner of the National Book Award which had sold 400,000 copies in

'A novel approach,' The Book Guild tell Adolf and offer to publish his new volume of Aryan ranting

paperback to a total of 14 different publishers and literary agents. They all turned it down. Its original publisher, Random House, used a form letter for its reply.

It's a cheap trick. All you need is a word processor, large envelopes, some stamps – and a pile of other people's books to copy.

But it's also an extremely effective trick. As a way of testing whether publishers really are interested in new writers, it is hard to better. And it's pretty good at establishing just how good they are at spotting world-class talent – or, in Adolf's case, world-class evil – when it fetches up in their morning post along with unpaid bills and invitations to other people's launch parties.

The scam was simple. Copies were made of five different pieces of writing. Hitler and Beckett; a section of Timothy Leary's drug culture 'classic', *The Politics Of Ecstasy*; an eight-year-old child's story; and, finally, the first chapter of the first winner of the Booker Prize, P H Newby's *Something To Answer For*.

The final results were a clear-cut victory for obfuscation. Harassed and overworked publishers' editors, sinking under the weight of recession, redundancies and shorter lunchbreaks, just didn't spot the ringers. Out of over 50 manuscripts sent out – to British publishers and one American vanity house – only one was spotted for what it was. A blatant piece of copyright infringement.

Adolf Hitler
Award-winning dictator
Book submitted: *Mein Kampf*

First adopting the pseudonym of Thomas Jeremy, Adolf Hitler composed a charming letter to publishers:

'After many years (how many I do not dare count) spent, like Karl Marx too, in the reading room of the British Library studying texts, I have now finished my life's work. Finally, I am ready. Before, I did not dare show my work to prying eyes. You never know just where your enemies may lurk. Here you see but

be shammed

the tip of the iceflow. Everywhere there are those who would spy and frustrate my aims. You will make money. Together we could change the world. Yours in the knowledge of final success.'

As well as a detailed synopsis – using chapter headings from *Mein Kampf* – he included four closely-typed pages purporting to be an extract from his manuscript. 'There are some truths,' the piece began, 'which are so obvious that for this very reason they are not seen or at least not recognised by ordinary people.'

Publishers certainly didn't recognise this truth. Virago having turned it down – albeit with the politeness and consideration which is clearly their hallmark – Faber & Faber bounced it back with a form rejection slip. Viking passed as well, using a phrase that would soon become very familiar indeed – 'not something we feel would fit well on our list.'

Hodder & Stoughton used a form slip to turn him down and Grafton also felt it wasn't something for their list, 'but thank you for approaching us and good luck with placing the book elsewhere.'

Then, most depressingly and in quick succession, came rejections from a pair of vanity houses. For those unfamiliar with the term, vanity – or subsidy or, as they prefer to be known, partnership – publishers only put out books if the author pays them to do it, a curious but time-honoured reversal of expected practice. Time-honoured because, as the vanity houses' blurb always points out, all kinds of famous writers paid to be published. Rudyard Kipling, Galsworthy, Edgar Allen Poe, Jane Austen (*Sense And Sensibility*), Edgar Wallace (*Four Just Men*) and Marcel Proust. Not forgetting, of course, that – in the words of one vanity house – 'Not all financed their own books. The great Honoré de Balzac' – as opposed to the mundane Bert Balzac? – 'had the publication of his early works paid for by his mistress!'

As fond as they are of the exclamation mark, however, these vanity houses just didn't go for Adolf. Dorrance is an English branch of an American operation which advertises in many English publications with the line AUTHORS WANTED: American Publisher seeks manuscripts for UK and USA. 'Beyond the scope of our representation,' they told Adolf.

The Book Guild, based in East Sussex, places ads asking: AUTHORS Are you looking for a publisher? But they just didn't want to know about Adolf. 'Not suitable for inclusion in our scheme.' Oh, the shame of it. Half a world conquered and he couldn't even get a vanity publisher to issue his most

famous work. Then, at last, *grüss Gott*, came a publisher who knew a work of vision when he saw it. Adolf drank in the words of acceptance – 'novel approach...writing is good...subject matter interesting.' He read on, filled with Aryan pride, seeking out the secrets of Adelphi Press.

'No man has the right to curse the darkness unless he is prepared to light a candle,' they told him. He nearly wept with empathy. Next he noticed their particularly moving rejection of a suggestion that books should be subsidised by the Arts Council. 'Isn't that one of the things wrong with Britain? How is it that everybody seems to expect the Government or some public organisation to finance their industry? Surely that isn't the right attitude for writers and publishers, the prime individualists!' Soaking in the luxuriance of both italics and an exclamation mark, Adolf was impressed. 'Call me old-fashioned,' he said to himself. 'But I always have been a bit of a closet Thatcherite at heart. Adelphi are my kind of publishers.'

P H Newby
First Booker Prize winner
Book submitted: *Something To Answer For*

Although no longer exactly a household name – despite still regularly publishing novels – P H Newby's heyday was the Sixties when his wryly comic novels attracted considerable acclaim and the very first award of the Booker Prize. Writing under the name R Perkins, he submitted the first chapter of his award-winning novel, *Something To Answer For*, a picaresque tale set in Egypt at the time of the Suez crisis. Claiming to have lived abroad for many years, he offered what amounted to '15 per cent of the entire manuscript'.

As expected, Virago rejected it as not being either feminist or written by a bona fide woman. Hutchinson used another favourite cliché. They felt 'unable to publish your novel successfully'. Gollancz didn't think it 'suitable' for their list. Nor did Futura. Hodder & Stoughton sent a form rejection as usual.

Grafton were more positive, asking to see the entire manuscript. And so did Faber – fortunately for their reputation as they were the original publishers. They weren't that positive though, asking for it to be accompanied by stamps to cover postage and adding 'the chances of publication are probably quite small'.

As for the vanity publishers,

Prize-winner P H Newby learns that his 'chances of publication are small'

Dorrance rejected it but the Book Guild asked to see more, sending their catalogue. So R Perkins wrote back, requesting prices and suggesting a social engagement.

'I've got a large lump squirreled away somewhere I wouldn't like the Inland Revenue to know about. How about a drink – or two? (I've heard about publishers' parties and always wished to attend one.) If you're ever up this way, let's meet. My local's the Carlisle.'

The Book Guild said the cost 'should not be more than about £6000 and probably less!' – don't they love their exclamation marks – but strangely didn't even refer to Mr Perkins's invitation to the drink.

Timothy Leary
Acid-dropped author
Book submitted: *The Politics Of Ecstasy*

Operating undercover as C Proud, Sixties LSD guru, Timothy Leary, began his letter thus: 'Ecstasy should be everyone's right. You know it. I know it. They know it. We all know it. It is time for us all to share. We need to enter our own molecules and take control of our own chemistry.'

The book he was offering was his best-seller, *The Politics of Ecstasy*. Its suggested synopsis included chapters such as 'The Magical Mystery Trip' and 'God's Secret Agent A0S3'. The sample chapter was headed 'How To Start Your Own Religion' and included such revelatory sentences as 'Karmic accidental differences exist in people's make-up' and 'Your mode of sexual union is the key to your religion'.

He told the publishers that his wife considered him 'the sanest, wisest man I've ever met' – an actual quote from Mrs Leary – and signed off 'Yours ecstatically'.

Right off, Optima knew what to do – pass on the book and pass the buck. They suggested he approach 'Arkana, an imprint of Penguin – they tend to publish more on New Age subjects.' Considerately, they gave Arkana's full address. So off the submission went. But no ecstatic luck this time either. It was back in three days with a curt rejection – 'not something we think would work for us.'

Timothy Leary discovers he's 'not entirely suitable'

Nor were Martin Secker & Warburg interested. 'Don't feel it would be something for our list.' Nor Hodder & Stoughton's religious books department – 'not entirely suitable'. True to form though, Virago were the most encouraging. 'Not right for our listing even though it sounds interesting.' But what of those fine people at the vanity publishing houses? Dorrance passed, the bastards. (Can you imagine the ignominy of being turned down by a publisher who you were actually offering to pay to bring your book out?) So did the Book Guild. Cloth-brained philistines, decided Proud.

But then, bingo, Adelphi Press welcomed him to their world. 'Your work is very interesting, with a lot of humour and

Young Daniel: his spy story shows sweeping 'talent'

you undoubtedly have talent.' Then, double bingo, all the way from New York, Vantage accepted him – dependent on the final manuscript. Thrilled, C Proud flicked through the Vantage catalogue. Oh, he thought, what joy to be published by the same company which handled *World War Three Is Inevitable*, *Being A Fire Fighter Isn't Just Squirting Water* and, most impressive of all, *Letters I Wish I'd Mailed To The Man Who Divorced Me To Marry A Waitress*. Now that's what he called vanity publishing.

He moved on to their projected sales figures. 'Sales of the average Vantage Press book vary widely. Some books sell a few hundred copies or less; some, a few thousand copies; a handful sell even more.' Now there was a prospect to cushion his twilight years.

And what about the PR campaigns they showed? C Proud decided he looked forward warmly to a publishing future in which he too could be photographed beneath local newspaper headlines of such powerful subtlety as 'Canadian Trappist Monk Co-Authors Worthy Book On Gospel Parables' – one of Vantage's major publishing coups of recent years. Such, such joy. C Proud felt profoundly moved, to nausea perhaps.

Daniel Silverton
Eight-year-old scribe
Book submitted: *Jewel Of The Seven Stars*

As eight-year-olds' stories go, Daniel Silverton's *Jewel Of The Seven Stars* was an eight year old's story. Spies, planes and football, that kind of thing. But he was hopeful. 'I've sent this to lots of publishers,' he wrote. 'None of them were interested. I really want to be an author, like Jeffrey Archer or Stephen King. Don't disappoint me.'

Viking's list was 'extremely full over the next couple of years'. Grafton felt that 'the market for this type of fiction is very difficult at the moment.' Hodder & Stoughton sent a form rejection but a helpful factsheet for would-be authors. Virago, as ever, were fulsomely polite in their turning it down. 'I'm sorry to give you this disappointing news but...we do publish predominantly female authors.' (As opposed to partly female authors, he assumed.)

Three vanity houses – Book Guild, Vantage and Dorrance – turned it down but Adelphi saw promise. 'Your work is interesting and you show talent.' They needed more however. 'Several short stories together will do.'

The last and most generous reply of all came from Victor Gollancz's crime department. It began with 'many thanks' and went on to detail various handbooks, magazines and shops which would be useful to a budding crime writer and finished with a charming postscript – 'I particularly enjoyed the reference to Peter Shilton.'

Samuel Beckett
Nobel prize winner
Book submitted: *Stirrings Still*

Using the pseudonym R White, Samuel Beckett wrote to a variety of publishers. 'As I heard I wrote,' began his letter and continued: 'A single page appeared. Then more. I send them. Shall you publish them?' He enclosed a story called *Stirrings Still*, two and half pages of very close typing. It started: 'One night as he sat at his table head on hands he saw himself rise and go.' It finished: 'Oh all to end.' It was archetypal Beckett, never likely to form the basis of a treatment for a new Carry On movie.

Martin, Secker and Warburg didn't think it 'something for our list'. Viking felt that 'prose of this type is best appreciated in small, one-off pieces, but to read this over a long period of time proves difficult, as it can be quite hard to maintain the rhythm and the flow of thoughts. Yours sincerely...'

Vantage, the American vanity house, returned it 'herewith'. Duckworth wished him success but didn't think, it – surprise, surprise – 'something we could fit into our publishing list'. Gollancz considered it carefully but decided they didn't want to see any more. Two more vanity houses – Book Guild and Dorrance – passed, making Beckett the only putative author to get a complete thumbs-down from them.

After sending a card to say they were considering it, Hodder & Stoughton finally said no. They apologised for the delay in replying but regretted that they did not feel able to publish it 'successfully in book form. I found the writing very unusual and idiosyncratic. I found the sentences distracting and felt that they pulled the reader back.'

And, finally, there was a reply from Beckett's own publisher, John Calder, the only one of all those publishers to recognise any of the manuscripts as the blatant pieces of larceny they were. The correspondent felt the occasion demanded verse: 'Even a page
    Can plage
    But plageing
Beckett
    Can only
wreck it.'

Beckett finds he's unpublishable 'in book form'

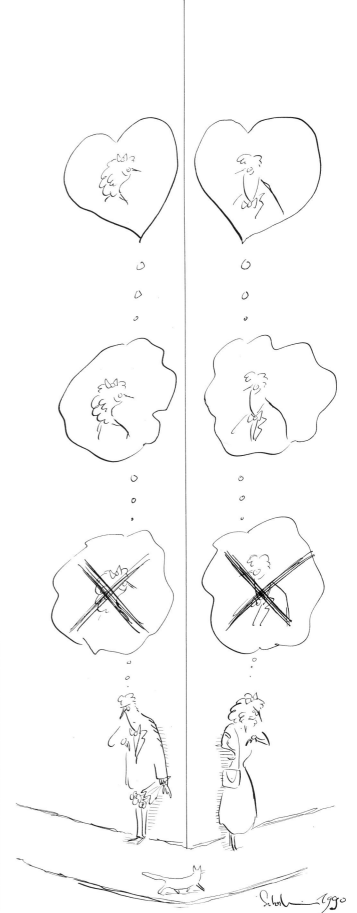

Currie

Having put her troubles behind her, the lovely Edwina Currie opens her heart to ANTON RUSH and fills in the Cosmo quiz

The world knows a lot about Edwina Currie. One could never call the Member for Derbyshire South publicity shy. But though she's never hesitated to tell old people to put their woollies on their heads, or berate Northerners for eating chips, her innermost desires have remained a secret.

Until now. For we asked the pouting harridan of the Right a series of questions specifically designed to elicit one, crucial piece of information: Are You A Good Flirt? First published by *Cosmopolitan* magazine in March 1988, this instant inquisition remains relevant today. And when we put Edwina through it over an intimate lunch, a mass of revelations emerged. Such as...

● Her earliest sexual activities took place under the influence of alcohol.
● She longs for sexy Janet Reger undies, and...
● She wears suspender belts.
● Now read on for more intimate – and entirely genuine – vindaloo-style revelations...

1. How did your father treat you when you were growing up?
a. He wanted you to achieve, fulfil your ambition, come top.
b. Much like your mother, as an extra agent for his domestic comfort.
c. Very susceptible to female charm, he complimented you on your appearance.
d. He was very critical of any signs that you were growing into an adult female.

Edwina says: It's **a.** He wanted me to achieve – he wanted me to go to Liverpool University. I could see no point in that –

I'd have to stay at home! My father said yes, that's exactly the point. Well, I damn well didn't want to stay at home, it was time to leave, fly the nest. My headmistress said if you get into Cambridge or Oxford it will be on the front page of the *Liverpool Echo* – and that's how I ended up at Oxford!

2. At school which extramural activity appealed to you most?
a. Acting, music, dancing.
b. Competitive activities.
c. Getting over the wall to meet the boys from the school next door.
d. Going off on your own to read or follow lone interests.

Edwina says: Yes, **d.** I was a loner as a kid. I went to the local library and started at A! Every time I found an author I enjoyed I read everything. When I was 14 I loved Hardy and wanted *Tess of the D'Urbervilles* for my school prize, they wouldn't let me have it because it had an illegitimate baby in it! You think I'm kidding, don't you? I got *Under The Greenwood Tree* instead.

'Is the curried teddy hot enough for you, sir?'

combing

3. Your early interaction with the opposite sex was:
a. A passionate one-to-one relationship.
b. Long talks on the meaning of life.
c. With a girlfriend or a crowd, teasing and taunting but never getting too close.
d. Difficult, because they were stronger, faster and more self-assured than you.

Edwina says: I can't remember – I probably wasn't sober!

4. Male colleagues flatter your looks and clothes, how do you respond?
a. You dress more severely; pull back you hair and work like fury to prove that a woman can work as well as a man.
b. You feel miserable and embarrassed.
c. Lightly but with appreciation; it all oils the wheels in the workplace.
d. You think they must be attracted to you, and consider starting an affair.

Edwina says: I think **c.** is the appropriate one, don't you? At the House men have often commented on how I look. A question from the opposite benches once began, 'May I

say how attractive you're looking today?' I replied by saying: 'You're looking pretty cute yourself.'

5. Which of the following do you think is your greatest asset with men?
a. The fact that you appear to be someone who enjoys sex.
b. Your intelligence and talent – you are a match for any man.
c. Your sympathy and understanding.
d. Your self-confidence – you are relaxed and enjoy being a woman in their company.

Edwina says: Someone who enjoys sex…Oh dear! Oh, all of the last three I should think! Am I allowed to do that? Rules are made to be broken aren't they?

6. An attractive stranger keeps staring at you across a crowded room. You:
a. ask someone to introduce you.
b. look away embarrassed.
c. hold his gaze just long enough for him to know you've noticed.
d. glare him out. People can be so rude!

Edwina says: No! I know what I normally do and it's not here – I just smile. It happens all the time. I was sent someone's telephone number on the back of a card at the Savoy one day. I put it in the back of my wallet and any time I'm feeling heavy and boring and dull it's still there! One of these days I must look him up in *Who's Who* and find out who he is.

7. You notice him first. How do you secure his attention?
a. Regale your companion with a dramatic story full of gesture and animation.
b. Flash a leg, run your fingers through your hair, and smile at him.
c. Cause a commotion, break something.
d. Pray silently.

Edwina says: Well, that's easy. I don't need to.

8. How many of the following do you have in the wardrobe:
seamed stockings (yes, got those!); **three inch heels** (no); **a very short skirt** (Oh no!); **something in black velvet** (yes!); **dangly earrings** (yes!); **a very wide belt that you pull in**

ILLUSTRATION: STEVE GOODALL

🦆 flirtysomething

Left: 'I'm sorry the Chief Whip is out. Thank you for your 0898 call...'
Centre: 'I haven't seen so many fresh fruits since I last flew Quantas'
Right: 'This piece is lethal at a range of half a mile. The gun's pretty hot stuff, too'

tightly (yes!); **suspender belt** (yes!); **a basque or a waspie** (no, too old for those); **silk teddy** (my daughter has – I bought it for her); **something see-through** (no!); **something strapless** (oh no, I've got narrow shoulders); **black leather skirt or trousers** (no); **blood-red lipstick** (yes definitely); **a hat with a veil** (no); **silk flowers for your hair** (yuk!).

a. 12 or more.
b. Between 6 and 11, but you'd thought of buying others.
c. Less than 6 – you'd never dare.
d. Less than 6 – you think the rest sound rather vulgar.

Edwina says: Definitely **b.** because I'd also like some Janet Reger underwear.

9. A man offers to help carry your supermarket shopping to your car. You:
a. feel offended and tell him you are quite as able bodied as he is.
b. say, 'No, I can manage thanks.'
c. dump all upon him gratefully, then offer to buy him a drink for his trouble.
d. surrender weakly and admiringly.

Edwina says: Anybody offers to carry my luggage for me and I'll say anytime, mate! So it's got to be **d.**

10. You are spending the weekend with your boyfriend's parents and it's separate bedrooms. What do you wear to go to the bathroom?
a. Slinky black satin and scent.
b. Your M&S paisley pyjamas.
c. A virginal Victorian style housecoat.
d. A towel.

Edwina says: All of them at once – it was freezing cold in the house!

11. How many of the following figure in your conversation with attractive men:
Your personal success (oh, all the time); **expensive things you've bought** (very often); **your distinguished friends** (no, not very often); **your financial schemes** (yes); **your inferiority complex** (no, I haven't got one of those, have I?); **your health** (oh, all the time I'm afraid); **washing machines** (NEVER); **ex-lovers** (NEVER); **AIDS** (occasionally); **world famine** (not too often).
a. Two or three as a last resort.
b. Four or more, mostly from the first half.

c. Four or more, mostly from the second half.
d. Four or more – but you can usually get people pretty interested in them.

Edwina says: It looks like **b.** There's a story connected with the AIDS campaign – I was asked if I would go on telly to do a piece on the kite mark for condoms – apparently we were importing a lot of stuff that didn't have a kite mark and was faulty.

Norman Fowler told me to play it straight – they had a piece of film showing how condoms are tested, did you know they blow them up? They fill them with water until they get that big (makes gesture to approximate the size of a prize-winning marrow). I'm not joking! I was finding it impossible to keep a straight face.

When I got back home, the phone was ringing and it was John Gummer and he was saying 'What are you doing playing with these things on TV? I turned on my TV while I was eating and you've ruined my breakfast – I simply couldn't touch the sausages!'

12. He is obviously attracted; where do you steer the conversation?
a. To subjects you can argue about?
b. To things you know you can shine at.
c. To things he can enthuse about.
d. Sex.

Edwina says: Well, it has to be **d.** really. No, it's all of them, I don't really see them as alternatives. Sex is something I can argue about, it's something I can shine at, it's something he can enthuse about, there we are!

SCORE Edwina, who once had the nickname 'Hot Stuff' isn't quite hot enough these days to be in the top category which *Cosmo* defined as 'not just flirtatious but ready for action' and 'an ardent admirer of Mae West.'

Still, settling snugly into the second of the four categories is no mean achievement. Edwina will be pleased to know that she is 'skilled in the verbal fencing that arouses interest and desire...' She also qualifies as a 'modern flirt', realising that 'combat can be very stimulating to sexual attraction.'

But before Cecil Parkinson gets to hear about those seamed stockings and suspenders, it should be pointed out that *Cosmo* also says, 'Although all men find you attractive you are very discriminating and only a special few come close.'

In other words, Currie may have plenty of sauce, but she's no take-away. 🦆

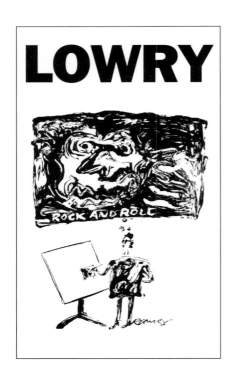

LOWRY

'He says if he concentrates hard enough he can remember the golden age of the Punch cartoon.'

'My muse didn't desert me! I deserted my muse!'

'You don't even MENTALLY undress me anymore, do you?'

'This place is really looking up — designer hoodlums!'

'It's a no-show, folks. Big Joe's had analysis and he doesn't have the blues anymore…'

'Just my luck — I developed a beer hump instead of a beer belly.'

Oil's well **That**

Are Britain's admen a much-misunderstood band of patriots? Or would they sell their granny for an Iraqi ad campaign? STEPHEN PEARCE and JOHN VOLAND put the agencies to the test

The news broke on Thursday 23 August, appearing simultaneously in the *Financial Times* and *Campaign*, the bible of the advertising industry. On page two of the *FT*, under the general heading CRISIS IN THE GULF, came a story by Alice Rawsthorne and John Thornhill headlined 'Plan for Iraqi advertising in Britain.'

It began, 'A number of leading London advertising agencies have been approached by a British businessman who says he is preparing an advertising campagin for the Iraqi government.' According to one agency, the man had described the Iraqis' budget as 'unlimited' and had promised that there would be 'no problem about payment.'

The businessman in question was one Stephen Pearce. Together with partner, John Voland, he had, it seemed, worked in the Middle East as a media consultant to the expatriate community. Now, the pair was back in Britain, with offices in the swish Chelsea Harbour

Plan for Iraqi advertising in Britain

By Alice Rawsthorn and John Thornhill

NUMBER of leading London vertising agencies have been roached by a British businssman who says he is preRing an advertising camgn for the Iraqi government. Ir Stephen Pearce, who aims to be acting as an intermediary for the Iraqi foreign ministry in Baghdad", confirmed yesterday that he had made approaches to "about a dozen" agencies. He said he planned to run a campaign in B...

'We're coming straight through the window with £500,000'

area of London. Were they pro-Iraqi, asked the *FT*? 'Good God no,' said Pearce. 'This is purely a piece of business.'

By lunchtime that day, Chelsea Harbour was besieged by the media. All the tabloid papers sent hacks in search of the treacherous duo, BBC TV wanted to get them on the evening news and admen were everywhere.

Pearce and Voland, however, had disappeared. They were thought to be in hiding. Except that they weren't. They were sitting in a flat in North London writing a story for *Punch*. This story, in fact ...

The situation was simple. Saddam Hussein is in desperate need of good publicity. And the British advertising industry, battered by the onset of recession, is in almost as great a need of cash. So, how would the agencies respond to requests for promotion of Britain's current Public Enemy Number One? We pondered the idea, flicked it back and forth, across and around the table, and then boiled up a plan.

Posing as media consultants who'd been working 'largely with ex-pats' in the Gulf for a number of years, we buzzed advertising agencies to tell them we'd recently arrived back in England at the behest of the Iraqi Foreign Ministry. We wanted to know if they'd be prepared to devise and place a 'balance redressing' publicity campaign for our media-unfriendly clients. We talked of full-page adverts in all the national newspapers, promoting the Iraqi government's opinions.

That would their reactions be? Could the creative whizz-kids be persuaded to sell their metaphorical mothers to the Arabs? Would principles and patriotism prevail over money-making? Would they at least run a few ideas up the flagpole for 'The Butcher of Baghdad'?

First port of call was advertising agency GOLD GREENLEES TROTT, the boys who once asked, 'Allo Tosh. Got a Toshiba?' Pearce spoke to Sue, who – on hearing this was 'a political matter' – put him first onto the accountant, then to Carol Pottinger, PA to the MD, who passed him to Nina Jasinski, new accounts manager. After hearing a précis of the Iraqi Campaign, Jasinski said 'You are talking to the right person. Go no further. Let's start backwards. What sort of budget are we looking at? Dates? UK Only?'

Pearce asked her to keep the matter 'close to her chest' and Jasinski wanted 'not to break confidence, but just bounce it off the chairman and come straight back at you and arrange a meeting for tomorrow or Wednesday'.

Later she phoned back to say that after high-level discussions GGT had decided it was not interested.

Next we tried YELLOWHAMMER, which gave a rather swift and proudly patriotic response. Pearce called its new business director, one Suj Summer. Summer said, 'I don't feel it

ends well

Pro-Iraqi ads shunned

A number of top London agencies have been left perplexed this week after being approached about a national press campaign apparently funded from Baghdad. The alleged aim of the ads is to put the Iraqi case in the Gulf crisis.

A company calling itself Voland Associates, it is working as

But the approaches have met with an uncertain response, as agencies believe they might be the victims of a hoax.

"This is so unreal we are having difficulty taking it seriously," says one. "The whole thing came completely out of the blue."

Others dismiss the idea even if it is genuine. "This is a highly political...

The Iraqi embassy in London says it is unaware of any planned advertising and Pearce Voland refused to comment.

Meanwhile British Airways has pulled its advertising campaign after the staff and passengers were taken "hostage" by Iraq when one of its planes landed at Kuwait airport (The ....

would interest us We currently work with the government through the Central Office Of Information and I think they'd probably take quite a dim view of it.'

Later Voland telephoned Summer and left the message, 'We'd still like to meet and swing some concepts with you'. There was no response.

Next up was BARTLE BOGLE HEGARTY. Voland called Andy Jackson, BBH's business development manager, announcing, 'We're coming straight through the window at you with a campaign worth £500,000.'

Jackson asked what the 'central objective' of the campaign was. Voland replied 'It's ever-changing, even over the weekend, but it's principally to off-set opinions currently being promulgated in the British media. Voland asked Jackson to 'please keep this very close to your chess-set'.

He replied, 'Absolutely. But in the meantime I need to mention it to my chief exec, Nigel Bartle. Although I have to say that it's not the sort of thing that we would really like to get involved in. We have a principle of no tobacco or politics. So I would really have to turn down your approach and say we wouldn't want to be involved.' To end he added, 'OK, good luck. I hope, whatever you get off the ground, it does something to defuse the situation.'

Given their Iraqi-Jewish background, we envisaged short shrift from the Saatchi Brothers and we were right. Voland phoned SAATCHI & SAATCHI's business development manager, Peter Burgess and announced to secretary Claire; 'I'm coming at you round the corner and through the window winging Peter a campaign.' Claire said he had 'just popped out for a second, try in ten mins'. When we got back he was on the phone. Claire said 'I'm just looking to see if he's coming off. He's having a cigarette now. Can I help?' Voland briefly outlined the Iraqi concept. Burgess swiftly returned a call declaring a categoric 'No!'

Desperate to get the flag up the pole ASAP, Pearce got straight on to Ian Waxman at ad-agency MARTIN WAXMAN

'We're on a roll, everything's in a go-mode and on the up and up! How are things at your end?'

ASSOCIATES. After explaining the concept Pearce added, 'We would need for you to do the whole job, top to toe.' Waxman replied, 'Let me speak to my co-directors and maybe we'll meet up on this.'

Voland called Waxman the following day, speeding; 'We've been on a roll, really, everything's in a go-mode and on the up and up! Can I ask you how things are going your end?'

'Umm, what – with business you mean?'

'No, no, as concerns the Pro-Iraqi Campaign. Whether we can arrange a meet and wing some concepts?'

Waxman replied, 'Ahh, yes. I have spoken with my co-director, and we felt we'd have to stick to our policy of not getting involved in political or sensitive matters. But I do have an associate who runs another media company – who may not have the same problems. Would you be averse to me mentioning it to him and getting him to contact you?'

The contact never came, but, ever determined, Pearce now telephoned Sarah Lang of ad agency J WALTER THOMPSON. He said to her: 'What this campaign will do is put over the points of view of the foreign ministry in Baghdad as thoroughly as possible. Now, if you're interested in doing this we could provide you with all the relevant glossy material to make up the adverts'.

Lang asked, 'How would we be paid?'

Pearce said, 'Money is no problem.'

Lang enquired, 'What's the point, the real object?'

Pearce told her, 'The thrust is to balance viewpoints being expressed in the British media currently'.

'Well, it's certainly an interesting strategy,' Sarah noted drily. 'What's the budget?'

'Whatever is needed to achieve the aims will be provided.

PUNCH

And Another Sting

☆ THE first casualty of war is truth and the noble Financial Times and the advertising industry's trade paper Campaign have fallen victim.
On the front page of Campaign and page two of yesterday's FT, were details of Iraq's attempt to hire a British advertising agency to polish its tarnished image in this country.
Unfortunately for all concerned, the whole brouhaha was a hoax perpetrated by Punch magazine to "test the patriotism" of the ad agencies. The agencies took it seriously — and tipped off the FT and Campaign who took it very seriously indeed

including J. Walter Thompson and Young and Rubicam, rejected the advances of the journalist who approached them posing as an "intermediary for the Iraqi foreign ministry in Baghdad".

Says Punch editor David Thomas, whose own (and true) version of events appears next month: "I'm not surprised by all the attention this story has received. The fact that British advertising agencies turn out to be patriotic after all is obviously a shocking revelation."

shocking as the

Magazine owns up to advertising spoof

By Alice Rawsthorne

PUNCH, the UK comic magazine, yesterday disclosed that it was responsible for the recent attempt to persuade advertising agencies to prepare an advertising campaign on behalf of the Iraqi government.
Two freelance journalists working for Punch approached the agencies using the false names of Mr Steven Pearce and Mr John Voland.

We're working to a whip-lash deadline'.

Lang pondered, 'I need to have a little think about this. Would there be an Iraqi briefing? It would help obviously to get as near as possible to the client, as it were. I'm not necessarily saying they're going to fly us out to Baghdad (laughs).'

Pearce replied, 'That could be arranged, if need be'; and asked for 'a decision by fax. It's quite possible we may not be by the phone tomorrow because we're winging here, there and all over the place'.

Lang's fax decision was: 'I'm afraid we would not be able to handle the advertising you describe because of its highly charged political nature. I wish you every luck in your quest. Regards, Sarah Lang.'

Pearce phoned to clarify Lang's position. She said, 'We have a policy that is quite strict but can be interpreted round the edges. That's why I had to consult. We think it could actually run us into some problems, being US-owned and with a lot of multi-national clients. We also do RAF Recruitment. Can I give you just a bit of advice? You're going to probably have the same results with any multi-nat agency, so I would go to a smaller local agency which will see some publicity advantage for themselves in it. Someone like Howell Henry.'

Finally believing our man had been found, Pearce immediately buzzed Zoe Day at HOWELL HENRY CALDECOTT LURY. She was otherwise engaged so he left a message.

Voland followed up the call, throwing himself into a creative fervour. He said to Day, 'My colleague Stephen Pearce handed me a note to get right back to you – we've been whirring with ideas – and off the top of my hair-style the two ideas are: blood-red spot-colour and camels – for half a million smackeroos.'

Day replied, 'I don't know what you're talking about!'

Voland said, 'Good lord, this is very bizarre, I've just been out – in congress. Maybe I should start from the beginning. Shoot straight through the window at you. This is about the Iraqi Press Campaign. We were hoping to discuss it with you. We're acting as intermediaries. We were actually in Baghdad for the last five years.'

Day riposted, 'Are you sure this isn't a wind-up? It's just

coming off four walls at me at the moment. No, no, go on it's alright. I'm with you now'. She gave no immediate decision, so later we phoned back and left the message 'Think camels!'

On calling YOUNG & RUBICAM, Pearce was not cognisant with the fact that the company handles the Royal Navy's advertisements and its New York wing handles the US Army's. He phoned Y&R's Paul Woolfenden.

Woolfenden phoned back and left two messages. Firstly to say that he thought it was a hoax, the second time to say that he realised it wasn't a hoax but that Y&R 'aren't interested.'

Fearing that we might have to execute the ads, we were meanwhile in phone-congress with Alistair Ferguson, account group director of corporate design consultancy SMITH & MILTON. Voland described the nature of the campaign and launch/press-pack and explained 'We're looking to get a real graphic sense to this campaign. Twirling a few concepts off the elbow, where do you think we should go from here in terms of Smith & Milton?'

Ferguson replied, 'Well, I could discuss it with the creative director, in terms of looking at page lay-outs. I don't think that's a problem. If you have copy and photography. We look at the likes of posters, for instance.'

Believing Ferguson to be a suitable visualiser, Voland phoned back five minutes later, leaving a message for him saying 'Think camels!'

Next up, Voland spoke to Amanda McGaughey at WOLF OLINS, the corporate identity consultancy. 'I believe my colleague Stephen Pearce was apparently in congress with you, vis-à-vis the Iraqi Campaign,' he quick-fired, 'The latest up-shot of it is that, talking off the top of my hair-style, we're talking blood red spot-colour, copy wise and camels.'

McGaughey replied, 'I'm not familiar with what you're talking about.'

But Voland was undaunted, 'Our primary idea is to have Ambassador Salihi arriving at the reception on a camel and we'd like to whirr the idea around with some colleagues.'

Feeling confident that the visual side of things could be handled by his partner, Pearce called Danielle Barr, managing director of the ad agency PUBLICIS. 'Is it basically a political campaign?' she quizzed.

'You could say that,' said Pearce, and then, after a pregnant pause, 'How does that strike you?'

'It's certainly the most interesting enquiry I've had today,' she noted. 'I'll have to think about it. I can contact the group chairman this evening. So you are asking us to do the creative work on behalf of the Iraqi government?'

'That is correct'.

'How do you feel about your involvement?' Barr asked.

Our man said 'Well, it's all part of the game really.'

Barr asked, 'Just as a matter of interest, do you think campaigns have the power to influence people and events of such a – if not critical – certainly sensitive nature?'

Pearce suggested, 'Well, I think what I think is neither here nor there, really. It's what the Iraqis think that counts.'

Barr went on to say, 'It's a very interesting proposition. I'll give you a response by tomorrow.' We have, as it happens, not heard from her since.

Spread-eagled over a creative barrel, we tried one last ad agency. COLLETT DICKENSON PEARCE. Pearce phoned Anne-Marie Yannaghas, explaining 'Pearce Voland did some work with the Iraqis and they've now asked us to try and arrange a press campaign for them over here.'

'Mmmm, interesting timing', Yannaghas noted.

'Now, loosely speaking,' Pearce said, 'what they want a company to do is balance anti-Iraqi viewpoints in the British media at the moment, and we wondered whether this is the sort of work you'd consider taking on yourselves?'

Yannaghas replied, 'Yes, of course. Do you have any idea of what the budget might be?'

'An upper limit of half a million, mainline money,' Pearce explained. 'Does that seem reasonable?'

Yannaghas replied, 'Of course. We'd be interested in having a conversation. Shall I send a brochure over? If you want to see a video of our recent material I could send a VHS.'

We thought we'd cracked it. We cried, 'Result!' We thought in a few days we'd be winging concepts in and out of CDP's window. We could see it now – a striking ad-image of Saddam Hussein riding into town on a camel, above the caption 'Don't Leave Me Ku-Waiting.'

However, the following day Yannaghas told Pearce on the phone. 'Having spoken to our seniors, they're not interested. So thank you for contacting us, but no, we won't be able to help you on this occasion. I'm terribly sorry, but it would conflict with some existing business. Sorry about that. Good luck.'

Thoroughly disheartened, we decided there was only one thing for it – we'd up the stakes and appeal to the pecuniary instincts. Voland faxed Yannaghas. 'Time being of the essence, we need to start flying on this one, so I have decided our best option is to double your usual commission.'

We knew it was all over, image-wise, for The Bogey-man of Baghdad, when CDP's new business director, Mark Tomblin, responded with a fax announcing: 'We have no interest in working on 'Project K', whether you double, treble or quadruple our 'usual commission'. We would not work on it under any circumstances.'

Sorry Saddam – we tried our professional, whirringly creative best. But it seems that this is one case where the British advertising industry puts patriotism before profits – where it places its country and conscience before its concepts and campaign coffers. We're bloody proud of it. 🐝

This article has been a John Hind and Steven Mosco production of an original concept by Pete 'Pol Pot' Silverton.

...and here are those ads you'll never see

ONLY Hussein can do this

SADDAM HUSSEIN. Softness is his strength

No F 15, no comment

I bet he drinks Carling Black Label

The budgie nibbled, Arthur liked it but the man from Del Monte, he said 'No'

HUSBAND

Tax appeal

'Hi, VAT Office. Listen, fancy kicking a man while he's down'?

'Next!'

'Darling, we've just worked it out. I pay more in taxes than Philip actually earns'

'I like to think I bring a touch of fun to the job'

'I'm afraid it's bad news, Mr Leekey'

Bend me, shape me

When David Bailey chose his 50 British beauties, POLLY SAMSON was one of them. So what would the plastic surgeons say when she told them: I hate my face, I want to look like Joan Collins?

The phone rang. 'Try and get yourself some plastic surgery,' said the editor of *Punch*. It seemed a rather drastic demand. Had I done something to offend him? Or had I looked particularly bad last time we met? 'No, no,' said the editor. 'There's money in it.' That sounded a bit better.

'We were thinking that you might like to visit some plastic surgeons. String them a line about hating your looks and see whether they are scrupulous enough to contradict you or they just go along with it and agree to operate.'

With a quick prayer for my acting abilities, I took the *Punch* shilling.

First, to double check that there really was nothing seriously amiss, I paid a visit to the Peak Health Club at the Carlton Tower Hotel to get the unbiased low-down on my physique and face.

After putting me through the rigours of questionnaires, callipers, lung-monitors and weighing machines they said that plastic surgery was not necessary, suggested that I could do with 'perhaps a bit more kip and food' and told me that anyone from whom I sought plastic restructuring should deliver me into the hands of a psychiatrist rather than a surgeon.

The Harley Medical Group's publicity blames 'sensational media coverage' for some public prejudices against plastic surgery for vanity or frivolous aesthetic reasons. They seemed to be asking for it. I booked an appointment.

'The good thing about working here is (hushed voice and giggle) – free treatment,' said the willowy young receptionist as I sat in the oak-panelled reception at the Harley Street clinic.

What free treatment had she had? 'Me boobs,' she said, proudly sticking her chest out. 'They're really groovy. I don't regret it a bit. But you won't tell anyone, will you?' She had also had an injection called a 'collagen lip pout', was considering having the skin around her eyes lifted and hoped that a surgeon would fit in a bit of free liposuction for her thighs (a particularly revolting operation that involves slicing through the flesh, vibrating the wound to separate the fatty tissue and literally sucking it out through a tube).

In return, I confided that I hated my face and was determined to have something done about it. 'But you have a groovy face,' she said and then, as though she had just committed an act of treachery: 'But of course, if you don't like it you should have something done.'

I was summoned for my consultation with Florence Campbell ('Good luck. You won't tell anyone about me boobs, now will you?')

I told her that I really couldn't live with my face any longer and that my husband wanted to pay for my treatment as a Christmas present. 'Yes, I see,' said Florence Campbell. As she turned a mirror to my face, I winced as though being shown Quasimodo's sister. 'It's particularly my nose I can't bear,' I said. Florence Campbell decided to take a risk: 'I have to say I find it rather pretty,' but added quickly: 'Perhaps we could refine it a bit.' She pinched my nose at the bridge and pushed up the tip making a nose that would have looked fine on a newly-born piglet. 'Yes, that would look quite lovely,' she said.

I agreed and asked what could be done about the rest of my face. Florence ran her hands along my cheeks and diagnosed triumphantly that I didn't have much cheekbone. I tried to hide my insulted feelings behind a mask of relief to have found someone so understanding. 'Perhaps cheek implants. Yes, yes they would look quite lovely,' she enthused while pushing at my face to show how gorgeous I would look. 'They would lift your whole face, make your eyes look lovely and big, add an extra dimension.'

Perhaps I was looking slightly queasy at the thought, so she added the clincher: 'They're very popular too. Lots of film stars have them done.' She explained how minor the operation was – the surgeon would simply slice through the top of my mouth and slide the artificial cheekbones into place. 'I think cheek implants would look quite lovely,' she repeated.

She recommended that I have my nose and cheeks done at the same time as it would save on the anaesthetist's fee. She showed me a colour brochure about the hospital and advised me on my post-operative diet: yoghurt, ice-cream, soups and juice – through a straw, of course, as I would have a sore mouth. I would also have bruising, a pair of black eyes, an internal nose shield and would only be a able to breathe through my mouth for a while.

But she made it sound most worthwhile and really nothing more traumatic than having a couple of teeth pulled.

I was told that the surgeon would be a Mr Stanek, 'one of the top rhinoplasty surgeons in the country' and to back up this claim and reassure me that my nose would be in the very best hands she produced a photocopy of an article from the *Sun* boasting that a comic actor called Stanley Lebor (who he?) had

had a nosejob by the very same surgeon.

I couldn't resist asking if while I was having the cheek implants and nose job there was anything else I should have done at the same time. Florence studied my face. 'No lines, nice skin.' Her eyes swept critically downwards. 'Perhaps some breast augmentation, that could look quite lovely,' she said.

We discussed the costs – £3090 plus £610 for the hospital. I told her that I couldn't make a decision until I had discussed it with my husband but that I was sure he would be relieved that they could help me.

She clearly still found my nose rather pretty, despite its need for 'refinement'. 'What does he think of your nose?' she asked. I told her that he agreed with me that it was rather unsightly, at which she looked delighted for me and said: 'That's good. So many husbands simply don't understand, do they, and say to their wives, "I like you just the way you are." '

My quest continued. I made an appointment at the Collagenic Clinic, also in Harley Street, and this time decided to be very specific. The receptionist showed me into the consulting room of Dr K Nulliah. 'Ah, Mrs Ellerton, I've heard all about you,' he said, incongruously.

'Now what is it you don't like about your body?' he said. I did my best to look startled, as though it must be obviously quite clear with my problem staring him in the face. 'Doctor, can't you see? It's not my body, it's my face.'

He looked apologetic, 'Ah yes, of course. Tell me about it.' I rummaged in my bag, trying to blush. 'I feel a bit of a silly doing this,' I said coyly. 'You see, I've brought a picture.' Dr Nulliah reassured me that it was a common occurrence. I rummaged a bit more and then triumphantly produced a picture of Joan Collins torn from a magazine. I lovingly

🐧 Plastic fantastic

smoothed it before handing it across the desk.

'I would like you to make me look like Joan Collins,' I announced. Dr Nulliah looked rather dubious. 'She is twice your age. It would be hard to make you look like her,' he said. I implored, saying how I had wanted to look like her for years and that my husband would pay whatever the cost.

We went through her features one by one. 'We could do the nose,' said Dr N. 'We'd have to narrow it, straighten it and implant a pointed tip.' I suggested that just having her nose wouldn't make me look like her and that perhaps cheek implants would do the trick.

Dr N contradicted the previous expert, advising me strongly against it. He told me that the techniques had not been perfected and the implants would be difficult to remove should infection set in. I most certainly should not entertain the idea of having such major surgery done at the same time as the nose operation, whatever the saving in costs.

Seeing how disappointed I looked, he brightened. 'What you could have done are injected silicon implants to the cheeks and chin.' He produced a brochure about the technique which explained how the silicon was simply injected without cutting open the face.

I clearly needed convincing, so Dr N produced a series of pictures of people who had had silicon injected into their breasts. He told me to imagine the same effects to my cheeks, which seemed a tall order.

'Would I look like Joan Collins if I had that done as well as the nose?' I asked. Dr N was clearly losing patience. 'Only Paul Daniels could do that. We couldn't promise to make you look just like Joan Collins – only a bit like Joan Collins. In the way that people look like Alistair Burnett or I look like an Indian cricketer but that doesn't make me an Indian cricketer, does it?'

I tried to look crestfallen and disconsolately repeated the words 'only a bit like Joan Collins'. Dr N was in his stride now: 'I mean, I don't wish to be unkind but you just don't look like her.' I looked deeply shocked at this revelation and he continued, 'Even if you have all this done, I have to be honest and say that people will not stop you in the street and ask if you are Joan Collins.

'Life just isn't like *The Life and Loves of A She Devil*.' I now looked so dejected as to be on the verge of tears and Dr N softened: 'I'm not saying you're chalk and cheese but even Jackie Collins doesn't look like Joan Collins.'

I asked him if there was anything else I could have done that would help me look more like JC: perhaps my lips could be altered? Dr N decided to indulge me. 'Your lips are very like Joan Collins's already.' I tried to look ecstatic.

Dr N was clearly ready for the next patient and so gave me the bottom line. The treatment that would make me look 'a bit like Joan Collins' would cost between £8,000 and £9,000.

I told Dr N that he must get really bored with people wanting to look like Joan Collins all the time. 'No, you're the first person who wants to look like her.' Incredulous, I pushed him: 'Whose picture do other people bring you if not Joan?' Dr N went into deep thought, 'Mostly Kim Basinger, because they want the collagen lip pout,' he said.

Dr N advised me not to go anywhere else as they might be less scrupulous. 'But I can tell you that even the Queen's plastic surgeon couldn't make you look exactly like her.'

We agreed that I would ring him if I wanted the surgery that would help me look 'a bit like Joan Collins'.

As he showed me out, he clearly felt that he couldn't leave me utterly without hope, 'I will ask around for you, obviously I get to hear of what's happening and what's possible. Now if you see Amanda she will, er, sort things out for you.'

'Sorting things out' wasn't exactly plastic surgery, but it left me £30 lighter.

As the Peak Health Club had advised me that I was 11.4lbs underweight, I couldn't resist a visit to a slimming clinic.

The advertisements for 'Just Slim' show a be-swimsuited thinny astride a bottle of pills. I made an appointment and was booked in to see a Dr Ailing.

The premises looked promising; the basement of a seedy concrete block in Vauxhall Bridge Road with Radio 1 blaring and dog-eared copies of *Best* and *Woman's Own* to read. The receptionist was keen to know where I had seen the ad, and in return for the market research handed me a form to fill in which advised me that my treatment would include a course of appetite suppressants, similar in structure to adrenalin. Apparently, 'the majority of individuals who take appetite suppressant medication will not experience any side effects at all and will generally feel better during treatment.' Sounded irresistible.

Money and pills changed hands while I waited and I nervously imagined what the sinister Dr Ailing would be like.

At last it was my turn. Dr Ailing sat behind a large desk. He looked kindly and perhaps a teensy bit overweight himself.

I thought I made a convincing case for my desperate need to lose half a stone. Dr Ailing looked appalled, 'If you reduce yourself to seven stone you would reach the level of a concentration camp victim,' he told me.

I protested and he asked me why I was so determined to do it. I toyed with the idea of telling him that I was up for the lead in the film of DM Thomas' *The White Hotel* but instead mumbled that my bones were deceptively light and that I was in fact very much overweight. 'Well you are not,' he snapped. My further protests got me nowhere. 'I will not prescribe drugs for you,' he said as he showed me the door and announced to the receptionist: 'No charge for this patient.' And that was that.

In the world of make-believe, a scruple shone in Pimlico. 🐧

'The Bells! The Bells!'

On 7 October the *Sunday Times*, edited by Mr Andrew Neil, was full of rubbish. Its magazine ran a ten-page series of pictures of the trash from superstar dustbins. Now here's the trash from Andrew Neil's dustbin. We removed it from the pavement outside his flat in Onslow Gardens, London SW7 at 10.00am on Wednesday 10 October. This garbage is absolutely genuine

NOW WHO'S BIN DONE?

ANDREW NEIL

Andrew Neil is bored with his bachelor pad, judging by John D. Wood's details for a £695,000, five-bed Chelsea mansion. The fun-loving, tri-wheat editor also binned an £80 bottle of 1979 Veuve Cliquot champagne; a bottle of Spanish red; two Romeo y Julieta cigar tubes, and two tickets to *Presumed Innocent* at the Odeon Haymarket. Neil acknowledges his Scottish heritage with Baxter's soup, and his waistline with Heinz Weight Watchers' baked beans and skimmed milk. But then, disaster! He just can't help porking out on Mr Kipling's Bramley Apple Pies and Country Slices. Neil doesn't recycle: note the piles of magazines and papers. But the most interesting revelations concern his personal grooming: a single empty tube of Clinique Non-Streak Bronzer for Men

PHOTOGRAPHY: SANDRO SODANO

Admission

What kind of upper crust club would CHRIS WARD asked the boys from the

ILLUSTRATION: MARK DRAISEY

Whichever way you look at it, John Major is quite something. What other Prime Minister has addressed a War Cabinet wearing a Marks & Spencer suit? A walking tribute to self-help, he pulled himself up by the bootstraps in a fashion that even the girl from

The Carlton

Annual membership: £475
Waiting list: Five years
No. of members: Undisclosed
Facilities: Dining, library, private functions

The Carlton is the only club – apart from the Chelsea FC Supporters' Club – to show much interest in John Major. In fact it's positively delighted to have him join its ranks, but then it would be, simply stuffed to the gills as it is with Tories.

'He accepted our invitation to become a member on 8 January,' says club secretary Robert Linsley proudly. 'It was announced in the *Times*.' And he adds, 'I see no possible cause for conflict with Mr Major's call for a classless society. He was, of course, proposed and seconded by existing members of the club, and then received at least 12 supporting signatures in the membership book.' Mysteriously, the usual five-year waiting list was reduced to a period roughly equivalent to 30 seconds.

impossible

admit a lad-made-good from South London?
blackball to rate John Major's chances

Grantham couldn't match. But even boys from Brixton may need a word in the right ear of the right right–winger in the right place from time to time and until that glorious day arrives when, like him, we too achieve M&S classlessness, Prime Minister John is doing his very best to ingratiate himself with the upper middle classes and the aristocracy.

Carefully adjusting his BetterSpex (£19.99 inc vat and lenses), he announced a Cabinet full of men all educated in public schools and Oxbridge colleges – not a single comprehensive or polytechnic education amongst them.

What he's managed to keep a little quieter is the news that he's accepted membership of the Carlton Club, that bastion of Toryism so *déclassé* it even let a woman, albeit Margaret Thatcher, in as a member.

Its invitation neatly avoided him having to face a rather stark reality – virtually no other Gentleman's Club would have him, either because he's too middle class, doesn't own any land, is not a successful business man in his own right or because he's just too boring.

Here *Punch* rounds up the clubs that wouldn't let him past the doorman (or even have him as a doorman) – and finds a couple that would.

Boodle's

Annual membership: £550
Waiting list: Six years
No. of members: 1,345
Facilities: Dining and snooker rooms.

You need to be invited to become a member of Boodle's, with several existing members suggesting your name. This is followed by a ballot procedure to discern your suitability and your eventual admission some six years later, if successful.

'We wouldn't want to invite John Major as a member,' says club secretary Mr R J Edmonds. 'Well, unless he had a dozen friends who were members there'd be no point. You see, this is a club of like-minded members who only invite their friends to join. Our members are all country gentlemen, you see.'

RAC

Annual membership: £500
Waiting list: Three years
No. of members: 13,500
Facilities: Dining, library

The Royal Automobile Club has no plans to rush an application form around to Number 10.

'Our membership,' explains a spokeswoman, 'tends mainly to consist of managing directors, lawyers, doctors, professionals, business people, judges and ambassadors.

'We probably would have politicians, but they'd be treated just the same as anyone else. They all have to be proposed and seconded and then wait.' Well, almost all. The RAC does make a few exceptions for people it really fancies.

'Members of the Royal family don't have to wait, they're specials. So are people high up in the motoring industry. But not politicians like John Major – they'd have to go through the same procedure as anyone else.'

Pratt's

Annual membership: £115
Waiting list: Six years
No. of members: Undisclosed
Facilities: Dining

Another haunt of politicians, Pratt's is actually privately owned by the Duke of Devonshire, a man who has yet to make public his views on our newly beloved leader.

'We have all sorts in here,' says a spokesman, making it sound like a clearing house for the dregs of humanity. 'Authors, parliamentarians, journalists...you have to get proposed and seconded and then get 22 signatures in the membership book before the committee puts you on the waiting list.

'But I've no idea if they'll be asking John Major to join. They certainly haven't yet, anyway.'

White's

Annual membership: Unknown
Waiting list: Unknown
No. of members: Undisclosed
Facilities: 'The usual'

'It's the usual procedure to become a member here,' says club secretary David C Ward. 'You're proposed and seconded by existing members, other members sign the book and then the committee considers your application.'

But what about that all-important invitation to dear, dear Johnny?

'Oh, well, I suppose that's up to the members really,' says Mr Ward defensively. 'I'm just the operational guy.'

The Beefsteak

Annual membership: £225
Waiting list: Five years
No. of members: Undisclosed
Facilities: Dining

'Unlike other clubs,' says secretary Mr E G Pool, 'members here don't hide behind newspapers, they all sit at the same table and talk to each other.

'We do have politicians as members, but the club wouldn't invite Mr Major to become one, although they might welcome him as a member. Or rather,' he adds in confusion, 'the members might. Although I don't know if anyone will be proposing him.

'In fact I have absolutely no idea, I simply don't know if he has any friends in the club or not. There are no exceptions to the rule – he'd just have to find friends to propose him, then the other members would sign the membership book for him if

HAEFELI

'You know perfectly well that when it says "black tie optional" only the dull, boring men with no personal sense of style will wear tuxedos'

'I have an extremely interesting job so I feel no need to be interesting in my own right'

DOABLE **DONE**

Club class

they wanted him as a member,' he ends, hurriedly. Mr Major shouldn't worry too much about what the members might write if he did get as far as this, though. 'All clubs try and avoid nasty publicity by having blackballs, and it's never happened in all my years at the club,' says Mr Pool.

MCC
Annual membership: £100
Waiting list: 20 years
No. of members: 20,000
Facilities: Tie, admission to Member's Pavilion

Perhaps John Major's dearest wish is to become a member of the MCC. Perhaps his best-kept secret is that he's been on the waiting list to become one since 1989 – where he'll stay until some time around the year 2009, according to club secretary Lieutenant–Colonel John Stephenson, a man who is resolutely unimpressed by the applicant's various promotions since his original application.

'We do have provision for electing applicants out of turn in the interests of the club, but becoming Prime Minister does not make membership automatic,' he explains tersely.

Like other mortals, John Major had to find four full members of the MCC, at least two of whom had to have known him for the last three years, to propose him for membership. His name then went before the committee, who agreed to put him on that lengthy waiting list.

Chelsea Supporters Club
Annual membership: £30
Waiting list: One week
No. of members: 18,000
Facilities: Cheap tickets

This is the other club apart from the MCC, according to those who've met him, which the Prime Minister, as a big fan of Chelsea, would like to join but dare not for fear of being mistaken for a football hooligan. He should be so lucky. Or interesting.

'Anyone can join Chelsea Supporter's Club – you just have to send us £30, which covers this year and next, plus four photos and we'll send you your membership card,' says the membership clerk. 'It takes about a week. I'm not allowed to say if any famous people are members, but John Major would be welcome to join.'

The Groucho
Annual membership: £275
Waiting list: Up to a year
No. of members: Undisclosed
Facilities: Bar, dining, private rooms

This is possibly the least likely London Club to consider admitting John Major, let alone allowing him to jump the queue. Even if by some fluke he did manage to find the requisite two members needed to propose and second him, he'd almost certainly fail to pass the scrutiny of the membership committee upon which sits Janet Street Porter, a person not famous for her love of the Grey One.

'We wouldn't ever say that we wouldn't let him in at all,' says a spokeswoman carefully. 'He could go through the usual application procedure if he wanted to.'

But the tone in her voice says it all. 'Most of our members are in publishing, film, TV, journalism, that sort of thing. There are also some architects, some people in property, lots of actors, musicians, dancers, even a few politicians. But we don't like people trying to jump the waiting list. We will try if, say, the proposer is one of the directors of the club and they're saying "Look, push this through, will you?" but it isn't the norm.'

'Mr Fagin? You'll be relieved to hear the social services have determined that the children in your care are not at risk'

First you buy the clubs. It's only social. You car hooked, honest. But finally you find you can't face hooked on the little white ball. ANTHONY GARDNEF

Fairway to

Golf Type No.1: Pringle single

With his pink sweater and yellow-on-purple check trousers, he's louder than Led Zeppelin. Mid-thirties aspirational, he does hand-brake turns as he arrives in his Sierra Cosworth. His first shot invariably has more slice than Mighty White and his swing often gets caught in his gold bracelet. But shame is not in his vocabulary. He spends a life failing to be elected to a posh club.

Hero: Greg Norman

The first golf club has just opened in Moscow. It's called the Tumba Club and costs 12,500 roubles to join. They'll regret it as soon as they realise what golf can do. There's little more frightening than a man in a Pringle sweater and fringed shoes coming towards you with a niblick – never forget the King of Malaysia once clubbed a caddy to death for sneezing at the wrong moment.

But Malays are not the only people to take golf seriously. One club in Ireland was so strictly men-only that at weekends women were not even allowed in the car park. When one member had a heart attack, his wife arrived at the club in the ambulance which had been called. When he had recovered, the member received a letter ticking him off.

Even modern warfare need not interfere with your golf. American servicemen in Kuwait were able to play in the desert using kits invented by a former Navy pilot. The kits included orange balls, boundary markers to define the fairways, doormats (to put under the ball before hitting it) and watering cans for the greens. The players filled the cans with oil which they sprinkled on the sand to form a surface firm enough to putt on.

You can see why golfers keep at it. Lee Trevino won $1.9m playing golf last year (and he's too old to compete in the biggest tournaments). Greg Norman won $1.165m and Wayne Levi $1.024m. And that's just playing. Nick Faldo is thought to have made £10m from sponsorship last year – as much as Arnold Schwarzenegger and Tom Cruise's earnings put together.

You can see why they need the money. Golf is not a pastime for paupers. The East Sussex National club, now under construction at a cost of more than £22m, will be asking members for £20,000 down in addition to the £1,000-a-year fee. A set of clubs can cost you £1,000, and that's before you splash out on a a diamond-patterned pullover, woolly-tasselled socks to keep your clubs cosy, ball-cleaning devices, golf-club letter racks or a Biffit practice kit (a ball attached to a bit of elastic). Once a man is smitten by golf, you need never worry about his Christmas present again.

Despite these drawbacks, golf is now the fastest growing hobby in Britain. (I will not dignify it with the name of sport.) Around 243,000 people belong to clubs, for an annual average subscription of £265. And there are an estimated 750,000 golfers who don't belong to clubs.

The effect of putting on the Brits

1. Golf UK 2000: Demand turns Avon into one big closely-trimmed fairway

2. Golf UK 2050: A nation of febrile matchplayers annexes Buckinghamshire

3. Golf UK 3000: North Uist is declared the nation's last golf-free zone

handle it. Then you get the Pringle. You're not the day without a pair of tasselled loafers. You're enters the frightening world of golf addiction

heaven?

Addicts already arrive at the links at four in the morning ready for the course to open at six. In Japan, you can wait for two hours just to get on a practice range, and some Japanese golfers practise for three years before they even set foot on the fairway.

There are already nearly 2,000 courses in Britain, but this doesn't seem to be enough. West Sussex Council, for example, now receives one application every day for planning permission to build new courses. According to the Royal and Ancient Golf Club at St Andrew's, 650 golf clubs are needed by the year 2000 to meet public demand. That's a new course every five days.

Since the average course covers between 120-150 acres there will be enough greens and fairways – assuming that the hopes of St Andrew's are maintained – to fill the county of Avon. Buckinghamshire would also be full by 2050, and an area the size of Warwickshire would be gone by 3000.

The Council for the Protection of Rural England is deeply concerned. Not only is it worried that the Yorkshire moors could end up looking like Surrey, but it fears the Trojan Horse Syndrome: wherever there is a putting green, a collection of club houses, chalets and conference centres cannot be far behind.

If you think that's bad, just consider for a moment the full-blown club and caddy meltdown scenario. In this, the demand for courses follows not a straight line but an accelerating, exponential, F-16 afterburner curve: the whole of Britain is transformed into one great golf course, with a 19th hole on every corner, putting greens where your office used to be and 15,000 Pringle sweater and tasselled loafer shops.

With this in mind perhaps, George Taylor, a lawyer, has founded the World Organisation For The Abolition Of Golf. He says more and more business leaders are sneaking off to the fairways when they should be in the office. You can help him:
● Write to your MP demanding a halt on course building.
● Hide any stray balls you find.
● Laugh when you see a man in fringed shoes.
● Pray for rain on the final day of the Open.
● Offer your children cash to refrain from golf before they're 21.
● Breed moles.

Remember the King of Malaysia's caddy. It could happen here, you know. 🦅

Golf pairs from Hell

● Alice Cooper *and* Ronnie Corbett
● Pamella Bordes *and* Julian Barnes
● Jimmy Tarbuck *and* Gerald Ford
● Bob Hope *and* Kenny Dalglish
● Terry Wogan *and* Bruce Forsyth

Golf Type No. 2:
Been there, Dunn it

Could swing before he could walk. By six, belonged to the junior sections of 14 clubs. By his early fifties, golf is the only thing left between his ears. Always arrives half an hour early – to change into a musty collection of green and brown valueless antiques. Playing off a steady 14 handicap, he scores 84 in summer, 85 in autumn and spring, 86 in winter. Dreams of showing the finer points of his off-drive to his grandchildren.

Hero: Ben Hogan

ILLUSTRATION: JULIAN KIRK

'You bet I'm bored. I must be the only boy in the world whose father bought him a model house boat'

'...and then there was Goldilocks. Now she was a meal to remember...'

'Winkie? What the hell kind of a name is that?'

'Well well ... look what dragged the cat in'

'Oh God! It's that dreadful pig we met on honeymoon last year'

Was it Bill or

MARCUS BERKMANN and BILL MATTHEWS offer up a complete and utter guide to thirtysomethings' favourite TV: flobbalobful Sixties and Seventies children's shows

One of the BBC's best-selling videos is *Watch With Mother*. This compilation, including *Andy Pandy* and the *Woodentops*, has sold 500,000 copies. But it isn't children who want to sing 'We like Muffin, Muffin the Mule.' It's their parents.

This nostalgia boom for adults eager to recapture their innocence is also having a far-reaching social effect. Whenever baby boomers and thirtysomethings get together, the conversation will inevitably turn to the

First test your TV skills with this quiz

1. Can you remember all the contestants in *Wacky Races*?

2. What is the difference between *Timeslip* and *Time Tunnel*?

3. Who roamed the Wild West – the White Horses or Champion The Wonder Horse?

4. Who was Captain Pugwash's long-standing enemy?

5. How old were you when you realised the Wombles didn't actually live on Wimbledon Common?

6. Was *Ask Aspel* a metaphor for patriarchy taming the shapeless chaos of the universe?

7. Was the bald, bearded presenter of *Fingerbobs* terribly uncool?

8. Roobarb and Custard: which one was the dog and which one was the cat?

9. In *Fireball XL5*, what was space officer Venus's pet called?

10. What did Marine Boy use to breathe underwater?

The answers are:
1. Penelope Pitstop, Peter Perfect, Dick Dastardly and Muttley, the Ant Hill Mob, Professor Pat Pending, cavemen Ug and Thug, and some ghosts (we can't remember them all either).

2. *Timeslip* was British with

Dennis Quilley, *Time Tunnel* was American with hilariously recycled footage from old movies.

3. It was Champ. (Extra points for knowing the dog was Rebel.)

4. Black Jake. (Incidentally, Pugwash's shipmate is now called Master Mates on a new video not Bates. And where's Seaman Staines gone?)

5. Over 12 is a bit shameful.

6. No, that was *Runaround* with Mike 'A-go, a-go, a-goooo!' Reid.

7. A most definite yes.

8. Roobarb was the dog.

9. Zooney the Lazoon.

10. He used Oxy-gum.

was it Ben?

...ame subject: what they watched as kids themselves.

Burning issues dominate: such as what was the gardener ...alled in *The Herbs*? (It was Sage. The others were Parsley the ...ion, Dill the Dog, Lady Rosemary and Lord Basil.) You may ...ave an IQ of 145 but it won't count for much if you don't ...now who starred in *Skippy*. (Ed Devereaux.)

The next dinner party you attend, be prepared to hum the ...heme tune to *Screen Test* (de-dum-de-dubbity-dum-de-dum-de-...um-de-dum-de-dum). Or compare the story lines of *Ivor The Engine* and 'steamin' and a-rolling' *Casey Jones*.

And don't forget to score Brownie points by remembering the ...ame of the old guy with the pipe in *How*? (Jack Hargreaves) or ...he silver-topped presenter of *Clapperboard* (Chris Kelly).

Young thrusting types will be of no use – they all think chil-...dren's TV started with Phillip Schofield. They haven't spent a ...hildhood memorising the cast of *Freewheelers* or Tony Hart's 'Sorry we can't return all your pictures...' speech from *Vision On*. And they don't have shameful memories of their mother shouting up the stairs, 'Haven't you finished your geography yet? *Junior Showtime*'s on in a minute!' But there is someone you can turn to for help – us. First complete the test. If you score less than five correct an-

Magpie's Mick Robinson and Susan Stranks – never quite had Blue Peter's bottle (tops)

Basil Brush: the fantastic fox who put the boom-boom into our hearts

...swers your social skills need a little fine tuning. Simply memorise ...the following handy info-packs for the inevitable occasions when ...these programmes crop up. And they will. Just introduce two ...people of Trivial Pursuit age and wait for that inexorable sound: 'We like Muffin, Muffin the Mule...'

Magpie

Seminal ITV magazine show – the *Blue Peter* for children who couldn't afford sticky-back plastic. To this effect, Thames inge-niously hired Susan Stranks. Her role as a sex object for nascent teens kept the show afloat for years, which was not surprising considering the only competition was Lesley Judd. In addition there was tall, enthusiastic Mick Robertson, whose Brian May haircut finds work even to this day in the backwaters of the Satellite Children's Channel.

Magpie is best remembered for its annual charity appeal – the idea was, as you'd expect, poached from BBC's *Blue Peter*. The total number of bottle tops, paper clips or unwashed socks sent in for the children of Ethiopia was represented by a horizontal red line on the wall of the studio. As the appeal proceeded, the line ran along the corridor and eventually all around the Thames build-ing. It was an inspired gim-mick, cleverly designed to deflect from the appeal's regret-table failure ever to collect as much as *Blue Peter*. Other presen-ters' names to drop: Jenny Hanley (blonde, wet), Tony Bastable (dark, patronising), Douglas Rae (Scottish, short).

Basil Brush

In 1964 Rediffusion ran *The Three Scampies*. This featured Howard Williams as a circus entertainer whose comeback plans are destroyed by his assistants – a hedgehog and a fox. Folk singer Wally Whyton was the hedgehog and Ivan Owen was the hand behind Basil Brush, 20th-century fox supreme.

With his buck teeth, snappy tweeds and ebullient impatience, Basil was destined for solo stardom. He did two years on *The David Nixon Show* – hosted by the Paul Daniels of the day – and then in 1968 *The Basil Brush Show* hit Saturday evenings on the BBC and 12 million people tuned in to see Basil boom-boom his way through a queue of straight men such as Rodney Bewes, Derek Fowles and Roy North. He kept it up till 1984.

You can impress people by telling them that Basil was 18 inches high and that he was elected to the Eton Library. But your best bet is to re-enact the show's high point – the story. This was where the straight man tried to read a story against a tide of Basil's irrepressible ad-libs.

Basil does have a reunion gig with Roy North scheduled for the ITV show *Motormouth*. But no videos of his greatest moments are available.

Captain Scarlet

With *Thunderbirds* finally exhausted as a subject of intelligent conversation, this later Gerry Anderson pro-duction has now super-seded it. Ten points if you can remember Captain Ochre, and a further five if you remember that the voice of Captain Scarlet was provided by Francis Matthews, who later played Paul Temple. ☞

One of Captain Scarlet's henchmen models the cosmic copper helmet

🐚 Cover puppets

The real thing: Blue Peter's Lesley Judd and John 'Go With' Noakes sport risqué Seventies bikini and briefs detail

Crackerjack funster and first-form heart-throb Ed 'Stewpot' Stewart

More of a mystery, though, is the way Spectrum's HQ managed to remain in mid-air indefinitely without any apparent means of propulsion. And the names of the angels? Melody, Harmony, Rhapsody and Symphony, not Theocracy, Coronary, Colostomy and Leprosy.

The Flowerpot Men

Although made in the Fifties, this was possibly the most psychedelic of all children's programmes. Bill and Ben, both of whom had been rendered unimaginably thin after many years of obvious drug abuse, each lived in a 'pot' and loved talking to their 'weed'. Such was the extent of their addiction that they spent virtually 24 hours a day in a deep coma, waking up only once a week at 1.30 in the afternoon to banter incomprehensibly in their patented 'Flobalob' tongue (untranslated to this day). After 15 minutes waiting for their Main Man (ie the gardener to return from lunch), the strain overcame them and they collapsed into catatonia once more. Somewhat subversive.

Mary, Mungo and Midge

Another vitally important children's show, mainly because nothing ever happened in it. A transcript of a production meeting has, in fact, recently come to light. It includes this exchange:

Producer: What shall we do this week?

Writer: Well, this week Mary, Mungo and Midge leave their flat, go down the lift, get out of the lift, go out of the building, come back, get into the lift again (with Midge sitting on Mungo's nose and pressing the right button), go up to their floor and go back into the flat.

Producer: Brilliant! Just the same as last week!

Hector's House

Biologists have long speculated over the nature of this *menage à trois*. And wondered what strange beast might have been created by the unnatural union of Hector the dog and Zaza the cat.

Hector's House can be read as prophetic political satire – Hector ('I'm a great big pompous old Hector') being based on Sir Geoffrey Howe. (Or was it the other way around?) Rumours that Kiki, the frog, was inspired by the antics of John Selwyn Gummer await confirmation.

Crackerjack

At a party, there is a strong probability that one of the guests was taken to see a recording of *Crackerjack* as a child. Even better, they appeared on it clutching a cabbage for every wrong answer. They will therefore have many amusing anecdotes to tell about the late Peter Glaze (such as the occasion he duetted with Don McLean on 'Pretty Vacant'). It's essential, therefore, that you nip in first with your own story, remembering that Eamonn Andrews, Leslie Crowther (when his hair really was that colour), Michael Aspel and Ed 'Stewpot' Stewart all hosted the show. Anyone who has kept their *Crackerjack* pencil is assured of social success, even though such a pitiful offering as a genuine prize would be death to any modern game show.

Scooby Doo

The first series, made over 20 years ago, is still worthy of proper discussion. Indeed, accurate impersonations of Scooby are obligatory at many top social occasions – the giveaway is the table of Scooby Snack hors d'oeuves. Hanna-Barbera's stolidly cheap animation required that, during the numerous chase scenes, only two backgrounds could ever be shown. Unfailingly, the villain when unmasked, a) always turns out to be the apparently amiable and helpful character they met at the beginning of the show, and b) always says 'If it hadn't been for you pesky kids...'

Trumpton

Modern success is naught without full knowledge of *Trumpton*, *Camberwick Green* and The Other One That No One Can Ever Remember. Key points to note are a) *Chigley*, b) Windy Miller and c) Pugh, Pugh, Barney McGrew, Cuthbert, Dibble and Grubb.

The narrator, of course, was Brian Cant of *Playschool* and, later, *Playaway*. All people under 35 are united by the fact that, at some vital moment, each of them realised that Brian Cant had a very unfortunate name.

Playaway's Brian Cant used textured shirts to charm his army of toddler fans

The Clangers

The theory that nothing ever happens in children's TV shows is further borne out by this series, which has nevertheless exercised a unique influence on modern culture. The character of the Soup Dragon, for instance, provided a pop group with their name, and the whistling noises made by the Clangers themselves were taken up by Roger Whittaker. What remains a mystery, however, is how these fascinating species managed to live on and inside a planet the size of a Malteser, while communicating in a language even less expressive than 'Flobalob'. Again, impersonations should be assiduously practised, as they go down very well at weddings, wakes and, of course, Masonic gatherings.

Playschool

With Brian Cant (see *Trumpton*), Toni Charles, Derek Griffiths and lots of other people who probably don't wish to be reminded of the fact. Although there were many quite splendid distractions – the arched window (far, far superior to the square or round), the clock that never told the time correctly (it was always 11.15 – whether am or pm was sadly never made clear), the game of guessing what was under the clock, and some gorgeously ghastly toys named Hamble, Humpty, Big Ted and Little Ted – the main appeal of the show was trying to work out whether the male and female hosts were more than just good friends.

Any useful information on this burning topic would be gratefully received.

Derek Griffiths – Playschool's answer to Sammy Davis Jnr

Top Ten Best-Selling Kids Videos

- Watch With Mother
- Andy Pandy
- Bill and Ben Flowerpot Men
- Bill and Ben 2
- Playschool
- Trumpton/Chigley
- Muffin the Mule
- Blue Peter
- Count Duckula
- Sooty *and* Learn With Sooty

And they call it puppet glove: Sooty firing on all cylinders

'We'll have to play at yours, they've repossessed my Wendy house'

'Oh look, darling, the children are playing junior doctors and nurses'

'Well, I can't stand here idly chatting'

HAEFELI
Company scars

'Must I actually smile when I say hello to you? Isn't it enough
that I acknowledge your existence?'

'That's Gary. My mother's training him to be my step-father'

'We're trying to raise him to be too polite to verbalise any of the prejudices we've taught him'

'Leglessness does not become you'

'Sometimes, Beverley, there is a fine line between conversation and interrogation'

'Straighten your tie, Stephen. The world is already filled with enough disorder'

How to be a has-been...
MILITANT

The hey day

With your snappy suits and ready smile you are the 'cuddly comrade' of British bolshevism. You oust 'the crypto Tory incumbent' and become the youngest town hall boss in Britain

The slippery slope

1. In a 'fraternal foreign power move' your borough is twinned with East Berlin...just before the Wall falls. You gain popularity by halving rents. 'How does he do it?' asks Paul Foot in the *Socialist Worker*.
2. By doubling the rates, house owners discover. The poll tax is introduced. 'No one will be prosecuted for non payment,' you declare.
3. No one pays. You borrow £3bn from the LeichensteinHandel bank. Dunn of the *Sun* puts you 'on the couch' and 'diagnoses' you a Looney Leftie. You 'reorganise the insulting names' of council dustmen and window cleaners. They strike.
4. 'Transparent wall sanitary engineers' and 'street orderlies' demand to be paid.

The futile gesture

5. You settle the dispute after a 'mountain holiday' in Leichenstein with the strike leader's daughter – a ghastly social climber. The *Daily Star* prints intimate photos of your 'militant's mounting holiday'. You deny all charges.
6. You tell Jeremy Paxman that to be 'with the people' you are taking a council house. 'With 20 rooms?' says Paxo. The PM asks, 'Is this man fit for office?' Chris Patten answers.
7. By disqualifying you. You march to the Town Hall. 'I had nothing to do with the riot,' you tell the press...
8. Just before it starts. You appear on Channel 4's clothes show, *VIP Suit*, and open an eaterie – the Radical Chip.
9. Soon it is radically bust. You stand for Parliament in a rock solid seat and are defeated by...

The killer blow

10...Eastbourne veteran Richard 'Who?' Hickmet. The police investigate your 'productivity' deal with the bank. 'I was fighting capitalism,' you say from Stringfellow's.

The cruel twist

After your assassination by 'persons unknown' the LeichensteinHandel bank pays tribute. 'He was a man we could trust,' says the chairman, announcing a profit rise.

MIKE CONWAY

ILLUSTRATION: ALAN DE LA NOUGEREDE

Worry now, die later

Muesli causes cancer: true! Drink'll wrinkle your winkle: it's official! The papers love a scare story. STEPHEN PILE faces down the fear and plunges into a decade of over-anxiety

Oh great. Terrific. Now Scotland Yard disbands its crack unit. All that worry. All those headlines. All those warnings from then Home Secretary Douglas Hurd ('We are in danger and it's not an exaggeration to say that crack is a spectre hanging over Europe. The outlook is bleak'). All those articles in the *Daily Mail* predicting ghettoes on fire and what happens? The police find 250 grammes of crack all year, which is not enough to fill a small handbag.

Why were we frightened in this way? Why did these experts get it so wrong? Why do we go on listening to them? Why isn't Douglas Hurd behind bars for spreading false rumours likely to cause public unrest? What is wrong with the British all of a sudden? Why are we panic stricken about EVERYTHING?

I don't want to cause alarm, but the latest research by leading scientists in Norway (it is always leading scientists and they are always in Norway or Alabama or somewhere remote) shows that a deadly new virus is sweeping through this country. Every adult in Britain is thought to be infected and those with the full-blown disease become near idiots unable to eat anything, drink anything, or do anything.

This is now identified in remotest Norway as a virulent new strain of the debilitating MIPA virus (Media Inspired Panic About Anything). It is interesting to note that in India, where they are dropping like flies, and Africa, where everything goes wrong eventually, there is not a single recorded case of this disease. Travellers report that inhabitants accept their fate with stoic resignation (interspersed in South America with random bouts of folk singing).

But in Britain, where most people have got nothing to worry about at all, apart from where to park the car without getting clamped, we are worried from dawn till dusk.

Who discovered the fear virus? The

disease came from America, where everything is banned sooner or later on health grounds. The first British carrier was Oliver Gillie after whom the acute condition, *Delerium Gillies*, is named. In the late Seventies and early Eighties he was health and hysteria correspondent of the *Sunday Times*, a didactic, joyless newspaper that likes to tell its readers of the many ways in which they could be improved.

Every Sunday morning there was a new outbreak of *Delerium Gillies* as he discovered that some fresh aspect in daily life was, in fact, lethal: butter, milk, cheese, beer, cars, sex, fluo-

ride, everything. (There is a saying, that you should not shoot the messenger for bringing bad news. But why not? If he comes week after week with gloomy, alarmist and totally unproven bulletins I can see no reason for such restraint.)

When Andrew Neil became editor, the *Sunday Times* carried on in exactly the same fashion except that a new puritanical spirit entered the weekly medical reports. Gillie was replaced by Neville Hodgkinson who has given his name to the condition known as *Hodgkinson's Spasm*. In his first weeks he told us that married celibacy was a good idea. The article carried a photograph of the heroically unmolested Mrs Hodgkinson and there was the clear suggestion that self-denial was of itself valuable.

'I've only got herpes!'

Over the weeks and months 'Mahatma' Hodgkinson told us we should be worried about holidays ('can damage your health'), alcohol ('threat to babies'), anti-impotence drugs ('safety warning') brain implants ('doubts linger'), condom failure ('leads to abortion rise'), dog poo ('parasites cause child blindness'), heart attacks ('all mother's fault'), and low-calorie diets ('dangerous') etcetera, etcetera, etcetera.

Mahatma's strangest report so far was the recent announcement that 'if you want to avoid cancer become a gypsy. The disease is almost unknown even though they ignore all warnings about smoking, drinking and eating the right foods.' The finding came, he tells us, from 'an informal study of 250 families attending the Appleby Horse Fair in Cumbria.' 'This,' says Mahatma, 'supports the view that cancer is a disease of location,' thereby worrying everybody who lives in a house. He then refers to 'a German theory that radiation seeping into homes from the ground plays a much bigger role in causing the disease than is generally recognised.'

How the virus works
After the 'Leading Scientists' and the 'latest research' at an obscure university on the other side of the planet and an outbreak of *Delerium Gillies* or *Hodgkinson's Spasm* we next see mass hysteria. Millions of hens are slaughtered, businesses are ruined and John Selwyn Gummer forces his daughter to eat hamburgers.

At some point in the following days a sensible counter claim is made pointing out that 90 per cent of the herds are completely free of Mad Cow Disease, for example, and only one cow per herd is even suspected of having it and even then there is no evidence apart from one mad cat in Bristol that the disease transfers to anything, let alone humans. But this is swept aside and ignored. By now, the whole population is suffering from Mad Cow Disease Disease.

In no time industry has come up with a wonder cure or marketable solution. But MIPA is a mutant virus that can change its form and attack anything it feels like. No sooner does some sweet soul suggest an answer to the problem than Leading Scientists do some more research in Norway or Alabama to show the cure is lethal and worse than the problem. Unleaded petrol causes cancer; decaffeinated coffee produces just as much cholesterol as the regular bean, but might also cause cancer of the liver; free range eggs are more likely to have salmonella than

battery ones.

Eventually, the patient reaches a state of total confusion. We had, for example, just got cholesterol down as a bad thing when *Hodgkinson's Spasm* struck again. 'Reducing cholesterol with diet does not save lives and may even be a threat to health, according to a new analysis by an expert in heart disease,' Mahatma writes. Suddenly it was described as 'an organic chemical' and profoundly beneficial. Now he is telling us that stress causes the heart attack and cholesterol is attempting to cure it. But Mahatma, the fridge is full of Flora.

Steadily the virus spreads, reducing people to jellies of alarm and confusion. And the strange thing is that just when our worry is at its peak we forget all about it and worry about something else: listeria, mad cows, cook-chill curries, chickens, pre-packed sandwiches, too much ozone in the levels, not enough ozone in the layer. In recent times the *Guardian*, the *Independent* and the *Daily Telegraph* respectively have told us that deckchairs are a peril, that cocktail sticks are deadly and that dancing causes a condition known as 'jazz ballet bottom'.

The latest evidence suggests that panics replace each other. We can cope with two at most and usually have a macro-panic and a micro-panic running in tandem.

The micro-panic: a case study
A classic micro-panic was Rottweilers which were introduced to Britain at the 1937 Crufts show. By 1959 these German cattle dogs were man's best friend and all the papers carried a heart-warming story headed: BRUTUS GOES INTO ACTION. It told how these helpful creatures were now on the beat.

Of course, PC Forsyth, of Wimbledon police station, told the press how the animal 'is bigger than an alsatian, has no tail and looks like a grizzly bear', but the overall tone was one of approval. On his very first day Brutus was covered in glory when he shot up on a roof and personally captured a youth

'He was best of this year's most feared breed!'

Panic attack

stealing lead. As late as 1982 one was commended for rescuing a seven-year-old boy called Darrel from a reservoir.

The message was clear: Rottweilers are a good thing and their popularity as guard dogs grew. In 1979 there were 1,033 of them in Britain. Ten years later there were 10,000. Then between February and June 1989 there were 12 newspaper reports of Rottweilers attacking children. Soon they were called 'Devil dogs' and photographed in exclusively demonic, snarling poses.

Total hysteria was reached within two weeks. The pinnacle came when Bobby Ewing from Dallas was bitten off duty by his pet Rot, Troy.

Two things are interesting about the Rottweiler scare. First, between March and June the reported potential weight of a Rottweiler in the British press increased from nine to 18 stone. Secondly, the reported number of Rottweilers rose from 10,000 to 50,000, a rate of replication that made the rabbit seem celibate by comparison. During this period there were calls for complete banning of the dog, their declaration as a dangerous animal in the same category as lions, and a psychiatric test for the owners.

But by October, the Rottweiler scare had completely disappeared from the press, resurfacing only for a mini-micro-panic in the spring of 1990. What had happened in the meantime? Had all 50,000 Rottweilers left the country? Today you and I feel no panic whatever about them. Why not?

The fear as fashion

If we can abandon scares so quickly then they are nothing more than fashions. Rottweilers, for example, enjoyed exactly the same popularity span as the Acid House craze (a fashion that became a fear). Salmonella lasted only slightly longer than Bros. Aids is the Shakin' Stevens of our subject, but both of them are coming up for retirement.

Macro-panics have a longer life. Ecological worries have been toddling along pleasantly ever since the late Sixties when Rachel Carson wrote *The Silent Spring* and terrified America with her description of how chemicals and pesticides affect our health, life and environment. But eco-terror lay dormant for years because we already had a macro-panic, thank you very much. We were worrying about nuclear catastrophe and the Soviet threat.

As soon as Mrs Thatcher had said she could do business with Mr Gorbachev and the Russians started disarming, eco-terror instantly filled the gap. Margaret herself cut the ribbon at the new launch and threw a bottle of champagne against the bow by saying that, 'We have been conducting an unwitting experiment with the planet'. This will remain our macro-panic for the forseeable future unless our Arab friends finally boil over.

And this brings me to the main point about these panics: they are always misplaced. Why have we spent the past decade worrying about Colonel Gadaffi when the worst he has done is introduce Derek Hatton-style suits into the Middle East? During the same period we have all been sublimely unworried about Saddam Hussein who turns out to be a second Hitler with enough mustard gas to wipe out not only Oliver Gillie and all his readers, but also the entire human race.

When Mrs Currie resigned we were in spasms of anxiety about salmonella. Egg sales slumped so badly that 400,000 hens had to be destroyed. We stopped eating omelettes and worried about mayonnaise.

But eggs disappeared from the news with Edwina. We have stopped worrying about it, even though the figures for salmonella in eggs are now higher than during the peak of the crisis. According to the Public Health Laboratory Service, there were

'Remember the good old days when we were terrified of Colonel Gaddafi?'

12,931 confirmed cases of poultry-related salmonella last year. This is 409 more than before the Government slaughtered infected flocks and introduced new hygiene regulations.

So we are not worried about eggs and Rottweilers when we could be, but we are worried about Aids even though there is more chance of the average Anglo-Saxon heterosexual being eaten by a shark. As with crack, the experts have had to back-track a bit here and lower the expected figures for new Aids cases from 30,000 a year by 1992 to 13,000. Other experts place it as low as 5,000 to reflect the fact that the rising curve has already begun to turn down.

Thanks to Aids, we have stopped worrying about herpes altogether, but the disease is now more prevalent than when we talked of nothing else. It is still incurable and still spreading. The latest figures show there are 20,000 new cases a year and the drug which treats herpes, Acyclovir, is Wellcome's single best selling drug with a global sale of £105 million a year.

Big worries to watch for the future include microwave cookers (only a matter of time before there is a mega-*Hodgkinson's Spasm* about this one), chlorine in swimming pools (scientists claim it strips the protective coating from your eyes) and that old favourite, sunbathing, which has not yet fully run its course. Already the *Sunday Times* has found that sun blocking creams don't work.

Should I worry about worry?

The latest research from Norway and Alabama suggests that the MIPA is genetic. If you are the sort of person who worries about this then there is not much that can be done for you. But the real sufferer here is science as the public realises that you might as well use a crystal ball if you want to find out anything about foodstuffs and health trends.

Fortunately for all you sufferers out there, the new deadly virus can be cured by common sense, moderation and a philosophical acceptance of our human lot. Of course, this will cost a packet in the shops, but drug companies are working on it even as we speak.

Fashionable fears: an easy-to-read graphic guide

A terrifying horror that may, like Aids, not be quite so bad after all: the white high-heeled shoe

Fear: **The Environment**
Status: Mega-macro
Date of origin: Early Sixties
Date of demise: Still going
Notes: Once only for radical weirdos, now universal
Equivalent fashion: Jeans
Equivalent rock group: The Rolling Stones

Fear: **Nuclear Holocaust**
Status: Macro
Date of Origin: Fifties
Date of demise: late Eighties
Notes: Once seen as inevitable, now (Saddam willing) passé
Equivalent social phenomenon: Rising house prices
Equivalent rock star: Roy Orbison (not passé, but passed on)

As vile as any rottweiler and, thank goodness, just as shortlived, the Beastie Boys

Fear: **The Rottweiler**
Status: Spasmodic micro
Date of origin: February 1989
Date of demise: October 1989 (occasional outbreaks in 1990)
Notes: Nasty, ugly things that attack children
Equivalent trend item: Masters of the Universe
Equivalent rock group: The Beastie Boys

Adam Ant: once feared, now forgotten

Fear: **Herpes**
Status: Shortlived micro
Date of origin: 1982
Date of demise: 1984
Notes: A brief cult fear soon superceded by a similar, but even more horrifying panic (Aids)
Equivalent fashion: The ra-ra skirt (superceded by marbled denim minis)
Equivalent rock star: Adam Ant (superceded by pretty well everybody)

Fear: **Sunbathing**
Status: Micro, but building
Date of origin: Eighties
Date of demise: No sign as yet
Note: Once thought of as a good idea, especially in the Sixties and Seventies, but now a major concern
Equivalent styles: Macramé plant-holders, flared trousers*
Equivalent rock group: The Moody Blues
* *Note:* whilst the flare has enjoyed a revival among certain younger elements (with whom, *en passant*, tanning is still in fashion), sensitive people still believe it to be unsightly and quite possibly carcinogenic

Flare-friendly warblers the Moody Blues: they and their misshapen trousers are now as passé as sunbathing

Fear: **Crack**
Status: Deceased
Date of origin: 1987
Date of demise: 1990
Notes: An artificially-imported trend from America that utterly failed to catch on
Equivalent fashion: The Dick Tracy/Breathless Mahoney look
Equivalent rock act: 2 Live Crew

Fear: **AIDS**
Status: Ex-Macro, now diminishing
Date of Origin: 1982
Date of Demise: Not dead yet
Notes: A super-maxi-mega-macro fear that seems (thank God) to be on the wane
Equivalent fashion: White high heels
Equivalent rock star: Shakin' Stevens

It sounds official but...

HARRY PHIBBS looks at the busybody organisations with suspiciously fancy titles

A dangerous political slogan at the best of times is 'something must be done', but in the present era of mushrooming pressure groups a legislative quick fix for any new problem becomes addictive. It is not merely that there seem to be more pressure groups than ever before; the real trouble is that they are becoming increasingly cunning. Mostly they are composed of a pretty unedifying collection of people. Usually self-appointed, some have a fanatical zeal that leaves objectivity a forgotten pursuit. Nevertheless, these groups are skilled at manipulating the media, and can wield an influence out of all proportion to their importance.

But how do they get away with it? One wheeze is to give themselves a name that indicates official authority of some kind even when they are a purely private organisation. This is not to say that officialdom should be trusted or that private organisations are incapable of authoritative expertise on a given subject. The *Guinness Book of Records* is an outstanding example of success in this regard. But the *Guinness Book of Records* has built up its authority on merit. Everybody knows it is a commercial concern; it does not go round calling itself the 'International Records Commission'. Elsewhere, there is room for confusion.

When I rang the British Safety Council for information about the organisation, its leaflets turned out to be mostly about its head, James Tye. One brochure features a photograph of him on every page. 'JAMES TYE IS THE MAN WHO MAKES THINGS HAPPEN' screamed the headline. 'World leader...publicist...activist...lecturer...' etc ran in similarly chunky letters along the bottom. BSC's 'Mr Safety' calls himself 'Director-General' and the council's literature prominently features a crest 'granted by Her Majesty's College of Arms'.

Over the years BSC has had its moments of controversy. In 1983 the *Observer* reported that representatives of British Safety Council Sales Ltd had been turning up at factories and businesses selling first-aid boxes and posters. Several company executives were indignant that they had been left with the impression that the BSC staff were government inspectors rather than sales reps. One cited a letter from BSC warning him that he should shortly expect a visit from their 'Inspectorate'. Mr Tye's subsequent complaint to the Press Council was rejected.

When I heard the London Food Commission warning against eating something I supposed it was a quango or some other official agency. I supposed wrongly. It is an independent and highly tendentious pressure group. Its only official connection seems to be a 'five year Trust fund' from the GLC in 1985. 'Projects' have included 'Food needs of black and ethnic minorities', 'Food as a trade union issue', and so on. Now renamed the Food Commission, it publishes a magazine which attacks the 'large food companies' – in one case for producing a milkshake with no actual strawberry although the label said 'strawberry flavour'.

Groups using 'National' or 'British' in their titles often sound official. It is to the credit of Mrs Mary Whitehouse and her National Viewers and Listeners Association that it is an 'association' rather than a 'commission' or 'council'. But it is still presuming a status it has not earned. It is really the Campaign against Broadcasting Sex, Violence and Swearing (and this despite Mrs Whitehouse's 1985 book, *Mightier Than The Sword*, having two of the three in its title). But it is a campaign with which many of the nation's viewers and listeners disagree.

When I rang to ask the group's membership figure I was quoted 170,000, but when pressed this turned out to be similar to trade union block votes at Labour Party conferences. The membership of affiliated bodies is added up: 75,000 from the Free Church of Scotland, 16,000 Seventh Day Adventists, etc. Their own membership (annual subscription: £2) is just 10,000.

Although 'Bureau' has an official ring to it, the National Children's Bureau, for instance, is purely independent. Groups whose names indicate they represent great sections of the population include the National Council of Women of Great Britain, the National Association of Home Owners' and the Consumers Association. Of these, the Consumers Association, while entirely unofficial, merits credibility through its near million membership (subscribers to *Which?* magazine are automatic members), but this is still only a small minority of British consumers.

'Unit', 'authority' and 'board' are other words to watch out for. Unit is a favourite amongst pressure groups such as the 'Low Pay Unit' and the 'Unemployment Unit'. Most pressure groups are left-wing although there are, of course, the Media Monitoring Unit and the Social Affairs Unit (whose head, Dr Digby Anderson, once claimed that he hadn't taken a bath since 1968).

SAU has published attacks on social workers, 'health' food and government advertising. In 1989 it argued that drinking alcohol is good for you – just a few hours after the Government had launched an extensive anti-drink-driving campaign. Even the right-wing *Daily Star* was moved call it 'dangerous nonsense' and urged its readers to 'pray that Dr Anderson doesn't have a death on his conscience.'

There is little danger of anyone imagining that any quango could have come up with some of these views.

Turn for our prank follow-up ☞

Custard perks –it *is* official!

We invented our own official-sounding sex institute to see who'd believe this outrageous claim. JOHN HIND and STEPHEN MOSCO report

On the morning of 12 March a press release arrived in the offices of Britain's national newspapers. It made some astonishing claims about male sexuality. Headed 'High alkaline diet linked with male genital growth', it announced the findings of a research institute in Switzerland. The institute reported how its researchers had been treating ulcer sufferers with a diet of custard, yoghurt and porridge when they discovered an astounding side-effect – a substantial increase in penis size. The press release quoted impressive statistics and heralded the psychological benefits of this growth for patients (and nationalities) with genital inferiority complexes. It also explained that the full report would be published shortly in a respectable medical journal. A phone number was given for 'Dr Lionel Greene', director of the Institute of Gastro-Sexual Studies, who was said to be on a London lecture tour.

There's no need to stock up on Quaker Oats though, as we can prove that Dr Greene is talking cobblers. We know because we made it all up.

With characteristic professionalism, the *Sun* was first on the story. The day after we posted our fake press release, reporter Phil Dampier left a message on the answerphone of Dr Greene asking him to return the call. Dr Greene did not do this for another 22 hours. But six hours after leaving the message, Dampier had a small story in the first edition, 'Porridge Is Good For Your Oats'. By the final edition, the story had aptly grown from four paragraphs to ten and knocked Elton's 'Battle With The Booze' from pride of place as the page-three lead.

Our spoof press release got the *Sun* treatment in one day flat. No word yet from Prince Charles, though

Phil Dampier had not neglected his own research. He had phoned Tony Blackburn who said, 'I eat lots of porridge and yoghurt and my member has grown by about half an inch a year. It is now over two feet.' Bernard Manning was non-committal about size but did say: 'For years I hoped my manhood would grow like Pinocchio's nose, but that didn't work. Now I'll stick to the porridge.'

By 3am, the story was being broadcast on LBC, a London commercial radio station. Presenter Mike Carson had chosen to discuss sex and porridge as his main topic on his phone-in programme, *Through The Night*. This was on the evening after the M4 multiple crash.

Carson was obviously in philosophical mood. 'It does seem a bit daft doesn't it,' he said after mentioning the story three times in 30 minutes. 'What they didn't say was that the men who were fed yoghurt were served by a busty lady.' He outlined his own acid/alkaline diet then launched into the phone-in. 'David in Beaconsfield. Are you a porridge eater?'

'Oh no, I'm not I'm afraid.'

'Oh dear,' Mr Carson lamented. 'But is the size of your manhood important enough to you to eat different things so that there'll be more of you?'

By lunchtime, an estimated 12 million *Sun* readers had contemplated the medicinal advantages of porridge. That afternoon, Dr Greene returned the *Sun* reporter's call.

'Hello Doctor,' said Phil Dampier. 'We had your story in about your institute this morning!' Dr Greene asked how the

up your lovelife

story had been treated, Mr Dampier seemed unable to find a copy of his longer piece. He chose instead to read the shorter, first-edition version. 'And, er, then we had a much fuller appraisal later on,' he said, 'naming the institute by name...What was it called again?'

Dr Greene now said that he was looking for British volunteers to come to Zurich, and Dampier immediately spotted the follow-up. 'I think we'd be extremely interested in writing about that, Doctor, and I think we'd also be extremely interested in coming over and covering the actual experiments...I'll come straight with you, Doctor – I'm actually the royal reporter. I was handed this yesterday because I was sitting in the office with nothing to do. I normally follow the royal family around. So, are we talking now about volunteers with ulcer problems or penis problems? Because obviously, being the *Sun*, the interest was in the side-effect on the penises...But really it's a dual-edged thing now, isn't it – it's both the ulcer and the penis. OK then, so we can say you're looking for 500 volunteers for penis-growth...Alright then, lovely, Doctor, lovely.'

That night the paper reported that 500 *Sun* readers were needed to help the institute's research. Below the page-three lead, about Cilla Black's new contract, was the story 'WANTED: 500 SOUGHT FOR PORRIDGE SWELL JOB'. It

read: 'The doctor who found that porridge helps men increase the size of their manhood, last night appealed for 500 *Sun* readers to take part in his research...' On page six, Franklin used the porridge topic for his cartoon of Prince Charles (see opposite).

Back on LBC, Mike Carson was still excitedly exploring the possibilities of porridge. 'Listen to this, you'll love this,' he enthused. 'Yesterday we ran this story about this professor who says people who eat porridge tend to, shall we say, develop more of an interest in, er, a certain area. Would *you* go off for a couple of months to Zurich and give them £1,000 just to see if, y'know, you sort of enjoyed eating porridge...Hello Adam, Have *you* got a bowl of porridge with you?'

Mr Carson was reluctant to drop the topic, which dominated all other issues, even marital rape. A woman caller said: 'I'm phoning about two experiences.' Mr Carson replied, 'What sort of experiences?...Oh, I thought it was more exciting. I thought it was to do with porridge for a minute.'

He then sprinted into a porridge frenzy, unfolding puns on the theme of porridge making you 'warmer' in the morning, even when callers dismissed the story as 'a load of cobblers'. 'Well it is, yes, it's all a load of...well, something else,' he conceded. Ninety minutes later, however, as the show was being wound up, the indefatigable Mr Carson was still promoting the good doctor's claims. Anyone for porridge? 🐍

IG-SS
Institute of Gastro-Sexual Studies
President: Prof. Lothar Kohl MD
Chairman: Dr. Bernadette Katz FRCP
Director: Dr. Lionel Greene DO, MRO
Dusourstrasse 356,
8008 Zurich, Switzerland.
Tel: 010 411 261 1520   Fax: 010 411 261 0191

What we said in our press release

❝ **62 per cent of ulcerated in-patients who adhered to a low-acid diet – custards, yoghurt, porridge – showed increases of up to 16 per cent in penile dimension** ❞

What the other newspapers said in reply

'Dr Greene' phoned a few newsdesks and medical correspondents to ask if they'd seen his research

● **Tony Walton, *Daily Star***
'Did I receive the press release? Y-yyyyyy-yyyyes. The story was definitely around the office for a couple of days. I don't think we ran it, although I don't know why...I think if and when we do we'll hang it very much on the same angle as the *Sun*.'

● **John Burke-Davies, *Sport***
'I suggest that if there's a report in the *Sun* that you're unhappy with you take it up with them, Doctor. Meanwhile, I'm always interested in good stories.'

● **Jenny Hoop, *Daily Mail***
'Oh yes, yes, I did get that, yes. I had a very good story on impotence this week, that only got a couple of paragraphs, so I think the issue's rather died a death for now. I don't think it's a goer before next week, if then.'

● **Annabelle Ferryman, *Observer***
'Ohhh! I did receive that story, yes. Much hilarity all round, I must say. I mean, it was widely read around the office and I understand a certain degree of scepticism was what most people read it with...To be

quite honest I won't be running it this week because I'm up to my eyeballs at the moment.'

● **Celia Hall, *Independent***
'Hello!!!...No, that didn't reach my cubby-hole. Various things might have happened, like – for instance – it hasn't arrived.

I think I would have remembered Institute of Gastro-Sexual Studies, and I would definitely have remembered male genital growth. But I'd be very interested in reading about that.'

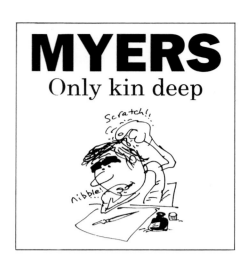

MYERS
Only kin deep

'You should be very proud, I hear your son's in advertising'

'Quite a nice day don't you think?'

'You may find our methods unorthodox but we do get results'

'I always show appreciation when he behaves well'

'Ignore him, he just doesn't take kindly to strangers'

'The boss's son? Next door down'

'Now I want a straight answer – that didn't get there by itself'

WHO GIVES A MONKEY'S?

A CRITICAL LOOK AT MODERN LIFE
by Richard Littlejohn

ESTATE AGENTS

If the cumulus of recession has a silver lining it is the misery rained upon estate agents.

Sales of striped shirts have dried up. Portable telephones litter every street corner. Motor auctioneers cannot give away repossessed BMW three-series convertibles.

During the recent cold snap, the only use being made of For Sale signs was as makeshift toboggans.

Now that you can pick up a 16-bedroom mansion in the Bishop's Avenue for what only a couple of years ago you would have had to pay for a lean-to in Rotherhithe, agents' commission has melted like the snow.

Then developers could buy an old tea warehouse for a song, bung in a few plasterboard partitions and an entryphone system, call it something like Gun Wharf and sit back and wait for mug yuppies to roll up in their Golf GTi's and hand over a King's Ransom for a slice of lifestyle.

Not any more. In some parts of Docklands, estate agents have taken to standing cardboard cut-outs in the windows of unsold properties to try to convince potential purchasers that they will not be living in a ghost town.

Desperate days require desperate measures. This is a job for Marketing Man. In a pitiful attempt to unload a lame-duck development in London's East End, Bow has been re-christened the Little Apple.

Adverts promise Manhattan-style loft living to anyone foolish enough to buy one of these flats in the romantic shadow of the A13 flyover.

The Little Apple? The Big Onion Bhaji might be more appropriate. Being born in the sound of Bow Bells used to make you an authentic Cockney. Now local residents are more likely to speak fluent Gujarati.

Comparing life in Bow to Manhattan is like reinventing Bridlington as Acapulco. The Roman Road is hardly Fifth Avenue although the danger of being mugged is about the same. Patel's Multi-Mart and Video Emporium doesn't exactly rival Bloomingdale's as a world's shopping mecca, either. You would need the gullibility of Trigger from *Only Fools and Horses* to swallow this pitch.

If you will excuse me, I am expected in the Windy City, as we must now call Muswell Hill.

Richard Littlejohn is a Sun columnist.

ILLUSTRATION: DAVID HENSLEY

The 1991 *Punch*

Robert Maxwell is a big man. Quite extraordinarily big. Vastly oversized. But no matter how gigantic Cap'n Bob may be, his ego is even more whopping. And last year it won the inaugural *Punch* Pro-Celebrity Trans-Atlantic Egothon.

We judged three finalists – Mr Maxwell, Donald Trump and Richard Branson – under a series of different categories, running from Dynastic Nepotism, via Over-Conspicuous Consumption, to Ethical Purity. In each category contestants were given marks out of ten, based on their behaviour as uncovered by teams of *Punch* researchers. The surprisingly self-effacing Mr Branson came third with 139 points, Trump ran second with 147 and the Bouncing Czech walked away with 160, thereby establishing

himself as *Punch*'s Mr Ego 1990.

As reigning champion Mr Maxwell qualified for this year's final, as did Richard Branson. But Donald Trump had less luck. The judges unanimously agreed that he was now just a mere shell of the rampaging self-publicist who thrilled and repelled global audiences at the tail-end of the Eighties. His place has gone to his ex-wife Ivana whose surgically-remodelled features and artificial embonpoint have rightly earned her front-page coverage the whole world over.

In, too, come a trio of contestants representing the multi-cultural fiesta that makes up our New World Order. On behalf of the repressed peoples of the Third World, let's hear a big cheer

Egothon

Our second annual search for the world's biggest ego

for Mr Genocide himself...Saddam Hussein! Nice 'tache you've got there, Mr G.

Representing endangered species – in this case, royalty – is the Duchess of York. And finally, it's a hearty 'Howay the lad!' to the pride of Newcastle, Paul 'Gascoigne' Gazza.

There was considerable debate in the *Punch* offices as to the lard-laden kickster's inclusion. Was it his fault that he was hounded by the tabloid press? Or was his tongue-tied ubiquity just a function of forces beyond his control?

But then we considered the facts. No one forced the man affectionately referred to by opposing fans as 'You fat bastard' to parade through Luton town centre wearing a pair of plastic strap-on gorilla's breasts. No, there could be no doubt that the air-gun-toting guzzler deserved his inclusion amongst our expanded field of six finalists.

With that decision, we repaired to the cuttings libraries. In-depth investigations began and the 1991 *Punch* Egothon was finally underway...

Please turn over

Egothon

Ivana and Bob: The two bouncing Czechs?

The runners	Historical role models	Heroism in sport
Richard Branson	Branson's father puts his son's adventurous spirit down to the fact that his grandfather's cousin was Captain Scott of the Antarctic. *8 points*	Almost in a class of his own, even if most of his heroic endeavours in hot-air balloons and speed boats have ended in disaster. Fortunately he has the resources to keep trying. *7 points*
Ivana Trump	Marie Antoinette (with a nose job), often compared to Imelda Marcos whom she makes look like a bag lady. *5 points*	Claims to have been a member of the 1972 Czechoslovak Olympic skiing team. The Czech Olympic Committee can still find no record of her existence. *1 point*
Sarah Ferguson	Queen Victoria, with whom she has discovered a series of 'spooky' parallels: Victoria was secretly a bit on the raunchy side, enjoyed the company of clowns and liked eating a great deal. *6 points*	Skiing, lots and lots of skiing. She also learnt to fly and paddle her own canoe. Got near to motor racing in the form of team manager Paddy McNally. *5 points*
Paul Gascoigne	The closest Gazza comes to having an idol is Stan Nixon – no relation to Richard Nixon, rather a soccer tutor and Gazza companion on many a fishing trip. *2 points*	Some great goals, but a large part of his fame comes from the World Cup blubbing. He also cried when Jack Charlton gave him a bollocking at Newcastle and when his plane hit an air pocket. *6 points*
Saddam Hussein	King Nebuchadnezzar, whose ambition was to re-build Babylon and be king of the universe. He also finds Don Corleone, of his favourite movie, *The Godfather*, highly inspirational. *7 points*	Grisly at best. He has authorised 30 different types of slow painful death ranging from gouging out eyes to roasting the players over a fire. *4 points*
Robert Maxwell	Himself. Revels in the remark made to party colleagues by Czech President Husak: 'You know what's wrong with our country? We no longer produce Robert Maxwells.' *6 points*	Bought Derby County, is director of Oxford and planned to underwrite the saving of Spurs. Blamed by fans for Derby's certain relegation as he banned transfers. *6 points*

Dynastic nepotism	Ogreism	High-profile love life	Rewriting history	Psycho-sexual fixations	Camera charisma
Though his kids are still young, Branson still felt he had to clear his marriage plans to long-time girlfriend Joan with his daughter. *4 points*	More like eaugreism. He foiled an intruder who broke into his Notting Hill mansion one bonfire night by throwing a bottle of water at him. *4 points*	None. This man's idea of scandal is marrying his girlfriend. *0 points*	No need. His mother achieved a certain notoriety by becoming a glider pilot at 18 by pretending to be a man. Also pre-empted John Major when he admitted to having no O-levels. *0 points*	Speedboats, helicopters, jumbo jets, you get the picture. His Chinese horoscope is the Tiger, the sexiest of bed-partners. Most suited to Horses, Dogs and especially Pigs. *6 points*	Normally excellent. Was upstaged after Mike Yarwood's comeback in New York ended in an on-stage walk-off. The connection? Branson was in town to promote new flights to the city. *6 points*
Called her daughter Ivanka and has already taken her to fashion shows. Her mother was ordered to spy on staff at her Trump Plaza hotel and write reports on their daily behaviour. *4 points*	Tentative. During her divorce with tycoon hubby Donald she cancelled a right to commit adultery agreement after just three days. But staff were quoted as calling her a 'despot'. *3 points*	Spent a fortune on plastic surgery to try to win Donald back. Cut a swathe through UK society seemingly in search of a titled hubby. Did manage dates with the Duke of Northumberland. *6 points*	Claims to have an interior design licence. How, is still a mystery to the American Society of Interior Designers. Promisingly, she is now working on her memoirs and film rights. *5 points*	Penis envy is possible as she used to enjoy a stroll up the Trump Tower, but preferred the less well-endowed Trump Plaza. *2 points*	Glamorous. Did fashion spreads for *Vanity Fair* and *Hello!* Unprovoked, she once clutched Norman Tebbit's hand at a London park photo-call. *6 points*
Has named her daughters after Queen Victoria's. Belonging to the royal family gives her a head start over the other Egothon entrants. *7 points*	Allegedly insisted that her mother curtsey to her after a restaurant lunch. Mitigating factor: this is normal protocol amongst the royals. *4 points*	Maximum points for marrying a prince. No papers yet speculate on her marital happiness. However, a Knightsbridge hotel room was recently reserved for her and the Dalai Lama, *Today* reported. *8 points*	Not much. She did reveal a life-long ambition to be a pork butcher while inspecting the Army in Berlin. And she had a migraine on the day of her wedding – but it quickly passed. *3 points*	Several frilly knickers and 'love-making litter' has been found in her grounds. So far, schoolkids have been blamed. In trouble with the Palace for flashing her thighs as she gets out of cars. *2 points*	All go since the *Hello!* baby pics and her weight loss. Her X-ray specs show her increased skill in getting photographed. As did her short hair cut. *8 points*
Allegations that his mother and sister receive £4,000 an hour for interviews brought lawyers out, but sister Anna, 'an actress', did land parts in panto and teenage TV drama *Byker Grove*. *2 points*	Some bouts of self defence, some bookings and a sending-off for swearing at the ref. Plus Neanderthal goal celebrations and membership of the Dennis the Menace fan club. *5 points*	A childhood sweetheart, a daughter of a scrap metal merchant, a dance with Mandy Smith and he asked a *Star* journalist to go fishing while in the nude. A tiddler, she said. *5 points*	There is so little of any interest, that the *Daily Express*'s full, in-depth, detailed history only stretched to three episodes. According to Wogan he could star as John Major in the film of the Gulf War. *2 points*	It's unlikely that Gazza would recognise any himself, but with communal showering, who knows? *0 points*	Tremendous stamina here. Opens dozens of places like pizza parlours attended by hundreds of teenage girls and plays golf with an exploding ball. *8 points*
Rampant. Most posts in government and business are given to relatives or close friends. His heir Uday admits to three killings. Made one man an airline director in exchange for his wife. *8 points*	Endless. Put his son on trial for kicking his food-taster to death, but the food-tasters' parents pleaded that Saddam should spare his son. Started branding Kuwaitis with the letter S for Saddam. *10 points*	A great fan of foursomes, he had his valet bring three girls at a time back to the palace for 'fun and games'. When his wife found out she had him shot – the valet that is. *6 points*	Gave himself an honorary degree. Claimed extravagant injuries in an attack on General Qassim. The truth is that Saddam was only slightly wounded and shot by one of his own men. *9 points*	Obviously trapped in the phallic stage. His attempts to build a 'supergun' were coitally interrupted by HM Customs. His official biography notes his love of guns at the age of ten. *6 points*	Paraded the most photogenic hostages in low-budget *Wogan*-style chatshows. Then held grand *This Is Your Life*-type reunions with the other fading ex-heads of state who flocked to Iraq. *7 points*
Two of the seven Maxwell children are joint managing directors of MCC. They are ominously described by Maxwell as 'the next generation'. *7 points*	Legendary. He harangued a *Sun*-buyer at Heathrow: 'Have you read the *European*? Why don't you buy a copy? Can you afford it or do you want me to pay for it?' *9 points*	Absolutely zero for the second year running, though he could be said to be conducting a public love affair with himself. *2 points*	Had Joe Haines write his life story in a brown-nosing biography. Modestly, Maxwell objected strongly to anybody hearing anything else (see legal wrangles). *8 points*	The yacht, the chopper, you name it. As owner of the sticker firm Panini, he has mooted the idea of adult stickers with peel-off clothes. *8 points*	Still no advance on official biography, in which he's pictured with 20 various heads of state. But his newspaper vending stunt in New York was shameless stuff. *7 points*

	Fear of being attacked	**Wardrobe excesses**	**Legal wrangles**	**Name & icon fetishism**	**Party animalism**
Richard Branson	His decision to spend a 6,700-mile round trip with one person must qualify him automatically. But he doesn't so much fear attack (he has no goon squads), as invite spectacular death. *2 points*	Cunningly casual, but deceptively expensive. One employee of his airline said: 'His jumper probably cost more than all our suits put together.' *3 points*	Keeps his lawyers busy only by signing contracts. A recent deal with Fuji for licensing Virgin artists will earn an estimated £85m. *2 points*	Has discovered that you can prefix almost anything with Virgin and still make some people feel uncomfortable – Records, Megastore, Airline, Games, etc. Not forgetting Mates condoms. *5 points*	Very low score. This is, after all, the man who flew in his 92-year-old granny, his mum, dad and aunt to a beach party in LA. *1 point*
Ivana Trump	Not pronounced, but does suffer from mild arachnophobia. *2 points*	In one year alone spent $1.5m on frocks and fripperies, though she refused to fly her private jet to the Paris couture shows saying, 'They'll have to come to me.' *8 points*	Issued a $10m writ over a new lipstick called Ivana. Noisy divorce with a £12m settlement. She rowed for seven hours over who got a car. *8 points*	Plans to launch her own 'Ivana' range of lingerie and luggage. Under US law Ivana is entitled to half Donald's worth. So she gets five of his ten Icon points from last year's Egothon. *9 points*	Spends vast sums throwing parties. Invitees vary – those with a title and bundles of cash stand a good chance of being asked. Is fond of lavish floral tributes in the $20,000 range. *5 points*
Sarah Ferguson	With her security, no problem. But, when a mentally-handicapped boy jumped around at meeting her, her bodyguards were rather taken aback. With good reason, the poor boy was jumping for joy. *2 points*	Some disastrous designer togs. Her matronly size 18 was the problem during her first pregnancy. Her recovery to a size 12 meant the papers went royal diet crazy. *7 points*	Sister Jane's marriage difficulties (children Seamus and Ayesha) did not stop Big F threatening to visit with a full complement of children. *4 points*	Several bonus points for calling her children Beatrice and Eugenie after Queen Victoria's. She also receives £18,000 a year from Sotheby's for letting them use her name. *2 points*	Revealed that 'some of my best friends have been alcoholics and drug addicts.' Proximity to such bacchanalia is sufficient, though her dad, Major Ron, is a good bet too. *5 points*
Paul Gascoigne	Gazza revealed in an LWT interview he dreads attack by a 'jealous nutcase'. Saddam-like, he surrounds himself with friends for protection. *6 points*	Voted Britain's Best Dressed Man, though by which group of myopics is not certain. Gazza wears leather jackets, gaudy tracksuits, and tacky nightclub outfits and a semi-shaved haircut. *6 points*	Lord Justice Harman decided he wasn't as famous as Wellington so he couldn't stop a quickie biography being called *Gazza*, despite the barrister's assertion that Gazza was a national hero. *5 points*	Pretty impressive. Apart from his recent book *Gazza My Life In Pictures* (text was too strenuous, one feels), Paul also endorses boxer shorts, football boots, shinpads, aftershave etc. *8 points*	Ranges from chewing dresses in nightclubs, stripping to the waist with a headband made out of toilet rolls, drinking foul cocktails and going to Dunston Working Men's Club. *6 points*
Saddam Hussein	Has his own food taster and special chair to prevent assassination by poisoned tack. Refused a call from George Bush believing he had a device that could kill him down the phone. *8 points*	His-and-hers cufflinks, a personal tailor, and his jacket lining is made from the same silk as his ties. His military outfits feature ludicrous cravats, and chunky drug baron sunglasses worn on parades. *5 points*	Legal difficulties stem from his definition of the law. Reported to have said: 'A law is a piece of paper on which we write one or two lines and then sign underneath it "Saddam Hussein".' *6 points*	His portrait is everywhere, on posters, murals, even on the dials of gold wristwatches. Muslims do not generally celebrate birthdays. Saddam made his a national holiday. *10 points*	Notorious for gate-crashing and bringing uninvited guests. Must be given credit for introducing such new words as CNN, Kurds and newscasters' favourite, Scud. *6 points*
Robert Maxwell	A raging Rosa Klebb complex means that any visitors to his opulent yacht, Lady Ghislane, are made to take their shoes off. *6 points*	Sensibly limited to changing his clothes every two or three hours. But he did don a baseball cap without any encouragement when in New York. *5 points*	Apart from the ongoing Pergamon dispute, Maxwell has tried and failed four times to injunct Tom Bower's unauthorised biography. Still suing for libel. *8 points*	Enjoys buying companies just to add the name Maxwell to them. Reportedly renamed Headington Hall, his council mansion, Maxwell Hill Hall. *9 points*	Enjoys a strange line in entertainment. At a party at Brighton's Grand Hotel, trade unions picketed to protest over Neil Kinnock's decision to attend. *6 points*

Global reputation attempts	But nobody asked (silly quotes)	War-mongering
Waived the £35K-a-week rent on his Caribbean island, Necker, for Princess Di. Good Queen Noor of Jordan gave him an audience after a donation of £150K to her country. *5 points*	'On paper I have the wealth of a small nation and if you're running a small nation, you have responsibilities.' *3 points*	Very low. Branson was balloon bound at the time of the Gulf crisis and claimed ignorance until mercy mission syndrome struck. *1 point*
Her bids to meet the Queen include the £300,000 sponsorship of the Royal Windsor horse show and the buying the £7.2m Mar Lodge hunting estate next to Balmoral. *5 points*	'Men are the last thing on my mind.' 'When people give me a punch in the nose, I react by getting even tougher.' *5 points*	Denounced love-rival, Marla Maples, as 'a slut, a bitch and a home-wrecker,' nearly putting her foot through the TV when she appeared on the screen. *5 points*
Very high. Interrupting Andrew's speeches did not go down too well in Canada. Famous in France for looking like her namesake, the Ferguson tractor. *9 points*	'I am not flavour of the month.' *3 points*	Fergie failed to devote herself to too much Gulf morale boosting (which could well be the reason it remained high). *1 point*
A *Daily Star* Gold Award, and the 1990 *Record Mirror* Poll voted him less likeable than Saddam Hussein. Down Under, Mel Gibson called him an 'idiotic buffoon'. *6 points*	'I'll see you in a minute, kids, I'm just going to get drunk.' 'I'm planning a mega-bender on Friday. You name it, I'm going to stuff it in my gob.' *4 points*	Much patriotic tub-thumping during the World Cup. He elbowed a Notts County player in the face and replied to a press question with: 'Do you want a bag in the face?' *6 points*
Obviously has a crusade to become a CNN anchorman. Big in Wales, where Kevin Davies had Saddam's face tattooed on his bum, according to the *Daily Star*. *10 points*	(To allied servicemen) 'The desert will swallow you up while your wives are being bedded by wealthy Arabs'. 'You have won... great Iraqis.' *7 points*	Too distressing. After a beating from the Allies, he has started on his fellow countrymen, the Kurds. Waged an eight-year war with Iran over a piece of swampland. *10 points*
Mammoth. But he erred in writing a foreword for a biography of Nicolai Ceausescu, lauding his 'tireless activity for the good of your country.' *7 points*	'You will not find my papers championing anything I'm in business for.' 'I am the *European*.' 'Even I can't be everywhere all the time.' *7 points*	The *Daily Mirror* backed the Gulf war except for Paul Foot. At the *New York Daily News* he promised 'no union bashing' then promptly laid off 850 workers. *5 points*

Results

BRINGING UP THE REAR with the wooden spoon is last year's bronze medallist, Richard Branson, with a lowly 59 points. Branson spent too much time in his balloon. Newcomer Sarah Ferguson polled a steady 76 points, but she was hampered by the Gulf War, when Buckingham Palace issued her a directive to lie low. Paul Gascoigne scored 77 points, mainly on the back of all his merchandising.

This year's bronze medallist is that woman scorned, Ivana Trump, who supersedes ex-hubby Donald, last year's runner-up. She scored 81 points. But this didn't compare with the two heavyweights duking it out at the top. This year's runner-up is last year's winner, Robert Maxwell, with a girth-swelling 105 points. But for all those 'ego has landed' jibes, Cap'n Bob couldn't keep up with the Beast from the East. The winner of the *Punch* 1991 2nd Annual Egothon is that mother of all egos, Saddam Hussein. He came, he saw, he invaded. And while he got soundly beaten in Kuwait, he came through where it really counts – in our poll. His total: a whopping 119 points. Saddam's consolation for defeat in battle is knowing that his self-importance, vanity, arrogance, bullying, selfishness, hypocrisy, mendacity, repugnance and sadism do not go unrewarded by us. But will he be able to hang onto his crown for the 1992 Egothon? See you then.

HANDELSMAN

'Nothing much. They've all gone to bed and
I'm just watching television'

'Dear Sir, My conscience forbids me to accept the Gold Card
you offered me. I am not the big success you take me for'

'I didn't even know there was such a thing as a Gothic novel'

'Supply? I have here a Mr Carlson, a former government
employee who never took a penny he wasn't entitled to. I'd
like you to issue him an extra-large halo with sequins'

'This fell out of your pocket. Always glad to
help a fellow marsupial'

I will strive at all times to be a wise
and just ruler, eating only those who
question my authority.

How to be a has-been...
BOXER

NEW BOXING CAREER
LOO CLEANSER—
IT SIMPLY GOES
DOWN THE TOILET
"It's Knockout"

The hey day

You get a crack at the much-loved champ, and floor him
in the first round. 'The old must make way for the bold,'
you swell. But it's all downhill from here...

The slippery slope

1. The old champ's career takes off. 'Why does he get to
open all the supermarkets?' you demand.
2. 'Have you ever looked in a mirror?' asks Jean Rook.
You go 'State-side to grab a belt'. You get a belt...
3. ...on your 'glass jaw'. Henry Cooper nicknames you
'Dozy'. A new manager takes you on. 'He's a financial
wizard,' you tell Reg Gutteridge. He sure is.
4. All your money disappears. You sue. The judge
throws the case out. 'Can't even spell his name,' he
sneers.

The futile gesture

5. You declare yourself 'open to challenge' and 'open to
payment'. The *Sunday Telegraph*'s Frank Giles says 'it's
the return of the prize fighter.'
6. 'I don't want no prizes,' you say. 'I just wants money.'
You get money. From your insurance company after
being KO'd in the first bout.
7. David Coleman rescues you. You join Bill Beaumont's
team on *A Question of Sport*. But find the auto-cue
'challenging'. You're switched...
8. To Ian Botham's team. You assist Harry Carpenter on
Channel 4's *A Bout Last Night*. Charlie Catchpole slags
it off. 'Harry and Dozy get slayed,' he quips.
9. You start 'building on your commercial potential' and
advertise loo cleanser. You appear on the *ITV Telethon*.
Michael Aspel asks you to nominate your charity...

The killer blow

10. But your memory fails: 'It's Alzheimer's disease,'
prompts the Asp. You attack boxing. Sarah Dunant
stares doe-like as you slam the sport on *The Late Show*.

The cruel twist

11. After your death, from Mad Boxer's Disease, Ms
Dunant forms 'Broadcasters Against Bouts' in your
honour. The Groucho Club regularly fills to watch
'boxing horror videos'.

MIKE CONWAY

ILLUSTRATION: DAVID LYTTLETON

Taken as

Why do idealistic left-wing MPs turn into paragon
CHRIS WARD charts the Labour Party's young turk

Something mysterious happens to Labour politicians as they make the journey between the back and front benches of the House of Commons.

Not only do they get a haircut, a new suit or frock and a pair of shiny shoes, their politics also suffer a significant wash-and-brush-up. Loony-left views magically disappear on the way down that shallow staircase. Student revolutionaries turn into middle-aged establishmentarians. Gay, black, one-legged single-parent supporters begin to play the white man.

The reason, of course, for this transformation is power. Suddenly they have a Portfolio, a suit allowance, a weekend at the Party's TV training camp and permission to sound off with the full backing of the Party – provided, of course, that they stick strictly to the Party line.

Not all who journey down to the Front Bench succumb. As we shall see, Dennis Skinner could, with hand on heart, say he's still the same bloke as Labour Party chairman that he was when he hewed coal from a Derbyshire mine – but most do. And, as a detailed example of the process this change involves, let's look at Labour's leader, the charismatic chrome-dome himself, Mr Neil Kinnock. This is his life...

Neil Kinnock, *Chapter One:*
A Totally And Utterly Angry Young Man

It's June 1970 and the carrot-topped, 28-year-old Neil Kinnock – former chairman of the Socialist Society at University College, Cardiff and a tutor organiser in Trade Union Studies – is elected to Parliament as MP for Bedwellty. Labour, however, lose the election and the young firebrand is condemned to the first of his periods in opposition.

By 1974, Labour are back in power, but the onset of political responsibility and the dawn of his thirties have in no way diminished our Neil's commitment to the cause of socialism. He campaigns in favour of paying companies not to export oil to South Africa and leads the opposition to the Lions' South African rugby tour...

In February 1975 he resigns as Michael Foot's PPS (in itself, a job with massive red cred) on the same day as a left-wing back-bench revolt, so as to maximise the publicity for the rebels.

His support for the poor against the unearned privileges of the rich and titled is demonstrated in 1976 when he condemns the decision to spend £500,000 on Gatcombe Park for Princess Anne as it could have provided houses for 50 homeless families. In April he refuses the offer of a junior ministerial post from Jim Callaghan.

In October 1977 our tempestuous young(ish) radical rallies support for the left-wingers of Newham North East who had campaigned for the long-serving right-wing MP Reg Prentice to be dropped. The following month Kinnock and Dennis Skinner become the 'loneliest men in Westminster' when boycotting the Queen's Speech in the Lords and staying in the Commons.

By now, Kinnock's reputation is secure. Left-wing, anti-royalist and willing to fight anyone in his party who can be accused of selling out to the centre, he typifies the radicals whose actions are steadily splitting the Labour Party in two. On 5 December 1979, he scuffles with Alf Morris, former Minister for the Disabled, in the division lobby. 'To say we had a fight is a mischievous exaggeration,' says Kinnock, but they had to be separated by Jim Callaghan and John Prescott.

Chapter Two:
Turn, Turn, Turn

The Eighties dawn in traditional Kinnock style. On 30 January, Jim Callaghan threatens to dismiss him from the Shadow Cabinet for not abstaining on a vote on nuclear weapons. Kinnock – like his wife, a committed unilateralist – voted to get rid of them.

But on 9 February 1980 there are strange portents of things to come as the *Guardian* dubs him a 'former darling of the left' and accuses him of 'having succumbed to ambition', after refusing to commit the next Labour government to restoring cuts in education.

He recovers some ground on 30 September 1980, calling for Eton and Harrow to be taken over by local councils. And on 27 October he speaks to the biggest CND rally since the Sixties.

On 13 January 1981, Kinnock calls the Duke of Edinburgh 'A world expert on leisure – he's been practising it for most of his adult life.' He turns down an invitation to the royal wedding. 'I am otherwise engaged, although I am not yet certain what that engagement will be.'

But then come more signs of a gradual shift to the right – or, at least, the not-quite-so-left. In 1981 he backs Silkin and Foot against Benn in the Labour leadership contest. Then in March 1982 he is challenged in his constituency by left-winger Ray Davies 'angry at his criticism of the left and his refusal to back Benn.'

Nor is Mr Davies alone in his criticisms. In September 1983 *Tribune* magazine calls Kinnock 'a shameless opportunist'. But this does not pre-

ILLUSTRATION: DAVID HENSLEY

red

moderation when they get a taste of power?
no fattened into pale pink turkeys

...ent him becoming leader of the Opposition in 1983. In fact, it ...nay be seen as his most convincing qualification for ...he job.

At first, his new-found power does not ...ramp his style. But soon, responsibility ...nd the need to compromise old ...rinciples if power is to be ...chieved have an effect. In ...ebruary 1985, he

urges local councils not to break the law in a campaign against rate capping. In June he repudiates a call by Scargill for more industrial action by miners. On 21 November 1985 he threatens to expel some Militant members. Then on 24 March 1986, he angrily rejects moves to commit a Labour government to removing all legal restrictions on strike action.

In September 1986 the Labour Party unveils its new, user-friendly, yuppie-style marketing logo; a red rose, conceived by none other than...Neil Kinnock. ☞

Diane 'Cornfield' Abbott; Paul 'The Judge' Boateng; Gordon 'Why Am I Here?' Brown; Gorgeous Neil Kinnock; Margaret 'The Cooing Dove' Beckett; Dennis 'The Mouth' Skinner

Chapter Three:
Principles? Isn't That A Clothes Shop?

It's January 1990 and Labour face a second decade out of office. Their leader tells David Frost he was never the darling of the party's hardline socialists – 'You know, the favourite lad of the left and all the rest of it.' He also explains that CND no longer advocates unilateral disarmament, that Labour no longer believes in the superiority of collective action and that he is one of nature's moderates.

On 24 February he faces the final insult: Dr David Owen endorses him as next Prime Minister.

But there is worse to come. On 16 April, Glenys admits the Kinnock family have 'never had it so good' as under Mrs Thatcher's leadership. The *Daily Express* reveals the Kinnocks' joint salary to be over £60,000, their house bought for £60,000 is now worth £300,000, they have two cars and 'regularly enjoy a two-week continental holiday in the sun'.

In April 1991, John Major tries to score points off Kinnock during Prime Minister's Question Time by pointing out the Welshman's absence from a debate on a bill proposing a barrage for Cardiff Bay. He has unwittingly played into Kinnock's hands. For the Member for Islwyn has a perfect excuse. Neil Kinnock, the man who attacked the gift of Princess Anne's house, who lambasted the Duke of Edinburgh and stayed away from the royal wedding was not in the Commons because the Queen had done him 'the enormous honour' of inviting him 'to spend the night in Windsor Castle'. Now *there's* maturity for you, boyo.

Having established the principles behind the great swing from mania to moderation, let's just take a glance through the personal histories of a sub-committee's worth of former firebrands – Margaret Beckett, Paul Boateng, Gordon Brown and Diane Abbott – to see how they have swung from deepest red to palest pink. Now you too can follow their progress with this handy *Punch* Moderate-O-Matic Guide...

Chapter One
Idealistic Youth

Margaret Beckett

1974 Wins Lincoln seat from Dick Taverne as Margaret Jackson.

1975 Tells *Guardian* she's 'Left-wing and proud of it.' Signs left-wing Commons motion calling for defence cuts and removal of American bases from UK.

October 1980 Elected to NEC.

1981 Attacks Neil Kinnock in vitriolic fashion for failing to back Tony Benn for Labour deputy leadership.

Paul Boateng

1978 Chairperson of Afro-Caribbean Education Resource Project.

1979 Appointed legal advisor, Scrap Sus Campaign.

1981 Becomes executive member of National Council for Civil Liberties. Also chair of GLC Police Committee and vice-chair of Ethnic Minorities Committee. Joins Labour Party NEC sub-committee on Human Rights.

January 1982 Writes and presents Radio 4 talk 'Rastafari: Black Redeemer' in praise of Rasta founder Marcus Garvey.

June 1983 As chairperson of GLC Police Committee says 'Campaign for Police Accountability is not about knocking police.'

September 1983 Accused of running up £234 bill in one week using official GLC cars.

Diane Abbott

October 1984 Denounces opponents of Black Sections as 'straightforward racists'.

December 1985 Declares, 'I am an extremist. I am extremely committed to race, to women's issues, to socialism.'

September 1986 Declares, 'I'm an old-fashioned, unreconstructed sort of Bennite.'

Jan 1987 Tells the *Sun*, 'All white people are racist,' and objects to Kinnock expelling Militant from Party. But...

April 1987 Issues statement of loyalty to Labour and Kinnock.

June 1987 Becomes MP for Hackney North. Leaves job as press officer for Lambeth Council. *London Daily News* declares she is 'ready to compromise in the interests of party unity.'

And n·

1970 Gives up job of 11 years as miner to be elected to Parliament after seeing 'A man from BBC' being shown round Bolsover with a view to becoming its MP.

1970 Refuses to adopt pairing system by which two MPs of opposing sides can both miss important vote. Told he'll have joined system within weeks – but still hasn't after 20 years. Time passes, leftwardly, then...

September 1986 Decries new Rose Party symbol to tune of The Red Flag at annual party conference. 'The People's rose in shades of pink/Gets up your nose and makes a stink.'

The Punch Moderate-O-Matic Guide

Chapter Two
The Turning Point

May 1986 Unions reported to be 'conspiring' to remove her from NEC for consistently voting against Neil Kinnock.

September 1986 Replaced on NEC by Shopworker's Union official.

March 1988 Quits hard-left Campaign Group when it decides to challenge Kinnock for party leadership.

November 1989 Joins the Shadow Cabinet. *Daily Mail* praises her 'formidable intellect'. A fellow NEC member says she used to be one of the 'most committed and ruthless of them all on the hard left.'

1984 Joins Police Training Council

September 1984 GLC records show he booked official cars up to 40 times a month. Other members averaged six.

July 1986 Claims his background 'Gave me a very strong emphasis on black consciousness and African socialism.'

October 1986 *Daily Mail* cleared by Press Council for contrasting 'what the paper claimed was the Boatengs' luxurious holiday in Rio de Janeiro with conditions and problems in Lambeth' where they lived.

April 1987 Issues statement of loyalty to Labour Party and objectives of Neil Kinnock.

June 1987 Elected to Parliament as MP for Brent South.

July 1987 Agrees to pair with a Tory MP 'as long as he is handsome.' *News of the World* reveals she spent 'more than £400 to lose weight at a top people's health farm' – Shrubland Hall, run by Lord and Lady de Saumarez.

September 1987 Declares the radical women's movement never really understood her because she was never one of them, exactly, and that although she was part of the faction that wanted a separate black group within the Labour Party she now, on most of the main issues, tends to agree with Neil Kinnock.

April 1988 Buys a £95,000 neo-Georgian mews house in yuppie Hackney – putting down £31,000 deposit.

Chapter Three
On Mature Reflection

November 1989 Tells the *Times* she sees no clash between her left-wing ideals and the Labour's 'New Realism'. 'It's extremely important never to lost sight of your principles, but it's also important to recognise that there is more than one way to put them into practice.'

October 1990 Described by *Observer Magazine* as 'a quiet, conservative woman'. Gives interview to *Daily Mail*, saying, 'Labour has made bad mistakes, especially in the '74 era. We were too idealistic…what counts in the future is getting value for money.' The *Sunday Times* says, 'She has been as gentle as any cooing dove with the merchant bankers.'

October 1987 Accepts lift from Oxford Union debate back to London in Edwina Currie's chauffeur-driven limo.

March 1988 Angrily disowns Labour's black caucus of MPs formed while he is in South Africa.

May 1989 Black militants disown him as a 'coconut' – black on the outside but white inside.

June 1989 Joins National Trust and spends holidays visiting stately homes.

7 November 1989 Neil Kinnock makes him the first black MP ever to be given a front bench post in his Treasury team.

August 1988 Spotted in another health farm: Inglewood Club in Berkshire.

June 1989 Referring to former jobs as press officer for Ken Livingstone and 'Red' Ted Knight says, 'I know what it is like to work for unscrupulous and power-crazy politicians.'

September 1989 Spotted again at Shrubland Hall.

December 1989 Writes letter to *Financial Times* containing phrases like 'The crucial issue is the determinants of the capital flows' and 'The outflow of portfolio capital at a rate equivalent to six per cent of GDP in the first half of 89…'

June 1990 Writes another letter to *Financial Times* saying 'The level of savings is crucial to economic growth.'

Dennis Skinner, the man who was Left behind

April 1987 Attacks Kinnock's trip to Washington and accuses him of seeking votes of 'yuppie readers of the *Independent* and the *Guardian*.'

July 1987 Offers new MPs crash-course on how to 'raise issues the Front Bench would prefer left alone.'

September 1987 Coins term 'Ramada Socialism' to describe how Labour MPs stay at a top hotel at the party conference. Checks into £15-a-night B&B.

March 1989 After Tory MPs propose a Commons motion congratulating Prime Minister Thatcher on birth of grandchild, adds amendment, '…this House hopes that the infant will learn to crawl as fast as the Honourable Members who signed the motion.' Ruled out of order.

September 1990 Describes Robert Maxwell and Norman Willis as a 'pair of sumo wrestlers trying to crush Arthur Scargill.'

November 1990 Says there is no difference between Heseltine and Thatcher. 'They are both peroxide blondes, millionaires and like getting dressed up.' *(Additional research by Steve Smethurst)*

'There'll be no more Saddam to kick around'

US Elder Statesman Richard 'Honest Dick' Nixon hits the
bovine scatology with General 'Borin' Norman Schwarzkopf

Chance would be a fine thing

The name Raymond Jones mean anything to you? What about Thelma Furness? John Byron? Believe us, without them you just wouldn't know the world around you. MITCHELL SYMONS and DUNCAN TERRACE on the little people that matter

You remember *It's A Wonderful Life*, the Frank Capra movie they show every Christmas, the one that gives you a nice warm glow. The story is this: believing his life has been a complete waste, a despairing Jimmy Stewart decides to commit suicide. Just in time, an angel comes down from heaven and shows him what life would have been like if he'd never been born. Without Jimmy there to save him, his brother would have died – that kind of thing.

It's a cleverly simple tale of ordinary people and how important they are in life's great masterplan. It also encourages a cleverly simple thought: what of all those other ordinary people without whom history would have been totally different?

We know the world would have been a better place if Mr and Mrs Saddam Hussein hadn't swapped precious bodily fluids that fateful night. And we know that if Mr Panayitou hadn't suggested an early night to Mrs Panayitou there would have been no opportunity for their son George Michael to popularise designer stubble. But what about all those Jimmy Stewarts out there? Isn't it time we stood up for all those otherwise insignificant people who acted as catalysts to history? Those without whom, for example, there would have been no JFK...

What is a Kennedy?

IN 1960, RICHARD NIXON WAS the Republican Candidate for the US Presidency. His opponent was John F Kennedy. Going into their four *mano a mano* network TV debates, Nixon enjoyed a clear lead in opinion polls. By the end of them, Kennedy had shaded it. He came across as fresher, much younger and considerably more vigorous. The reason? Nixon had just been in hospital for a knee operation while Kennedy had the sort of all-year tan we would nowadays associate with Essex car salesmen. Even more importantly, Nixon spurned the ministrations of The

Unknown Make-Up Artist: accordingly, his five o'clock shadow became 'an issue'.

But what if...

The Unknown Make-Up Artist had persuaded Nixon to submit to her powders and brushes? He would not have looked quite so dreadful and would thus been elected President.

So...

...although Kennedy came close to winning for the Democrats in 1960, he never got another shot at the presidency. He remained Senator for Massachusetts until a Democrat President gave him the chance to follow in his father's footsteps as the Ambassador to the Court of St James's. He never went to Dallas and is still married to Jackie.

Having won the presidency by a whisker, Richard Nixon immediately set in motion his campaign for 1964. As a perennial winner, he never felt the need to go in for the sort of tactics which led to the Watergate scandal and, after an easy victory, retired in 1968 to become an elder statesman.

And so...

...no US troops were even sent to Vietnam – experts agree JFK only committed troops because Krushchev made him look a pussy at the Vienna Summit. Which meant that Dan Quayle never had to field questions as to why he joined the National Guard instead of the army.

Also, not having been traumatised by their failure in Vietnam, America didn't have to invade Grenada just so they could win a war at last. And more importantly, Marilyn Monroe – not having been murdered by Kennedy people frightened of a scandal – had another career as the blonde bitch in *Dynasty* and is now making a fortune out of the geriatric fitness vids she promotes on chat shows.

Since his brother never became President, Robert Kennedy never became Attorney General and the Democratic Party – having lost with JFK – wouldn't rightaway give another Kennedy the chance to take on the Republicans at presidential level. He too is still alive, in New York, where he continues to practise law and adultery in equal measures.

Edward Kennedy succeeded JFK as Senator for Massachusetts. On 18 July 1969, therefore, he was with his ☛

two elder brothers instead of Mary Jo Kopechne. As she therefore didn't drown, the Democratic Party was accordingly free to make Edward its 1976 presidential nomination. He easily beat the Republican candidate, Ronald Reagan.

There being no Watergate scandal to expose, Carl Bernstein is still hanging round the Metro Desk at the *Washington Post* and Bob Woodward didn't become a household name. This meant that all subsequent political scandals never had to endure the suffix '-gate' – Irangate, Manuregate, Cow & Gate, etc.

Lee Harvey Oswald, Jack Ruby and Sirhan Sirhan all, quite properly, remained consigned to total anonymity.

What is a Beatle?

ON SATURDAY 28 OCTOBER 1961, Raymond Jones, an 18-year-old print apprentice, went into the NEMS record store in Whitechapel, Liverpool and asked the man behind the counter for a record he'd never heard of. The record was 'My Bonnie' by The Beatles and the counter man was Brian Epstein. Intrigued, Epstein went down to the Cavern Club to check them out, take over their management and help create the legend of the Fab Four.

But what if...

...Raymond Jones had gone to Boots instead? Epstein would never have met The Beatles and they would have faded into obscurity.

So...

...after a year or two more gigging at the Cavern and half-hearted, unsuccessful attempts to get a recording deal, John called it a day and The Beatles split up. He married Cynthia, fathered three children – including Julian in 1963 – and became a commercial artist who supplied the occasional cartoon to regional newspapers. His guitar stayed – but only ever left its case for the occasional jamming session with Paul or George. He'd always had a tendency to plumpness and the family saw to it that he became fat enough to curb his intended forays into adultery – until he ran off to London with a sushi bar waitress who encouraged him to revive his interest in musical talents. His Saturday night rock group can still be spotted in South London wine bars, playing John's beloved R&B standards. And, as far as he's concerned, the Dakota is just an ancient two-engined prop plane.

After the break-up, Paul moved to London where he worked as a commercial songwriter. Each year he enters the UK heats of the Eurovision Song Contest. Unfortunately, his songs – 'Mary Had A Little Lamb', 'Silly Love Songs' and the like – are always rejected as 'too deep and complicated' for the contest. He married in the early Seventies and has never been unfaithful to his wife – like him, the sort of vegetarian who eats fish and the occasional free-range chicken.

After initial despondency at the break-up, George realised that he was now 'liberated to do his own thing' – a phrase he'd picked up from a Timothy Leary paperback he found on a secondhand bookstall behind Central Station. He took a job in his local library and worked on his music in his spare time. Then, in the late Sixties, he made a journey to the Far East, returning with a deep love of Indian music and his new Indian wife.

Today they run an organic health-food shop in Henley-on-Thames in the shopping mall that was built on the site of the old Regal Cinema.

The Beatles' premature demise meant very little to Ringo because, of course, he never actually joined the group, Pete Best being the drummer at the time they weren't discovered. He settled down in Liverpool with Maureen Cox and together they opened a hairdressing salon. After a few years they promoted Cilla White (who, as a hairdresser, never found the need to change her surname to Black) to chief stylist because of her ability to persuade the customers to 'promise to come back next week and tell me how you got on'. Nowadays Ringo's greatest love is to read Thomas The Tank Engine stories to their youngest child, conceived in the reconciliation which followed his battle with the bottle and infatuation with that Barbara from the local amateur dramatics group.

Brian Epstein continued running his store and 'came out' at the end of the Sixties. Today, he is a retired businessman living in Marble Arch, within walking distance of some of the best bridge clubs and 'cottages' in Britain.

And so...

...Merseybeat never happened and nor did 'The Sixties' and nor were there any Rolling Stones. Mick Jagger became an English and cricket teacher in a boys' grammar school and Brian Jones started his own swimming-pool servicing company.

The most tragic result, however, of Raymond Jones's choosing Boots instead is that we were never treated to Linda McCartney's one-fingered piano solos.

What is a Simpson?

IT WAS THELMA, LADY Furness, who introduced Mrs Wallis Simpson to Prince Edward, the Prince of Wales.

But what if...

...Thelma had stayed in that night? Prince Edward would never have met Mrs Simpson and therefore wouldn't have abdicated from the throne.

So...

...although Edward continued to associate with older married ladies, he succumbed to political pressure to find himself a wife who would provide him with heirs. Although not a popular King – due to his supporting Hitler's proposals for a negotiated peace in 1940 – he reigned until his death in 1972.

Mrs Wallis Simpson, never having been exactly a one-man gal, set out to find a titled husband, intending to settle for nothing less than a Duke. Which is just what she ended up with.

The Queen Mother remained the Duchess of York. Without the pressures of kingship, her husband Bertie lived until 1981. Accordingly, the Queen Mother never became The Nation's Favourite Grandmother.

As she was only the King's niece, Princess Elizabeth never ascended to the throne and was able to give her full attention to the day's *Sporting Life*.

As Princess Elizabeth's son, Prince Charles did not have to bear the impending doom of heirdom, never had to marry a woman with whom he evidently had nothing in common and never had to go and watch Dire Straits at Wembley.

Lady Diana Spencer married an ex-junkie aristo; Prince

Edward became a theatrical impresario; Prince Andrew joined the Royal Navy, having married the actress Koo Stark; Sarah Ferguson started an agency supplying chalet girls for ski-ing holidays; Princess Margaret married Group Captain Peter Townsend and lived happily ever after; and Edward Fox never portrayed Edward VIII in *Edward And Mrs Simpson*.

And so...

...more obliquely, in 1957, King Edward preferred Rab Butler (an arch-appeaser like himself) to Harold Macmillan when the monarch was asked to find a successor to Anthony Eden. As Butler then lost the 1959 election, Gaitskell became Prime Minister – which ensured that Jenkins and Crosland were in a better position to succeed him than Wilson.

FALKLAND ISLANDS
(ISLAS MALVINAS)
(To United Kingdom)
1 : 5,000,000

What is a Thatcher?

IN 1764, COMMODORE JOHN Byron (the grandfather of the poet) led an expedition to the Falkland islands. He arrived there in 1765 and claimed the islands in the name of King George III. The Islands have been British ever since.

But what if...

...Commodore John Byron's boat had sunk in the Bay of Biscay? The islands would now not be British.

So...

...any number of sheep are now Argentinian.

And so...

...there was no Falklands War. General Galtieri is still running Argentina, not having screwed up over the Falklands, and, without the help of the 'Falklands Factor', Margaret Thatcher didn't win the 1983 General Election. Unemployment, cuts in public services and a recession were enough to make even die-hard Tories switch sides, creating a hung parliament.

The Conservatives were the largest party but were without a majority, and so, given that there was absolutely no way that Labour would form a coalition with the Alliance the result was a Conservative/Alliance coalition. Roy Jenkins, the leader of the SDP, refused to join a coalition headed by Mrs Thatcher and a compromise leader had to be found. Step forward, Peter Walker. Roy Jenkins became Home Secretary, David Steel became Energy Secretary and David Owen went to Defence.

The Labour Party became even more dejected than it usually was. The left seized on the election as a vindication of their belief that socialism mustn't be compromised. Tony Benn succeeded Michael Foot as leader and there were massive defections (Smith, Kaufman) and resignations (Healey, Hattersley).

Peter Walker continued as leader of the Conservative Party until he was succeeded by Michael Heseltine. John Major is today Shadow Sports Minister.

At the next General Election – held in 1987 – the Alliance was seen as a credible Government and duly won. The two Alliance parties merged, with Jenkins as Prime Minister and David Steel as Deputy Prime Minister/Home Secretary. Shirley Williams was given the chance to ruin Education once more and Bill Rodgers became Foreign Secretary. As for Dr David Owen – don't you remember? He stormed out of the Cabinet over the Westland Affair and never again held high office. He is to retire from politics at the 1992 General Election. 🐍

More Great Moments in History That Never Happened

■ **Adolf Hitler,** having failed as a portrait painter in old Vienna, moved to Buenos Aires where he launched himself as sportswear couturier. Here, his great friend, Diego Maradona Senior, models his ground-breaking designs for Boca Juniors

■ **No one** having turned up to see his band at the Maritime Hotel, Van Morrison joined the church. His congregation speak highly of his scat version of 'The Sash My Father Wore'

■ **Miss Margaret Hilda** Roberts went far in her career as a research chemist employed by the London Rubber Company. Here she is shown at the launch party for their 1987 safe sex suit

■ **Stormin'** Norman joined the RSPCA instead

A Viz-ible difference

An entire generation is growing up whose reading matter is limited to trashy comics with names like *Viz*, *Zit*, *Pus* and so forth. Any publication that wishes to survive into the 21st century will have to adapt to this new trend. STEVE PUNT and TONY HUSBAND have been looking at the news-stands of the future

Marxism Today tomorrow

Ee-zee-read economics from the new **Economist**

Those schedules explained by your post-literate **Radio Times**

A message with meaning from **War Cry**

A charming, Grade II-listed **Country Life** with panoramic views

At last! The truth about the **Independent**

GARDENING

ook up into the garden of the night. Many years ago, when the earth was still flat, there was only the sun and a few planets to take care of. Later, at the time of the early stargazers, the universe was still neat with nicely defined borders - but after Copernicus and Galileo things really began to get out of hand. The number of stars increased, orbits became elliptical and new planets were discovered going round our sun. Sir Issac Newton, Astronomer Royal at the time of Charles II, watched as the universe burst forth with uncontrollable fecundity - probably under the influence of that jovial but licentious monarch.

Today, Joddrell Bank reports total chaos - partly because we have stopped looking at the sky and now only listen to it with radio and gamma telescopes. Stars are very quiet and very devious - they must be watched carefully at all times or the universe will become completely overgrown.

Someone needs to go through the heavens with a pair of shears and a stiff broom. The sky needs thinning out. And while they're about it they should take up a shovel and flatten out the earth. It's about time a few people fell off the edge...

SNORT!

Meteorites are a dreadful source of worry to the folk of Glasshouse.

Lovely for the roses!

Planet Rollo benefits from its position near the constellation Taurus the Bull.

Huge bees the size of helicopters visit Planet Nectar.

suck suck suck suck

Bah!

Help!

Weeding the garden is a never-ending challenge on Ranuculus.

Planting in Black holes is a constant source of disappointment to Mr Spiney.

Aaaargh...

oops...

Eat my dust.

Stupid clod!

Sod you, you sod!

Fertile imaginations - various soil types exchange insults on Compost W

USEFUL TIPS FOR CULTIVATING
PLANT PEOPLE

this packet contains **1 FAMILY**

How do you do?

Be careful not to let the seeds escape. Sow in a shallow tray and remember to provide entertainment.

The young plants must be vigorously pruned in order to promote healthy growth in the coming year.

a — SEEDS WONDERING

b — PRUNING

me me!

hurrah!

Keep still...

c — HARVESTING PLANT PEOPLE ON NIMBOS:

Just a minute...

? Here, I say!

dum de dum

Heads may be sauted for a tasty side-dish, limbs shredded and woven into a sturdy napkin. Internal organs may be soaked and fermented, producing a delicious aperitif.

This is intolerable!

The remains of Plant People make a rich compost — very little is wasted on Nimbos, the ecology minded planet.

glub glub

How to be a has-been...
HEADMASTER

The hey day

You're darling of the headmasters' conference and a dab-hand with the crenulated cane. You retire to 'aid the country'. But it's all downhill from here...

The slippery slope

1. You appear on BBC 2's *Mortar Board*. 'One in seven state school pupils is functionally illiterate,' you slam. The *Independent*'s Ngaio Checker agrees...
2. That one in three of your former pupils is really illiterate. You hit back: '50 per cent went to Oxford,' you gloat. 'Yes,' says the *Daily Express*'s Ian MacGregor.
3. 'Oxford Prison.' You launch Standards In State Education.
4. 'He should be in a state institution,' says NUT chief Doug McAvoy. Standards In State Education...collapses.

The futile gesture

5. You apply for the job of HM Inspector of Schools. You get an interview...
6. With HM Inspector of Taxes. 'It's all charitable,' you plead.
7. 'Except him,' sneers Peter McKay. You go to Scotland. 'To teach them proper education.' You leave...
8. At the request of a lynch mob. You form the Union of Non-Striking Masters.
9. 'Striking was all he ever did,' says an old boy of your school.
10. You present quiz show *School Buoy Ahoy*. But become too close to...

The killer blow

11. The buoys. You retire to 'fish and think'.

The cruel twist

After your death, from bamboo cane poisoning, your memoirs *Please Sir, More!* are published. The Chancellor's tenant buys your cane for an undisclosed fee.

MIKE CONWAY
Next week: How to be a has-been Punch letter writer.

ILLUSTRATION: DAVID LYTTLETON

Just how bad is the current unemployment crisis? What will people do to get work? JOHN HIND and STEVEN MOSCO placed a series of bizarre job ads to find out who would write back and say: 'Give us a job...

I could

The Employment Department Group is currently running an advertising campaign for their Jobclub. It has a picture of an earnest young man, head tilted optimistically upwards. 'I WILL get a job,' he's saying. 'I WILL get a job. I WILL get a job.'

With unemployment on the rise, is the Jobclub's gritty spirit increasing too? How much are the general public prepared to do for work? And how far will they respond to a boss's unsavoury needs? We devised a number of demanding, not to say demeaning jobs in order to assess what people will tolerate for a weekly wage.

Multiple whippet-walker
Number of applicants: 1

We placed the following advert in newsagents and post offices in north London:

'Canine Operative required to walk 17 whippets, morning and/or afternoon. £3 per hour. We provide the pooper-scooper. Please apply, noting experience and suitability, to...'

The only response was from a South African woman, aged 21 but with 'no experience of whippets'. She said she was 'prepared to do anything while in London.' But on being told the

do that

next day that there were now 27 whippets to walk, she changed course. 'To be quite frank,' she announced, 'I think I've secured a posting as a pizza waitress in Cricklewood.'

Compliant Feminine Personal Assistant
Number of applicants: 23

We placed the following advert in the 22 October edition of the free magazine, Ms London:

'The MD of a growing media concern seeks a PA with a difference. You will be traditionally feminine, attractively dressed, ALWAYS smiling, and good at making coffee. Salary will compensate for this pressurised position.'

We heard from 23 potential PAs, but no 'feminine' men, and the 'On Top' staff agency said that they could provide 'many suitable girls'. As to the applicants, for the purposes of this feature let's call them Amanda, Samantha, Vanessa, Joanna, Stella, Belinda, Melissa, Rosa etc. 17 said they were 'single' and 18 addressed the letter 'Dear Sir' rather than 'Sir/Madam'. Only one jester wrote, 'Dear Cur or Madman'. ☞

🐾 Funemployment

The first female from the pile exclaimed, 'I will have you know that I am constantly smiling and brew the best coffee this side of Australia!' She noted her leisure interests as 'car repair, weight-training and collecting matchboxes.' A 22-year-old from Essex played the aesthetics card – her escapades in Beauty Therapy and Cosmetology at the London Institute of Beauty Culture ('my greatest asset').

Another 'passionate worker' began her letter by relating her experiences as communications assistant at a police station. 'I believe the post you advertise is ideal for me. It will enable me to utilise my feminine traits to the full.'

Others sailed in with examination statistics. Stella had 'a Grade 2 CSE in Office Studies and piles of personality.' Helena had 'nine "O" levels, three "A" levels, an MA and ballroom dancing qualifications.' She admitted that 'I am actually very good at making coffee and the fact that I live locally will help to keep a smile on my face.'

The most exotic applicant was a 24-year-old multilingual woman who listed London and Paris addresses. She reported that she had the French equivalent of ten 'A' levels, a year's 'au-pairing experience' and her hobby was 'reading philosophy'. Her CV looked as if it had been designed by a computer graphics consultancy. Another respondent – 'an-prefect' – offered references for her 'first-class coffee making skills'.

The oldest applicant, a 40-year-old mother of two had – since becoming 'fed up with dirty nappies and bottles' – been working for 'a rather suffocating firm marketing room-deodorisers.' She said she felt 'the way you have worded the ad makes you seem like a very nice man – a very, very nice man! I enclose my CV and would like to be considered for a position under you.'

The most suitable married applicant was the 29-year-old PA looking for a '1-1 role' with her employer. 'I always strive to run a smooth office,' she explained, 'thus allowing my boss to be truly free of the mundane – allowing him to immerse himself in importances. I would very much like to have the opportunity of meeting you and going through my particulars. I would like to show you what a lovely cup of coffee I make...I would appreciate it if you would run your eyes over my resume.'

Three short sharp letters arrived too. More precisely, from:

One non-humorous feminist: 'If this is a joke, it's in very poor taste. If not, you should be ashamed of yourself, and I can only hope you get exactly the bimbo you deserve.'

One humorous feminist: 'The wording for this post is illegal, offensive and makes bad business sense. I would have phoned you to tell you this direct but as I am always smiling in a traditionally feminine manner it makes verbal communication uncomfortable. Must go – the coffee's almost ready. Yours faithfully, Melissa Fotherington-Pile.'

And one (hopefully) humorous feminist: 'I might just castrate you, you snivelling little ****.'

Maggot-sifter
Number of applicants: 1

We felt that this task should be placed in professional hands, and contacted a north London employment agency we'll call 'Get Staffed'.

Posing as a maggot farm with staff problems ('They leave once they realise how unpleasant it is'), we emphasised the duties and working conditions. And then inquired whether they could find us a suitable candidate...strictly for night-shift work. We called the post 'Chrysalid Sifter and Grub Sorter'.

'Will he primarily have to sift the maggots from rotting chicken carcasses?' enquired the agency rep, then passed us over to another Get Staffed branch. Here we were told within 90 sec-

---

'I wish to register a complaint...'

IT IS REASSURING to see that the watchdogs of commercials are as vigilant as ever. After the publication of our advert for a compliant PA (see page 25) we received two official letters of complaint.

The first came from the Advertising Standards Authority. This was not too chastising. It said that they had 'advised the complainant we will not be pursuing the matter...there does not seem to be a complaint under the terms of the British Code of Advertising Pratice.' But they did say that they had referred the complainant to the Equal Opportunities Commission.

This 'squealing' resulted in the letter from the Equal Opportunities Commission in Manchester. Ms Joy

PA

The MD of a growing media concern seeks a PA with a difference. You will be traditionally feminine attractively dressed always smiling and good at making cofee. Salary will compensate for this pressurised position. Write with cv stating why you think you would be suitable to

**The MD, RFI Communications
Suite 3, Midhurst Mansions,
Fortis Green London N10 3E2
(No Agencies)**

Murphy of their Dirty Harry-style Advertising and Law Enforcement Unit had this to say:

'Section 38 of the Act makes it unlawful to publish or cause to be published an advertisement which indicates or might reasonably be understood as indicating an intention to breach the employment provisions of the Act' – which pretty much covers the whole issue. Ms Murphy also drew our attention to a case taken to the Industrial Tribunal in October 1990. She quoted the findings. Namely that 'The advertisement was heavily facetious in an attempt to attract attention. In our view the advertisement with its eye-catching flippancy was discriminatory and the application succeeds.' She also enclosed a leaflet, *Men's Jobs? Women's Jobs?*, and left us with the hope that we would give 'positive consideration' to their 'guidance'.

The oddest application to our campaign, however, came from a *Private Eye* reader who had seen the *Sewer and Sewerage* ad reprinted in the magazine's joke clippings section. Scary.

onds, 'Don't worry. We can help you with anything, sir. I actually have a man who would be ideal for you. Would you like him to start tomorrow or Monday?'

Sewerage journalist
Number of applicants: 14

Posing as a soon-to-be-launched trade paper, we placed the following advert in the 22 October issue of UK Press Gazette:

'Editorial staff and freelance writers required for SEWER AND SEWERAGE, a new trade paper for the effluent disposal industry. Applicants should have a keen interest in the subject and its related products. Send CV, reasons for your suitability, and three ideas for articles.'

Before long, an assortment of applications from aspiring cloacal correspondents arrived through the post. 'I would like to contribute an article about tertiary treatments,' wrote one sewerologist. 'The disposal industry is beginning to look at dosing excreta with ultra-violet light. How does it work? What does it cost? Meanwhile, the polymer industry developed new designs and materials that will allow it to take a market sewerage share from large diameter concrete pipes. Pros and cons?'

One woman wrote, 'I have had a very successful career in journalism which has covered Toiletary Services and Middle East sewage magazines. I have also worked on a number of construction industry titles with a sewerage flavour...Three ideas which come to mind for your title are 1) Clay versus plastic piping? 2) Drain filters and enzymes, 3) Don't drink that water! I hesitate to expand on these themes because I know only too well that ideas are often asked for simply so they can be utilised!'

More bemusing was the enthusiasm of one applicant whose two stated qualifications for the job were that he had 'once lived in Letchworth Garden City, where the refuse company Shelvoke and Drewry is situated' and that 'my son-in-law has descended to the bowels of the earth to test underground workings.' The gentleman then expressed concern over 'the "Turtle" craze of entering sewers,' and interest in compiling an article on 'the unique range of equipment in North Hertfordshire now used to combat "The Odour Factor".'

One northern agency offered their 'undiluted journalistic services' but the most enthusiastic was a Canadian.

'In my heart of hearts I know *Sewers and Sewerage* is my home. I offer these possibilities:

1) Biologically Better Bugs. The University of East Anglia has been given £300,000 to test 'environmentally-friendly microbes' in raw sewage. It was my understanding that this was what anaerobic digestion was all about, but perhaps they have something new in mind! Worth checking out.

2) The Price of Purity – a regular series on different international effluency constituents, with an eye on both primary and secondary sedimentation.

3) The grand opening of the Ontario Water Resources Commission's stunning tertiary treatment sewage plant (I have a photograph of the mayor drinking the final effluent!) These are, of course, very much "off-the-top-of-my-head" suggestions.'

As if these splendid ideas wouldn't be enough to convince

RAW MATERIALS

MAGGOT-SIFTER

FRESH MAGGOTS TO GO

any editor of this man's suitability for a posting, one footnote was added: 'Let's make this a magazine to be proud of!'

Tele-rep for coffin-makers
Number of applicants: 2

It was now time to try and entice the workforce with a real dead-end job. We decided to record the demand for coffin sales jobs, and placed the following advert in shop windows around north London:

'Enthusiastic, tactful people required to sell coffins over the phone. You get a healthy profit because we under-cut the undertaker. If you think you're suitable for this job, please write to The Personnel Officer, Tele-Cask Ltd.'

The response was not encouraging. Our cards in the windows brought just two replies. 'I was very interested in your direct-sales approach,' wrote one gent. 'And after reading Ms Mitford's book *The American Way of Death*, I was already aware of the huge profits to be made from the death industry.' The other hopeful was particularly candid: 'I've sold encyclopedias, hi-fi, shoes, watches and insurance, but coffins would be a challenge to relish. Please send me details immediately.'

We wrote back explaining our 'revolutionary new direct-sales approach to funeral marketing'. Our coffin consultants-in-waiting were told how it involved telephoning potential clients to offer a range of services – from a budget-priced weekly 'Coffin-Club' to a deluxe burial service – and offered full training for 'potentially difficult situations'. Adding that Tele-Cask (pioneered in the USA) had 'many satisfied customers', we ended with an upbeat line: 'Let's see if we can help each other to succeed in what is anything but a dying business.' Only one reply arrived. 'I have had 27 years sales experience across the field,' he wrote, 'and I can confidently state...I will boost your coffin sales-figures beyond all targets.'

Unfortunately, we'll never find out now if this determined man really could be the number one reliever of the bereaved's wallets. ▓

ILLUSTRATION:PAUL CEMMICK

The incwedibly stwange Jonathan Ross

He's a famous face. But no one watches his shows. So why, asks CHRIS HORRIE, has Channel 4 just signed up Jonathan Ross and his 'wacky' chat show for another ten weeks?

That Incredible Shrinking Audience

The Last Resort	**2.6m**	(1988)
The Incredibly Strange Film Show	**2.7m**	(1989)
One Hour With Jonathan Ross	**1.2m**	(1990)
Tonight with Jonathan Ross	**1.5m**	(1991)

(*This is a Channel X claim. For full investigation see overleaf.)

According to the legend, Jonathan Ross began his celebrity career by accident. Earning his crust as a humble TV researcher (an honourable profession based on scouring the entire world's media in search of something original-looking to copy) he came across the *David Letterman Show*, an American chat-show sometimes described as 'wacky', and suggested that Channel 4 should copy it. Since 'wacky' is Channel 4's middle name the suggestion was snapped up.

At this stage Jonathan had no intention of fronting the show. It was only after the search for a British David Letterman collapsed in the normal Channel 4 chaos that he volunteered, at the 11th hour, to step into the breach. And there he was – Mr Ordinary Bloke, complete with cheeky chappy smirk, endearing lisp and self-deprecating style.

But this was January 1987. Nigel Lawson was pumping rocket fuel into the economy with various interesting results. Not the least of these was a new epidemic of tabloid greed hysteria focused on the new phenomenon of the 'Yuppie'. Since Jonathan was under 30, wore a suit and was on the telly, he became, as the *Times* put it, 'the personification of ambitious Yuppie values'. In tabloid terms this translated as at last a Yuppie the punters have heard of. Hallelujah!

The *Sun* and, in particular *Today*, instantly appointed Ross Chief Yuppie and reported on his earnings and lifestyle with psychotic attention to detail. Hapless readers were bombarded with factoids such as his supposed ownership of '100 designer suits' (the *Sun*) and his penchant for 'burgundy Comme Des Garçons socks and Gianni Versace trousers' (*Today*) as part of the standard overkill treatment.

In the posh papers Jonathan expressed astonishment at the scale of tabloid interest. But if it increased his stock with TV companies, advertising agencies or anyone else interested in paying for a slice of the 'personification of ambitious Yuppie values', he wasn't complaining.

Soon advertising agencies were offering serious money, to coin a phrase popular at the time, to associate with Jonathan in the hope that some of that Yuppie magic would rub off on them. First into the ring was Harp lager.

A spokesman said Jonathan had been chosen to front the ads because he was popular with the 25-34 age group. Thus another valuable piece of the Jonathan Ross legend was put in place – his 'perceived ability to win a committed young audience' as

caweer of TV's

SCRIPT EDITOR ON THE FLOOR PLEASE...

CUE: SPONTANEOUS APPLAUSE, WHISTLES, 010101, etc.

JON: WELCOME INDEED LADIES + GENTLEMEN TO ANOTHER HALF-HOUR OF TOP RANK ENTERTAINMENT (APPLAUSE)

independent media pundit Martin Rowe puts it.

Julie Pickford, producer of *Tonight with Jonathan Ross* says that his youth appeal is based on an 'alternative approach to the traditional chat-show format. He's still irreverent and fresh, with an air of unpredictability and a genuine interest in things like obscure and cult films.'

More than this he's 'honest and straightforward' to work with and 'certainly not the sort of prima donna you get in the TV industry. There's absolutely no difference between his onscreen and offscreen persona.'

Humility is certainly an asset in an industry which, critics agree, works best when serving up ritual humiliation. From smarmy game show hosts to *All Right On The Night* and from hit comedy shows to Jeremy Beadle's sundry activities, TV thrives on the public's ecstatic delight at seeing other people making absolute pillocks of themselves.

And it is easier to take the piss out of others when you take the piss out of yourself: 'I hear you drink your own urine,' Jonathan once said to Sarah Miles, a guest on *The Last Resort*. 'I hear you eat your own shit', she shot back. And folks still say TV has killed the art of conversation.

Perhaps the great thing about watching prime time chatshows is that you know where you are. There is sometimes the simultaneous and mildly disturbing experience of knowing where you would rather be. But no matter. Chatshows are comforting.

Mocking the chatshow format has become the 'last resort' of the media scoundrel. Trying to make the format 'edgy' (one official description of *Tonight With Jonathan Ross*) is a cruel and pointless sort of joke – like trying to spike the nation's Horlicks with amphetamine sulphate.

Jonathan Ross described *The Last Resort*, his first chatshow series in 1986 as 'silly and surreal'. The idea of an anarchic chat show sending up all the conventions might have pandered to the daringly wicked sophisticates making up the late-night Channel 4 audience. Most prime timers, on the other hand, probably think 'surreal' is the generic name for cornflakes.

But if there is a danger of confusing the punters, the effect on Mr Ross himself has evidently been even more marked. He has become a walking mass of contradictions. An ideological minefield. In making the transition from what he is pleased to call cult status he has also changed from Yuppie role model to ☛

Above: Chatsmith Ross probingly interviews his big name guests

Right: The thinking man's Wogan gets to grips with key issues

Below: Mrs Jane Ross assumes shiny-thighed aerobics tableau

post-Yuppie role muddle.

At one time, for instance, it was a media commonplace to say he was the new David Frost. Mr Ross seemed to agree. 'If you have to compare me to anyone, I suppose I aspire to achievements of David Frost,' he said in June 1988. But eight months later he was complaining that the comparison was invidious. 'I'll never be another David Frost,' he chirped. 'Whatever people say.'

On the more general topic of intellectual tone he veered about just as wildly. 'Sometimes I feel I am not fit to hold a conversation with an intelligent adult...I've lost the art of intelligent conversation,' he told us in March 1987. This revelation was followed by spells as a nationally networked radio show specifically hyped as providing a lot of 'intelligent conversation'.

The following year he reversed the equation by promising clever stuff and delivering crass stupidity. 'I'd like to try something more intellectual. I wouldn't mind trying my hand at the odd political interview,' he said before publishing the entirely mindless *Go To Bed With Jonathan Ross*. This was a classic of the worn-out genre of disposable Christmas TV tie-in picture books.

The new enthusiasm for political interviewing didn't last long either. 'I can think of nothing more boring than being like Jeremy Paxman,' he said last, before changing tack again and tossing the occasional heavy political comment into the 'anarchic' mix of *Tonight With Jonathan Ross*.

Politics is one thing, and money quite another. What really sent tabloid Ross-watchers reeling was his zig-zags on the related subjects of product plugging and advertising.

Here he started by occupying the moral high ground. 'I have no objections to plugs as long as they are honest,' he sniffed soon after the launch of *The Last Resort*, pointedly observing that *Wogan* had become 'one long commercial.' In August 1987 Ross went further by vowing, at least according to the tabloids,

That Ross ratings investigation in full

❓ Does anyone really watch Jonathan Ross? Or is he just an invention of the marketing men? There was only one way to find out: ask the ratings people.

TV ratings are a tricky business. The Channel 4 press office won't give you any figures directly if the show isn't in the top 30 – which none of the three weekly episodes of Ross's current show are. Only the company producing the show, Channel X in this case, can give out those figures – but only if they want to.

Channel X were very helpful and polite. They said the average figure for the current series was 1.5m. The week we phoned, the lowest rated show in the Top 30 was Oprah Winfrey at 1.59m. This

meant 1.5m wasn't far behind. So we phoned the British Audience Research Bureau (BARB) – the official monitors of TV audience figures.

The people at BARB explained that only Channel X could give out those figures. But on voicing some concern at the quoted figure being 'alarmingly high,' they offered to dispel our confusion. The first figure they gave was for Friday 11 January. That day's show began with 1.1 million viewers at 6.30, rising to 1.3 at 6.45pm. Then to illustrate how averages work, they quoted Wednesday, 9 January. And were the figures around the 1.8 mark? No. They were 1.3m rising to 1.4 at 6.45m. BARB said breezily, 'So yes, you see, they *are* averaging 1.5m.'

The same week's Channel 4 figures saw ratings of 2.27 million for that soggy old chestnut *Voyage to the Bottom of the*

Sea, a similar figure for a repeated nature documentary about snakes in *The Survival Factor* and a whopping 2.9 million for *Great Plant Collections*, which was a repeat wander around Birr Castle in Ireland.

But who does present *Great Plant Collections*? And why isn't he a sharp-suited mega-star with his own production company and a wallet full of advertising contracts? After all, he can attract nearly twice as many punters as Jonathan Ross. The man in question is Roy Lancaster. And who's ever heard of him? As our favourite star columnist might say, it's a funny old world...

he would never do TV adverts.

But then he immediately signed for a series of Harp Lager ads, appearing on the cover of the *TV Times* with a can of Harp placed nonchalantly in the background before the deal was made public.

In the opinion of the *TV Times* ('Furious' – *Today*), at least, this did not constitute an 'honest plug'. Mr Ross described the whole episode as the work of a commercial 'arsehole'; an arsehole who turned out to be his personal business manager.

As for actually appearing in the adverts, the tabloids, he explained, had got it all wrong. What he meant was he wouldn't appear in absolutely every single advert on TV without exception, or without being paid. Which is obviously a very different thing – although an additional series of adverts for a building society started to cast confusion on even this.

But Mr Ross did at least seem definite about one thing when he started out. He would not front *Wogan* and that was final. The show, he said, had 'lost its way' and could not be rescued. And he just wasn't interested in the larger audience *Wogan* would give him. He even told the *Times* that he had 'no burning ambition to remain in the public eye.'

Soon afterwards he was proclaiming an exactly opposite desire to 'see if I can do real television and draw audiences of 15 million.' In another U-turn he then turned down an offer from London Weekend Television to do just that, revealing that television exposure was all very well but 'not what I thought I wanted. It's not unpleasant, but it's not what I was after.'

Then in a rare attack of temporary consistency he also turned down an offer to do *Wogan*. 'I want to develop my own ideas, and not follow in another's footsteps,' he said before the inevitable rethink led him to do the show for three weeks in 1990.

After the agonising over whether to *Wogan* or not there is the question of what to do, or not to do, while presenting it. The key concept here is how much blandness to include – a brilliantly fertile area for more dithering bemusement.

In April 1990 he announced that *Wogan* was bland because it was on three times a week. Bland was sort of bad. Six months later this was reversed with the announcement: 'Bland does not mean that it is not good television.' So bland was good. Sort of.

By now the endemic confusion had spread to his personal life, which had been transformed by marriage to Jane Goldman, an award-winning teenage rock journalist. At first this did not change much. 'Right now we are not thinking about children. Jane is still very young,' he told us. A couple of month's later he explained his need for a £250,000 income on the cosy and contradictory grounds that 'we are planning to have a family in the not too distant future.'

Given this impressive record of consistent inconsistency Mr Ross's thoughts on the future are a matter of some importance. As a useful sideline he could present himself as a modern reverse Nostradamus. Whatever he says you can put money on the exact reverse taking place.

In October his business partner at Channel X TV said: 'We're quite good at making disposable TV. But we could be disastrous at doing anything else.' Discounting the ever present possibility of double bluff, this would appear to signal an imminent move out of television in order to be 'good at something else.'

This is not a bad idea. Perhaps the idea of delving deeper into politics is not so daft as it first seems. Mr Ross would be great at any job that requires saying one thing and then doing exactly the opposite. 🐾

WHO GIVES A MONKEY'S?

A CRITICAL LOOK AT MODERN LIFE
by Richard Littlejohn

BREASTFEEDING

I didn't notice her at first. The bloke sitting next to her on the Moorgate rattler was monopolising my attention. He had two ponytails – one just below the crown and the other in the nape of his neck. When he bent down to adjust the laces in his Doc Martens, he looked like a rhino.

By comparison, the young woman with the Bart Simpson barnet and so many earrings she resembled a curtain rail, appeared almost normal. It was her reading matter which fascinated me.

She was engrossed in a weighty tome entitled *The Politics of Breastfeeding*. Unless it was a Jonathan Miller-style pop-up book, it must have contained at least 500 pages. Even assuming there are burning ideological arguments at stake, I can't see quite how you make them last 30,000 words.

Nor could I understand why this particular young woman would be taking such an earnest interest in the subject. No one could possibly imagine her actually producing an infant to put her theories into practice. She was the type of woman who considers sex sexist. Not even a man with two pony-tails could ever be desperate enough to agree to fertilise her.

Yet it is this sort of hideous harridan who insists on the right to breast-feed in public, even though they demand the abolition of Page Three on the grounds that displaying bare bosoms degrades women.

You can't imagine Luscious Linda Lusardi whipping out the breasts and refuelling her sprog in between her avocado prawn starter and her tournedos Rossini.

It's only natural, they argue. So are all manner of other bodily functions but we do our best to draw a discreet veil over most of them. You don't get CAMRA demanding urinals in public bars so that they can recycle their Dogbolter without putting their glasses down. And no-one insists their local curry house installs vomitoria next to the help-yourself buffet or replaces its gilt seating with commodes.

I await the publication of *The Politics of Puking*. It will probably be by a man with two pony-tails.

Richard Littlejohn is a Sun columnist.

HONEYSETT
Home and dismay

'It's the only sure way of getting him up in the morning!'

'Isn't it usually the breasts they enlarge with silicone?'

'I would have preferred the royal handshake'

'It's no good, we'll have to find a horse'

'It was bad enough when he just had it combed forward
to hide his bald patch'

'Can't you go outside like any normal streaker?'

WHO GIVES A MONKEY'S?

A CRITICAL LOOK AT MODERN LIFE
by Richard Littlejohn

Hotel menus

Imagine rolling home from work and being asked by your spouse what you fancy for supper.

'More Fun Than Jogging,' you reply. A perplexed look would be the best you could hope for; a smack in the face with a Le Creuset marmite is a more likely response.

But that is how you are expected to tell the Holiday Inn, Birmingham, that you would like them to bring a cottage cheese and fruit salad to your room.

There is a growing trend among hoteliers to give ever more ridiculous names to over-elaborate dishes. Room service menus are the worst offenders.

They might argue they are only trying to bring a little wit and escapism into the humdrum lives of the commercial travellers – sorry, sales consultants – who comprise the bulk of their custom. What other explanation could there be for the Holiday Inn's Movie Mogul's Menu?

The idea is that you tune into the in-house video channel, relax and summon a gourmet meal. Sounds romantic, the sort of thing Gérard Depardieu might do at the Cannes Film Festival, sprawled on silk sheets while some adoring tottie slides caviar and passion fruit between his lips.

The squalid reality is an overweight machine-tool company representative squatting on his bed in his Y-fronts eating turkey and almond curry with his fingers, while dribbling over the Playboy Channel.

From the Movie Mogul's Menu (quite genuine) he can begin with 'terrine of veal complemented by a spinach cocoon of sweetbreads and sherry-soaked mushrooms amidst a chervil salad.'

He can then graduate to heavy duty dishes such as *Sirloin Stallone* (prime Scottish steak, lots of blood), *Lamb Fillets Coppola* (you'll love the smell of napalm), *Piggy Hitchcock* (you must be a psycho), or a close encounter with *Salmon Spielberg* (don't forget to phone home). How about a *Chicken Welles* ('You're the third man to order that tonight, sir')?

When you get home this evening, try asking for a *Prawn Connery*. Or maybe *Foie Oliver Reed*. What do you mean you don't know how to cook it? It is an enormous liver, heavily battered and pickled in vodka.

Richard Littlejohn is a Sun columnist.

Feuds

MIKE CONWAY reports columnists' favourite

Everyone loves gossip columns. Editors like the way diarists can break juicy news stories which, for a variety of reasons, not least legal, they were previously worried about touching. Nigel Dempster, for instance, recently saved the British tabloid press from 'Allies Intensify Bombing' boredom by revealing Lord Althorp's affair with Sally Ann Lasson. It was a 'naughty but nice' scandal, just far enough removed from the throne to be safe.

But what about the gossip columnists who write the diaries? Do they take themselves seriously? More importantly, do they take rival columnists seriously and admire their fellow toilers in Gucci-land? Well, no. They hate each other.

Or rather, Ross Benson and Nigel Dempster do. Over the last few months, a bitter feud has developed between the two diarists on the *Daily Express* and *Daily Mail* respectively. In their gossip columns they regularly accuse each other of inventing stories and lifting 'exclusives', spicing it up by flinging personal remarks across the middle-market divide.

Diarists such as Mrs Betty Kenward of *Harpers & Queen* would not be 'delighted' to be caught in this crossfire. Everything in her 'Jennifer's Diary' is viewed in a roseate haze. Her New Year's greeting, for instance, was 'may 1991 bring peace and prosperity throughout the world.'

The Peterborough diary in the *Daily Telegraph* and 'Londoner's Diary' in the *Evening Standard* are different again. Both columns feature male-orientated stories concentrating on the minutiae of public schools and Pall Mall clubs. Their accounts of academic scheming and Etonian worthies are a world apart from the 'weddings and wenchings' so zestfully catalogued by Mr Benson and Mr Dempster.

All those adulteries, divorces and joyless marriages. All those gone-wrong children, insane relatives and vulgarian parties. And all those poisonous little paragraphs about retch-making rich-raff. These are the preoccupations in the battleground between 'the haughties and the naughties'. At least, they are when the diarists can draw themselves away from their feud.

Artillery fire at the moment is focussed on hair. Mr Dempster recently called Mr Benson a 'poor old pompadoured poltroon' for printing a piece based on a fictional Sally Ann Lasson column in the *Tatler*. Mr Benson showed a picture of Prince Charles's bald spot and mischievously asked: 'Is this a picture of my so-called rival? No. Too much hair.'

'He can say what he likes about me,' said Mr Dempster from his Kensington offices. 'I only attack his column when he puts in lies dressed up as fact. He filches his material from all sorts of American magazines and even British ones. I'm

Ross Benson On Mr Dempster

'It all started just before Christmas at the Hacks' Lunch when I rose to thank Nigel for making the Benson column look so good that year. Blood-red mist appeared in front of his eyes. He started spewing abuse and then trooped off to write an attack.

He calls me a pompadoured poltroon in the fade-away Mail because he isn't as young and hirsute as I am. In fact, he spent a fortune trying to restore the thatch on his bald pate. It failed, naturally.

We're like battling warlords in ninth-century China. So he thinks I've never been near a shell? How about covering Beirut, Iran/Iraq, San Salvador, the Falklands...? Dempster has always wanted to be an international reporter but they won't let him out of the office. You can quote everything.'

ILLUSTRATION: FIONA DUNBAR

corner
on the gossip targets – each other

just trying to make an honest journalist out of him, but unfortunately failing.'

'The boy's deranged,' said Mr Benson from his Blackfriars eyrie. 'I would hate to have to get up in the morning and think that I wrote a column like the type of column written by Dempster. It's a fricassee of dead dog. If he launches a Scud, we'll fire back a Patriot.'

Military terminology comes easily to Mr Benson, a former war correspondent – he was International Reporter of the Year in 1983. In his younger years he also acquired a reputation as something of a ladies' man. These days he sports his trademark all-year suntan and is happily married to Ingrid Seward, the editor of *Majesty* magazine.

Mr Benson took over as *Express* diary figurehead with the demise of the William Hickey column in 1987. This was marked by Mr Dempster theatrically dancing a jig on a coffin outside the *Express* offices.

Mr Dempster had already proved himself adept at self-publicity before he became named diarist on the *Daily Mail* in 1973. One highlight was a *Woman's Own* article on 'Mr Dempster's average day'. This had a photo montage similar to the opening credits of *The Saint* or *Jason King*. Squash, swimming, shaving, a lunch with someone 'newsworthy' like Lord Lichfield and the champagne nightclub circuit were all featured.

This mood of benevolence didn't catch on. In 1977 the *Sunday Express* covered Dempster's wedding to Lady Camilla Harris. The headline ran: 'Ex-Hoover salesman weds heiress.'

Mr Dempster and Mr Benson's current feud merely continues this grand tradition. It is a little bit of Fleet Street surviving in the new, widely-dispersed, 'international-style' Lubiankas.

There is also a suggestion of intrigue. How did Mr Dempster discover that his rival had to look up 'pompadoured poltroon' in a dictionary? Did he have a mole in the Benson team?

'No,' replied Mr Dempster slightly surprised. 'He told me over lunch.' They didn't actually meet each other? 'Oh yes,' confirmed Mr Benson, 'we meet for lunch regularly.' This was bizarre. So they didn't hate each other? 'There's nothing personal in it,' confirmed the aspiring Swift, Mr Dempster.

Despite the bile, it is somewhat disappointing that they don't hate each other. But you should hear what they say about the glitterati scribe of *Today*, Chris Hutchins...

Turn over for more exclusive revelations on the nibs who tell the yobs about the nobs ☛

Nigel Dempster on Mr Benson

'I called him a pompadoured poltroon because I consider gossip columns to be the equivalent of 18th-century pamphlets, and that's a pamphleteer's phrase. Even then he had to go to a dictionary to find out what it meant.

He's only speaking to his own readers on the downmarket Express, which makes bogus claims, like claiming to have revealed the Althorp affair. Other newspapers credited me. My column is home-grown and home-researched.

The Express used to send him to various parts of the world because they couldn't think of anything to do with him. He claims to have been a war correspondent but I doubt he's ever been near a shell. If he stops telling lies about me, I'll stop telling the truth about him.'

And now that diary

Mail Diary

NIGEL DEMPSTER
Daily Mail

Leading players Princess Margaret, the Tennants, Harold & Antonia, nearly Royals (preferably insane)

Formula 'Already the proud parents of [*enter children's names*] , the noble couple are expecting their [*number*] child at the [*private hospital*]'

Typical Quote 'Lord Macduff – the Duke of Fife's son and 36th in line to the throne – resigned from Bell Lawrie & Co…and is now seeking an alternative career'

Favourite Phrases
'Another diary scoop…'
'They declined to discuss the matter'
'She mused'

Little Foibles
Likes the Queen (eight mentions in one month)
Praises his own work: *Nigel Dempster's Address Book* is 'Warmly recommended!'
Promotes his own horses
'Isn't life grand,' he declares when they win

Pet Hates Ross Benson on the 'downmarket *Express*'. Was furious when Benson didn't credit him for the Althorp adultery scoop

Witty Flourish
'[Benson]…would be better employed plugging half-empty restaurants in St James, owned by his friends, as he did last week, to guffaws from the trade'

Inspirational Novelist
Late Evelyn Waugh (*Brideshead Revisted*)

The Diary

ROSS BENSON
Daily Express

Leading Players The Queen, Monaco royals, fallen Australian press baron 'Wokka' Fairfax, various Euronobs, Mrs Thatcher

Formula 'My picture shows [*titled bride*] plighting her troth to [*nouveau riche*] groom on [*date*] at the delightful country church of [*posh shire address*].The bride's father [*eccentric peer*] is worth [*sum in millions*]'

Typical Quote Prince Philip is described as 'a European Prince of indeterminate appelation – who was not even a real Mountbatten (it is the bastardised name of his mother)'

Favourite Phrases
'I can disclose'
'I understand'
'As I exclusively revealed'

Little Foibles
Really loves the Queen (40 mentions in one month)
Promotes her horses

Pet Hates
Nigel Dempster on the 'fade-away *Daily Mail*'. Was furious that 'minions' in the 'crumbling empire' were lifting his exclusives. Loves quoting Lord Rothermere, who said the *Mail's* Diary was akin to 'old, cold fried potatoes'

Witty Flourish
'A so-called rival diarist has produced a tome he calls his *Address Book*…'

Inspirational Novelist
Early Evelyn Waugh (*Scoop, Vile Bodies*)

Confidential

CHRIS HUTCHINS
Today

Leading Players Glitterati, Hollywood stars like Stallone etc, New Money, Pamella Bordes, Viviane Ventura

Formula 'At a glittering reception last night in [*hotel*], [*list of celebrities*], danced the night away to [*ageing rock band*]. Overheard speaking to [*big celebrity*], [*small celebrity*] said [*feeble quote*]…'

Typical Quote 'President Bush teased the world's press…by delivering a V-sign and asking them what they thought it meant. "Peace?" offered one hack…'"No," said Bush. "That's how Julius Caesar ordered five beers." Geddit?'

Favourite Phrases
'Following my forecast it would happen…'
'An amusing anecdote'
'How embarrassing'

Little Foibles
Thinks Queen is a rock band.
Promotes Bordes

Pet Hates No one. But would dearly love to join big boys Dempster/Benson's mutual animosity society

Witty Flourish '(Ritz design group) millionaire Michael Bancroft confides that he is often to be found sporting his wares. "When I go out in temperatures below zero, I will obviously be wearing my thermals," he barks. Now we know'

Inspirational Novelist
Jackie Collins (*Hollywood Wives, Rock Star*)

Londoner's Diary

RORY KNIGHT BRUCE
Evening Standard

Leading Players Crazed restaurateurs, Jeffrey Bernard, minor Scottish aristos, the *Spectator*, debs you've never heard of

Formula 'Handsome old [*Etonian*], a [*wannabe film maker*], met his soon to be wife [*the deb you've never heard of*] at [*smart Oxbridge College*] May Ball. He was seen last night…'

Typical Quotes 'I've been flicking through my copy of Kingsley Amis's memoirs…' 'When Lady Parsons switched on her television set to watch her husband, Sir Anthony, she was horrified by the photo on the mantelpiece…'

Favourite Phrases
'He tells me'
'I hear that'
'Jolly sounding'

Little Foibles Blasé about the Queen (once wrote that Prince Charles might suffer the fate of Edward II)

Pet Hates People who say he's obsessed with Etonians

Witty Flourish
Prince Philip 'may have been introduced to (his uncle) Lord Milford Haven's pornography collection, which included such works as *A Tale of the Birch* and *Lady Gay: Tales of Fun and Flagellation*'

Inspirational Novelist
P G Wodehouse (*Young Men In Spats, Psmith Journalist*)

data in full

Peterborough

ROBERT HARDMAN
Daily Telegraph

Leading Players The recently deceased, Tory grandees, Lord Dacre, *Debretts'* editor, huntin' shootin' fishin' folk

Formula 'Eyebrows were raised last night at [*haute bourgeois arts event*] when [*mildly risqué scene*] occurred. But the organiser tells me [*press officer's comment*]. How intriguing!'

Typical Quotes 'Having royalty as neighbours, one might think, would do wonders for property prices as well as social one-upmanship on the local sherry circuit'
'Andrew Robathan has landed the plum job of succeeding Nigel Lawson as MP for Blaby...He was educated at Merchant Taylors' – where his ruddy complexion earned him the nickname Rosy...'

Favourite Phrases
'There will be puzzled looks...'
'A mite baffled'
'Appalling'

Little Foibles
Is read by the Queen
Chases hearses

Pet Hates John Major's 'classless' society (too lofty to attack Dempster and Benson)

Witty Flourish 'A bottle of whisky, a ream of Basildon Bond and 50 first-class stamps will be awarded to the newly-sacked entrant who has suffered from the worst excesses of bad news-speak'

Inspirational Novelist J R Hartley (*Fly Fishing*)

Jennifer's Diary

BETTY KENWARD
Harpers & Queen

Leading Players Any host who invites this 83-year-old trouper. Anyone in bridal dresses

Formula 'One evening I went to a delightful party given by [*Hon Mr & Mrs Double-Barrel*]. I was so delighted by the [*describe flowers*]. Guests included [*list everyone, including the 'delightful' caterer*]'

Typical Quotes 'I was so happy to meet Duque and Duquesa San Carlos... as I first knew Alvaro San Carlos when he was a schoolboy'
'Her full tulle veil was held in place by a lovely diamond bandeau'

Favourite Phrases
'Delightful party'
'From the Dorchester I went to Claridges'
'Other guests included'

Little Foibles
Thinks she is the Queen
Attended the 'Brent Walker Festival of British Racing'

Pet Hates Has none. Far too busy being 'delighted'

Witty Flourish (Accidental) At one 'luncheon', she said, 'I did not know any of my fellow guests, who were mostly from the promotional and cosmetics worlds'

Inspirational Novelist Barbara Cartland (*First Class, Lady?, A Virgin In Mayfair*)

And now Haldane's view

'So Nigel Dempster rang Noddy and asked him if it was true that he and Big Ears were sleeping together...'

'Apparently a famous gossip columnist lives here'

'At the moment I write the odd poison pen letter but eventually I'd like to become a fully fledged gossip columnist'

KEN PYNE

Park Larks

'I'm afraid you've failed as a human being'

'No, nobody pays – everybody breaks in'

'He was devoted to that Rottweiler'

'They'll throw away the key'

'It's a new idea to stop the British being filthy'

GAZZA

he laughs, he cries he dribbles!

We *do* need another hero. JASPER REES charts the Gazza phenomenon

here have been two crucial moments in the arc of the Gazza comet. The first was his switch from back-page star to front-page hero. The second was his switch to centre-page idol. Gazza's tears made him famous, but his grin made him loved. Immortality requires more than just sporting drama. When Terry Butcher's bloody England shirt made the front page, no one wanted to mother him. When Gascoigne's girlfriend trouble hit the headlines, Fleet Street's grande dames fell over themselves to sound off faster than you could say facelift. Gazza was *blessed*.

There was a time, after the Danish midfielder Jan Molby emerged from his month-long sojourn at her Majesty's pleasure, when the Liverpool fans on the Kop used to chant, 'He's fat, he's round, his car's in the pound.' The unkindest thing you could say about Paul Gascoigne is that he is two-thirds of the way there. He is as fat as the cheque Spurs will receive when they sell him. And he is as round as the football he plays about so deftly. But he has not, so far, driven a car through a built-up area at 90 mph while under the influence of a reaction-dulling fluid.

This month's trendy fear is that he may, sooner or later, let all the attention get to him. Retired players have leapt onto the Gazza bandwagon by issuing unprompted warnings via the tabloids. Ray Clemence, Howard Kendall and Jimmy Greaves all 'roared' that they feared for the lad. Kevin Keegan issued an 'astonishing' caution to his one-time boot boy at Newcastle. 'He could finish on skid row,' thundered the diminutive permster. 'Gazza's in London and that's a different kettle of fish. There's no hiding place for him.'

There is no more drably over-used word in football than pressure, but pressure is what Gascoigne has been getting used to – ever since his Newcastle days when Vinnie Jones manually

applied quite a lot of it to his nether parts.

Until Gascoigne burst into tears in Turin, that was the single most memorable image we had of him: sinewy, log-like neck, bulging chops, rock-hard chin and cavernous mouth collectively wracked with, presumably, pain. Lower down in the frame his testicles were wrapped in the hands of a man who was taking his reputation as the football league's premier nutcase rather too literally.

So victimisation is not new to Gascoigne. And it is hard to

imagine that there will not be more of it in the season to come. Gordon Taylor, chief executive of the PFA, warned against it, ingenuously asking the Division One's hard men to lay off Gascoigne. Less disingenuously, he also asked the refs to protect Gazza if his plea to the crunchers fell on deaf studs. Taylor is widely regarded as English football's most sensible personage, so this seemed like a sensible request. Whether the likes of Vicious Vincent, back in the First Division with the regrettably promoted Leeds United, will pay heed is open to doubt. You don't, after all, get the chance every Saturday of the season to break the legs of one of the best players in the world.

But whether other people look after him or not, Gascoigne still has to look after himself; something he is good at only half the time. Gordon Taylor's plea rather irrelevantly compared Gascoigne's situation to that of politicians three times his age, but more aptly to that of George Best. For now the similarities are all positive: the young Best also had the world at his feet; it was only later that he also had the bottle at his mouth.

The sportsman Gascoigne most resembles, however, is that beefy epitome of John Bull defiance, Ian 'Guy the Gorilla' Botham. Guy and Gazza have a lot in common. As athletes they are only good when they 'turn it on'. Without inspiration flair players are nothing, they fade away. The temperament intrudes too much (witness Gazza's pink-faced impotent rage all through the recent Spurs-Arsenal derby).

But neither Gazza nor Guy has angst like George Best. Guy and Gazza are not tormented. They are more of the fighters and stayers school – lad's own heroes who don't *hide*. All fired up and fiercely patriotic. George Best was never a mainland prole with a nickname who would battle to the death. He was adored, but not as 'one of us'. (Botham only slipped from his People's Choice position when he got boorish and headbutted members of the public.) Gazza like Botham looks like his fans. It's all in the haircut.

For the doubters who suspect that Gascoigne has all the markings of a sportsman about to go off the rails – genius, money and, without a ball, no control – one can riposte that unlike Alan Hudson or Charlie George or the gifted players who were under-used by England managers, he has a quirky way with self-publicity. Admittedly, the crying jag was not scripted, but as spontaneous stunts go it worked with everyone but the referee who booked him.

In the offices of Collett Dickenson Pearce, the London advertising agency which rushed out an ad of Bobby Robson smoking a Hamlet cigar, half the staff have a picture of Gazza weeping above their desks. If it works for people in the cold-hearted image-mongering business, it is always going to work for us more gullible mortals.

It even worked for Professor Karl Miller, the editor of *London Review of Books*, who unironically put Gascoigne on the cover and effusively described him as a 'Priapic monolith in the Mediterranean sun'. (As wrongheaded assessments of a man with a daft bogbrush haircut go, this one is right up there with Hunter Davies's pre-World Cup rationalisation for Gascoigne's absence from the England team: 'He happens not to be good enough.')

Other television appearances have also worked their charm. When

"DAFT AS A BRUSH"
R ROBSON 90

GAZZA nicknames

Dazzler Gazza
Laughing Gaz
General Gazza
Bawl Boy
Teargaz
Guzzler Gazza
Gazza the Great
Gazza-nova
Red Legs (as an apprentice)
The Clown Prince of Soccer

GAZZA pricetags

Tabloid cost estimates of Gazza during World Cup (Spurs bought him for £2m in the summer of 1988)
£5m 24 June 1990
£6m 2 July 1990
£7m 6 July 1990
£8m 8 July 1990
£15m 10 July 1990 (Not so outrageous. On 27 August 1990 Spurs rejected an £11m bid by Juventus)

GAZZA headlines

Dog of war with face of a child
Gazza is ours say acid fans
Gazza gets a cake in the mush
Gazza's bigger than the Beatles
Gazza is told to sling his hook
Gazza: I got booked for smiling
Gazza owes it all to gran
Gazza: I hid in car boot
Tears we go Gazza
Watching my lad Gazza could kill me
Gazzumped!
Venables: Hate mob said I'd blown £2m on a fatso

GAZZA quotes

'He was never fat when he was little.'
Gazza's mum Mrs Carol Gascoigne

'There was no evidence that he was ever on course to become Bamber Gascoigne.'
Daily Express on Gazza's schooldays

'He was always Paul or Gassa then, not Gazza.'
Childhood pal Keith Spraggon

'I went up to him outside the bar to have a word with him and he suddenly laid into me.'
Tony Marshall, unemployed Geordie

🐾 Ball Boy

Gazza was a guest on *The Jonathan Ross Show*, at a time when Bobby Robson had yet to decide about even considering him for Italy, our hero admitted that he was keeping too high a profile for the manager's liking. 'I don't know why you agreed to appear on the show then,' quipped an amused Ross. But the interview – and the one with Wogan – depicted him as shy and engaging; not the kind of guy to round off a night on the town with a punch-up (as our hero reportedly did before his Cagliari flight).

In another post-match interview with the BBC, Gascoigne answered the suggestion that he bubbled over too often by pointing out that he was only a young lad, which seemed an immeasurably mature thing to say. The rest of the England team, lest we forget, appointed him spokesman to the press in Cagliari. Though we should also not forget that this is the same young lad who, after David Platt had scored against Belgium, shaped up to hug his besuited manager but opted to kiss him on the forehead instead. And the same young lad who returned to Luton Airport from Italy with a large pair of fake breasts strapped to his chest.

Soon after the Ross interview the young lad got his chance against Czechoslovakia. He didn't so much book his ticket for Italy as hijack the plane. The rest, as writers on any subject tend to say when the occasion suits, is history. Albeit a history we would all like to rewrite slightly. Already Gascoigne has broken off the engagement with his childhood sweetheart Gail Pringle and been linked with a 'part-time model' called Heidi`.

But what of the future? There are inordinately high expectations of Spurs this season, which ignores the fact that they are essentially the same side which belatedly scraped up to third place in the First Division last May. Gascoigne is still virtually a one-man midfield, Lineker a one-man attack, their defence a four-man colander.

But whatever happens to the club, the season is of intense personal importance to our hero: if he can build on what he achieved in Italy, he can be certain of going to Juventus or Marseilles or Barcelona or some other such dementedly spendthrift Mediterranean club. It is doubtless of no small importance to Spurs, which tends to put a premium on keeping the bank account full rather than the trophy cabinet, that he raise his price to somewhere near *Today*'s restrained evaluation of £15m. (Roberto Baggio, the world's most expensive player, cost Juventus half that.)

In the meantime, he has taken the financial precaution of patenting his own nickname, so that in the unlikely event of your wanting to market a product called Gazza, Gazza himself takes a cut. This sets the imagination to work: what artefact would most aptly bear the name? Gazza toilet brushes modelled on his haircut? Gazzler chocolates? A cover version of Smokey Robinson's hit, 'Tears of a Clown', which has already been used to caption a Gazza T-shirt? What about Gaz, the washing-powder that removes those tricky tear-stains? Or perhaps a range of absorbent handkerchiefs to mop up at those mopey moments?

For now, the rag he is promoting goes by the name of the *Sun*, which became his best friend in the World Cup, to the extent that for the whole month of June its back page bore his nickname like a trademark. But if the bookings start piling up, as in pre-season friendlies, if the on- and off-the-pitch misdemeanours accumulate with Botham-like regularity, the newspaper without scruples may yet become his worst enemy. And it may be that, like Best, Higgins, Botham, or any of sport's flair players, only Gazza himself can play in that position. 🐾

GAZZA quotes cont.

'Tomar no cu!' (Up yours, pal!)
Mirandinha, ex-Newcastle team mate

'The *Daily Star* today honours his courageous exploits by awarding him our coveted Gold Award.'
Tabloid consolation after semi-final defeat.

'Whether it's France, Espana or Italia, Gazza will always razza dazza.'
Russell Grant's in-depth World Cup horoscope

'It's nothing to do with age, lack of maturity, being silly, losing his head, arguing with the ref, committing petty fouls, all of which are true. He happens not to be good enough. End of story.'
Spurs fan Hunter Davis on why Gazza shouldn't be in England's World Cup team

'Fierce and comic, formidable and vulnerable, urchin-like and waif-like, a strong head and torso with comparatively frail-looking breakable legs, strange-eyed, pink-faced, fair-haired, tense and upright, a Priapic monolith in the Mediterranean sun – a marvelous equivocal sight.'
Professor Karl Miller, editor of the London Review of Books

'Mr Gascoigne does not quite fit the Greek ideal of the godlike athlete. It seems he has a weight problem and undeveloped muscles. Yet even in his wilder apparently boorish behaviour, there is something mythical which would strike a chord with the ancients.'
John Casey, Fellow of Gonville and Caius College, Cambridge

GAZZA cash-ins

Have a guzzle with Gazza
Win some drinking time with Gazza – Newcastle Brown Ale of course

Grabba Gazza T-shirt
Photo of Gazza crying, and 'There'll always be an England' logo

Grabba Gazza Poster for just £1
Sun charity fund-raiser

'I have a reet treat for you'
Gazza launches Soccer Sticker Collection

Have you got the next Gazza in your home?
Competition to track down the future cheeky soccer crazy lad who captures the nation's hearts

Gazza's Story – the video
Narrated by Danny Baker with whom Gazza duets 'All you need is love' – if not necessarily a decent voice

GAZZA
he scores off the pitch too

After the goals, the girls. But who is the Clown Prince's real love?

The ex-girlfriend

Gail Pringle, Gazza's fiance, gave him the shove soon after he returned from Italy. 'How I lost Gazza to the world' was the *Mail on Sunday's* comforting tactics. 'When we were together we just rented a video and picked up a bottle of Asti Spumante and a Chinese takeaway,' said Gail. 'If he had been the postman or something we would have been happy forever.'

The new girlfriend

Gazza was soon linked with beauty **Heidi Shepherd** after she delivered a fax machine to the Gazza family home. Gazza cried, 'All this talk about another girl is lies, lies, bloody lies. People are making me out to be a bastard – and it's not true.'

The new girlfriend's ex-boyfriend

Gazza was told that he wouldn't 'score in bed with my beauty' by insurance salesman **Bruce Walker**. Bruce – Heidi's ex-boyfriend – was 'broken-hearted' over her supposed new romance. A *News of the World* exclusive eased the grief.

'I was shocked to find she'd got a new bloke,' he said, sipping a Southern Comfort and nursing his pet Persian cat. 'Then, on top of that, to learn it was GAZZA! I can't compete financially with Gazza – let's face it, who can?'

Our portly Geordie pranksters pull another old trout

The would-be mothers

After the front-page brouhaha, came the ultimate star treatment. The tabloids' women columnists were sufficiently engrossed to put aside their Oil of Ulay. At least, long enough for them to move in and deliver *their* views on Gazza's love life.

Jane Gordon, *Today*
'You might have thought down-to-earth Gazza would have been warned about girls like Heidi. Girls who describe themselves as 'part-time models' on the strength of one picture published in *Amateur Photography*. I suspect that Heidi is more Fiona Wright that Miss Right.'

Jean Rook, *Daily Express*
'Already the hospitable Mr Gascoigne is tossing back Pernod-gin-vodka-blackcurrant-lemonade cocktails, and flinging round macho remarks like: "The most important thing in my life now is to be one of the lads." Someone should blow the whistle before it's too late.'

Lynda Lee-Potter, *Daily Mail*
'The important thing for him to accept is that his confused feelings are utterly normal. He needs a sensible, down-to-earth, lovely girl who's not afraid to tell him the truth and won't treat him like God.'

Carole Malone, *Daily Star*
'Being one of the lads is all right if you've got a woman at home who loves you. When all you've got is a bunch of boozing buddies who will drink as long as you're paying, life can get unbearably lonely.'

And now the *Daily Mirror*'s Anne Robinson, who writes:
'If I was [were surely?] Gail's mother or Heidi's mother I'd be relieved to see his backside out of Gateshead for good.'

The true love

All this maternal solicitude is somewhat misplaced. As Gazza's mum said, 'He never had much time for girls. It was always football.' So who is Gazza's true love? After England's defeat by Germany, the *Sunday Mirror* kindly shipped out roly-poly Geordie **Jimmy Gardner** (see left), Gazza's best pal.

Fifteen-stone tarmac layer Jimmy – nicknamed the Legend – has a special bond with Gazza: practical jokes. The lit Catherine wheel in the window of Jimmy's Cortina? 'We killed ourselves laughing,' chuckled joker Jimmy.

What about the Christmas when they threw darts at each other? 'We didn't mean any harm,' chortled the lard-laden Legend. 'Luckily I've got a bit of fat on me and it didn't hurt. I got my revenge by sticking one in his cheek.'

Or how about those airgun hi-jinx? 'When I bent over,' recalled the Tyneside Titan, 'Paul shot me in the backside from 15 yards. It was a good laugh – I only felt a tingle.' Gazza and Jimmy are a lovely couple. As Jimmy summed it up: 'I'd do anything for Gazza, because he'd do anything for me.'

ROSS
Smarty arties

'Whoops, must get that laser fixed'

'Much obliged'

*'Oh, how embarrassing, there's a woman over there wearing
the same cosmetic surgery'*

'I think, initially, we should clear up the issue of what can and cannot be treated by homeopathy'

'Get a job'

'It's cold tonight. We've got another tramp frozen to his cider'

MAGGIE

The Man Who Gives It To You Straight

WE WERE SADDENED when members of Parliament chose once again to reject the death penalty.

We have always been one of the most prominent supporters of capital punishment.

Perhaps if MPs had shown some guts for a change, we would not have been forced to watch helpless over Christmas as the well-known businessman Mr Ian Beale tried to kill Simon 'Wicksy' Wicks.

The threat of the rope would surely have made Mr Beale think twice about his crime.

Life can often be difficult in the East End, and that's why our Tory Government began the Docklands initiative.

But Mr Beale should remember that nobody got anywhere in life by moaning, whingeing, and trying to cut other people's brake cables.

Mr Beale will no doubt say that he was trying to murder Mr Wicksy because *EastEnders* has fallen

Butcher Beale should swing

behind in the opinion polls. But, as we tried to tell our colleagues, we were often behind in the polls yet always came back to win.

Soap

Mr Beale would do better to support our many initiatives in London's East End.

He should remember that *EastEnders* was itself set up under a Tory government, as were *Neighbours* and *Coronation Street*.

Can anybody give me the name of a successful television soap opera that has been created under a Labour government?

THAT WAS THE WEEP, THAT WAS

★ **THE CELEBRATED FOOTBALLER** Paul Gascoigne wept when he thought he would miss the World Cup final. He has since resumed the game to become Britain's best-loved player.

We, too, wept when we were forced to miss our big final, but we are now forced to watch the game from the terraces.

As I often say, it's a funny old world, isn't it?

Why we're the best writer for the job

★ **SOME OF OUR COLLEAGUES** have advised us that the New Year may be the right time for a fresh columnist to take up the pen.

They say that although our first two columns were hard-hitting, radical and witty, we may now have run out of steam.

Some have even suggested we are out of touch with our readership and that a column by Mr Michael Heseltine could attract more readers.

Nonsense!

We fully expect to be giving our views on the controversial issues of the day well into the next century. We will be writing on – we write to win!

THE TARBUCK STOPS HERE

★ AFTER 11 HAPPY YEARS of government, we were saddened by the carping at the very reasonable list of honours that we submitted.

An Earldom for our son, Mark, seemed a very small price to pay for the way he was constantly by our side as we strived to put the Great back into Great Britain.

The honour for Dame Samantha Fox seemed only fair after the way she stood up to the trade unions at Wapping.

And how will we now repay the unswerving loyalty of Sir James

NO OTHER WRITER'S A PATCH ON THATCH!

Every cloud has a hi-ho silver lining

DAVID QUANTICK on the pitfalls of student discos

My moment of greatness as a student DJ came the night I rode the graduate wheels of steel on behalf of something called Rock Soc. Any collectively feasible activity in a university is perverted into a 'society', a term which is one remove from 'hobby club', and rock music was not exempted. In this case, the 'Rock' bit signified one thing. Namely, that the hairy denim-and-PVC-leather-look acne-farmers who comprised Rock Soc didn't listen to anything other than very slow records by long-haired white men with loud guitars, preferably made after 1970 and never released as a single. These buffoons made trad jazz buffs look dangerously experimental.

Also they didn't dance. As I played their scrupulously requested tunes – Quo, 'Sabbaff', Purple, the whole dismal crew – three or four of them would shuffle about the dimly lit parquet dance floor, disco lights exploding above them, in the manner of roadmenders fixing invisible shovels. Sometimes during a solo one of them would appear to be carding wool, his hands moving back and forth unsettlingly.

It was an evening in hell. They hated me and I hated them. Finally someone appeared with a Led Zeppelin album. 'Play "Stairway to Heaven",' he demanded. Now 'Stairway To Heaven' is rubbish for dancing on two counts; first, it starts off as a slow folk ballad about a woman who lives in a hedge, and then it turns into a blethering thing with tempo changes. You can no more dance to 'Stairway To Heaven' than you can shave with it.

But then students, more so than the average punter, regard their discos as battlegrounds. Recently filled with A-levels and a lot of clever college nonsense, students see the disco as a place to educate their friends ('It's not the original version, is it?'), impress their loved ones ('God! Can't you do the Mud walk?') and, like all off us, live out their fantasies through music ('I met a! Gin-soaked Bar-room queen! In Memphis! Doo de doo!').

To this end, they spend their evenings thinking of increasingly obscure records to request ('He hasn't got any Mahavishnu Orchestra') and ever more scurrilous attacks on the records being played. The latter habit is spectacularly vexing. Just when you have finally found a record that more

than 20 people are prepared to dance to, some halfwit English Literature student with a Stone Roses CD and a slender volume of verse in the folds of his kagoul will come up, spill beer on the console and shout, 'Why are you playing this crap?'

Bizarrely, all students think that the greatest record of all time is 'Hi Ho Silver Lining'. This is clearly absurd. 'Hi Ho Silver Lining' (rendered as 'HI! HO! SILVER LINING!') is like 'The Birdy Song' with guitars, a shouted, laddish nonsense and the over-educated equivalent of a terrace chant. It is by Jeff Beck, a man who has spent much of his career being touted as a great guitarist by people whose only knowledge of his work is 'Hi Ho Silver Lining'.

Despite this awful anthem, students are, surprisingly, not really prey to generalisation. There are students all through this land and none of them are quite the same. In Oxford, grovest of groves of academe, old Etonians in mortarboards waltz May Ball night away to the amusingly retro sounds of Showaddywaddy and Marillion; while down the road at the Polytechnic, a thousand Fred Perry-ed business students lift a happy leg to U2 and the great empress of pop, Kylie Minogue. And while the thuggish rugger buggers of Glasgow howl happily to Deacon Blue and The Skids, the coffee-klatsches of the Slade Art School will only tread the floor to the sophisticated rhythms of Miles Davis, Charlie Parker and Gary Numan.

What degree students are taking also influences what music they like. How else to explain the fact that any jaunty pop record with shouting on it will immediately be bought by geography students? (Madness's chart career was, tragically, entirely dependent on good A-level results for people interested in contours and grain exports). And one would have thought that a 20-year-old forced to read Baudelaire all day would, in the evening, opt for the happy music of Barry Manilow, but no; the resoundingly glum strummings of Suzanne Vega are toppermost of the poppermost with the Unhappy French Poetry Brigade. The connection between science and heavy metal is clearer, since both attract people keen to wear jet boots and battle

Jeff 'Just don't ask me to play that bloody song again' Beck

The hair remains the same. Those be-bearded Led Zepsters get ready for another woman-in-hedge-style songfest

huge space monsters for the love of large-breasted warrior women; but why do only mathematics students demand to hear Sting? Whence the deep love of would-be lawyers for Motorhead? And why do Christians dislike everything?

What life behind the armour-plated, beer-smitten console finally proved to me was that students really are not like the rest of the world. They are as arrogant as a child prodigy on the flimsy pretext of being quite good at German. They have an innocence rare among 20-year-olds; cosseted in halls of residence and looked after by adults at an age when most people are making the tea for some nasty bald git, students charmingly believe that they have been thrust into the real world. This is why students are simultaneously so annoying and so fascinating. They are, after all, the only community in the world who consider 'Stairway To Heaven' a suitable record for dancing.

10 GREATEST STUDENT RECORDS

1. Jeff Beck: 'Hi Ho Silver Lining'
Goth and Sloane, Sociologist and Anarchopunk united in one floor-smashing primal stomp, roaring through clouds of sweat thus:
'You're everywhere and nowhere babe/Something something in your hippy hat/ And it's HI! HO! SILVER LINING! something something something HI! HO! SILVER LINING! / La da da, da da dada da da'.

2. 10cc: 'I'm Not In Love'
Ironic tune and clever words make this the student slowie. Truly the undergraduate's answer to 'The Lady In Red'.

3. Tom Robinson Band: '2-4-6-8 Motorway'
Plodding beat and easily memorised chorus lead into eminently mimable guitar solo while many opportunities about for fake working-class shouting.

4. Dexy's Midnight Runners: 'Come On Eileen'
Starts in amusing square dance fashion, has easily roarable chorus, and gets faster and faster in the manner of fondly-remembered Music And Movement broadcasts (with Eric Dobbin). Splendid opportunity for participants to fall over.

5. Gary Glitter: 'I'm The Leader Of The Gang (I Am)'
Through this record, even the dimmest of students can begin to comprehend the notion of 'camp', reeling about to a song which is completely undanceable, contains eight choruses and no verses and has a really exciting motorbike noise at the start. Also ideal for multiple toppling.

6. Beastie Boys: '(You Gotta) Fight For Your Right (To Party)'
Sums up limits of graduate political involvement. Can wave fists in air, look aggressive and let off steam against parents. Also drums so loud that even Gyles Brandreth could strut his funky stuff to them.

7. New Order: 'Blue Monday'

The nearest most students get to proper dancing, 'Blue Monday' is the best-selling 12" single of all time and the only 12" single ever owned by geography students. Insistent and glum, it reminds them of their courses.

8. Blues Brothers: 'Everybody Needs Somebody To Love'
The Blues Brothers' record fulfils the following needs: it is a song from a cult film, a Sixties song, a song made famous by a black man but remade faster and louder by white men, and best of all, a glorious opportunity for FANCY DRESS.

9. Gary Numan: 'Cars'
Another FANCY DRESS classic, albeit of minor appeal. Only dedicated individualists dressed up for it; but both of these individualists and rugby players combine in the frightening Thunderbirds/semaphore signalling dance routine that accompanies it.

10. Slade: 'Merry Xmas Everybody'
Trunks are packed. Railcards dug out from wallets. Vast amounts of filthy laundry are loaded up to be taken home. Christmas is imminent and to celebrate, the students are standing on the dance floor, shouting and doing a weird dance where they stand in a circle and kick their legs up in the air. Why this is no-one knows, but it was probably introduced by Prince Albert.

10 WORST STUDENT RECORDS

1. Lynyrd Skynyrd: 'Freebird'
Grim ballad with inane lyrics that mystifyingly turns into a screaming instrumental. Undanceable and unlistenable.

2. Led Zeppelin: 'Stairway To Heaven'
Pretty much the same as 'Freebird' only thankfully minus the absurd Beverly Hillbillies accents. Great one to fade out during the solo.

3. George Michael: 'Careless Whisper'
A clever slowie. 'Guilty feet have got no rhythm' sings George. Nor, coincidentally, have student feet.

4. Pink Floyd: 'Another Brick In The Wall'
The idea of 200 well-educated young people chanting 'We don't need no education' and 'Hey! Teacher! Leave those kids alone!' is absurd beyond language.

5. U2: 'I Still Haven't Found What I'm Looking For'
Again, about as relevant to the lives of future would-be professional doctors, accountants and lawyers as Elizabethan plainsong. Also sung in a horrible whiny voice.

6. Bruce Springsteen: 'Born To Run'
Spectacularly irrelevant (though 'Wendy' is quite a popular name among students) to student life, impossible to dance to, composed largely of shouting and motorbike noises and liable to over-excite the punters. Worth playing, however, just to hear 60 law students shouts 'Tramps like us!' Indeed they do.

7. Phil Collins: 'Groovy Kind of Love'
Encourages kissing among students. Features man who used to be Genesis, who were the top student band of the 1970s. From a dire film liked by students because it's got Julie Walters in it 'and she's really good in Victoria Wood'.

8. Bob Marley: 'One Love'
Dismal meaningless hippy burble with irritating chugalong beat that only serves to wrongly convince students that they can dance and that they like reggae.

9. Dire Straits: 'Money For Nothing'
Student loans, ha ha. Students love it because it features Sting on backing vocals and the lyrics are Mark Knopfler griping about how people think he is paid lots of dosh for doing sod-all the live long day. Students readily identify with this.

10. Jeff Beck: 'Hi Ho Silver Lining'
'HI! HO! SILVER LINING!'

The old pals

Who can you call a friend these days? Someone famous and useful, says ERIC STRATTON

The concept of friendship used to be pretty straightforward. A friend was someone you'd been to school with, a workmate or a neighbour. Your spouses knew one another. You chatted on the phone; had dinner; went on holiday together – all that sort of thing. From time to time a friend might do you a favour, but that wasn't the reason for your relationship.

Nowadays, the laws of the marketplace have intruded into friendship as they have done into every other aspect of our lives. The idea of 'a friend in need' has taken on a whole new meaning. A friend is someone who might be useful. You don't even have to know them particularly well. You just have to turn a profit.

One expert practitioner of the art of modern friendship is Piers Morgan, the rosy-cheeked, public schoolboy pop columnist on the *Sun*. So deeply chummy is the genial Mr Morgan that whenever he meets a juvenile chart sensation, he is photographed with his arm dangled over their shoulders. The celebrities, with admirable professionalism, refrain from wincing excessively.

The extent of Morgan's professional sycophancy was revealed on New Year's Eve last year, when the *Sun* ran a full-page story headlined, 'Who Is That Poser With Piers Morgan?' The tooth-laden, globetrotting, incongruously besuited Morgan was seen getting matey with an astonishing array of publicity addicts.

These included (with Piers's own comments in brackets)... Kylie Minogue ('She chatted to me in Birmingham about boozing, drugs and blokes'); Phil Collins ('He threatened to cut my head off in Osaka, Japan'); a Mutant Ninja Turtle ('Sewer glad to see me in London'); Charles Bronson ('I trembled when he insisted on meeting me at a Hollywood bash'); David Bowie ('Polite, funny and full of hilarious anecdotes when he kicked off his tour in Canada'); Gloria Estefan ('I gave her flowers at her Miami home'); Mike Tyson ('Interviewing him in New York was my most dangerous task'); M C Hammer ('I proved U can touch him'); Jonathan King ('He tried to strangle me at the

Above: Waiting on a friend with Mick and Keith – the ultimate in long-term friendship for fun and profit.
Below: Smiling unknown Jack Turner (third from left) scores with his celebrity amigos Jeff, George, Eric, Ian and Elton

Stones' Philadelphia gig'); Sean Connery ('Wasn't happy to see me in LA'); and Frank Bruno ('I showed him my picture of Tyson').

As if to complete the illusion of mutual affection, Mr Morgan delights in reprinting the Christmas cards and jolly messages he receives from the stars (or, to be cynical, which the stars may or may not dictate to their press officers). When the celebs need a kind word, or a friendly shoulder to cry on, Piers Morgan is the man to whom they turn.

If they want a quick Buddhist chant, however, they go to Lynne Franks, the PR dynamo behind Katharine Hamnett and Swatch watches. Ms Franks has often been heard referring to 'her new best friend' and is, as Americans say, plugged into the network. Her friends include Sir Ralph Halpern, Lenny Henry and fellow Buddhist, Sandie Shaw. The benefits are mutual. Lynne gets showbiz glamour, Ruby Wax gets a whole load of material for her act.

Less fashionable figures have learned to play the same tricks. Richard Branson and Margaret Thatcher became friends, for example, when they picked up pre-scattered litter together in a park. He was the woolly-jumpered tycoon going corporate; she was the Iron Lady needing to show she cared. This handy alliance lasted long enough to make its point then quietly, but rapidly faded. But they had been friends.

Similar alliances flourished between the Iron Lady and such corporate mastodons as Lord King and Lord Hanson. But it took Nancy Reagan to raise the art of profitable intimacy to its highest point. She ensured that her entire life – from free haircuts, through complimentary couture to her million-buck Bel Air retirement home – was paid for by a combination of power-crazed billionaires and publicity-hungry tradesmen, all desperate to cash in on proximity to the presidency.

Away from the corridors of power, the book world is one in which mutually-beneficial friendship has been raised to the status of an art form. Literary backscratching – 'You praise my novel, I'll praise yours' – oils the wheels deliciously ☛ *(page 177*

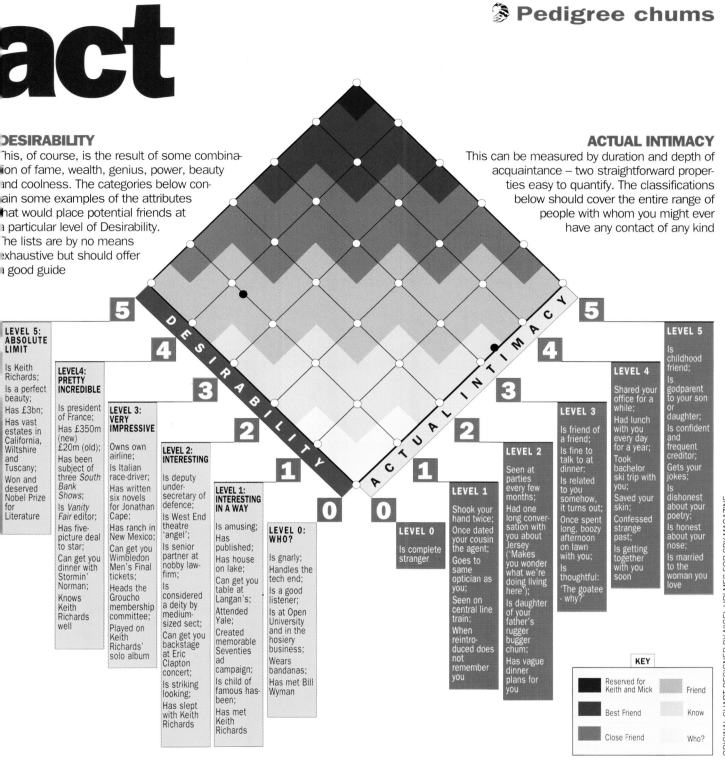

DESIRABILITY

This, of course, is the result of some combination of fame, wealth, genius, power, beauty and coolness. The categories below contain some examples of the attributes that would place potential friends at a particular level of Desirability. The lists are by no means exhaustive but should offer a good guide

ACTUAL INTIMACY

This can be measured by duration and depth of acquaintance – two straightforward properties easy to quantify. The classifications below should cover the entire range of people with whom you might ever have any contact of any kind

LEVEL 5: ABSOLUTE LIMIT

Is Keith Richards;

Is a perfect beauty;

Has £3bn;

Has vast estates in California, Wiltshire and Tuscany;

Won and deserved Nobel Prize for Literature

LEVEL 4: PRETTY INCREDIBLE

Is president of France;

Has £350m (new) £20m (old);

Has been subject of three *South Bank Shows*;

Is *Vanity Fair* editor;

Has five-picture deal to star;

Can get you dinner with Stormin' Norman;

Knows Keith Richards well

LEVEL 3: VERY IMPRESSIVE

Owns own airline;

Is Italian race-driver;

Has written six novels for Jonathan Cape;

Has ranch in New Mexico;

Can get you Wimbledon Men's Final tickets;

Heads the Groucho membership committee;

Played on Keith Richards' solo album

LEVEL 2: INTERESTING

Is deputy under-secretary of defence;

Is West End theatre 'angel';

Is senior partner at nobby law-firm;

Is considered a deity by medium-sized sect;

Can get you backstage at Eric Clapton concert;

Is striking looking;

Has slept with Keith Richards

LEVEL 1: INTERESTING IN A WAY

Is amusing;

Has published;

Has house on lake;

Can get you table at Langan's;

Attended Yale;

Created memorable Seventies ad campaign;

Is child of famous has-been;

Has met Keith Richards

LEVEL 0: WHO?

Is gnarly;

Handles the tech end;

Is a good listener;

Is at Open University and in the hosiery business;

Wears bandanas;

Has met Bill Wyman

LEVEL 0

Is complete stranger

LEVEL 1

Shook your hand twice;

Once dated your cousin the agent;

Goes to same optician as you;

Seen on central line train;

When reintroduced does not remember you

LEVEL 2

Seen at parties every few months;

Had one long conversation with you about Jersey ('Makes you wonder what we're doing living here');

Is daughter of your father's rugger bugger chum;

Has vague dinner plans for you

LEVEL 3

Is friend of a friend;

Is fine to talk to at dinner;

Is related to you somehow, it turns out;

Once spent long, boozy afternoon on lawn with you;

Is thoughtful: 'The goatee - why?'

LEVEL 4

Shared your office for a while;

Had lunch with you every day for a year;

Took bachelor ski trip with you;

Saved your skin;

Confessed strange past;

Is getting together with you soon

LEVEL 5

Is childhood friend;

Is godparent to your son or daughter;

Is confident and frequent creditor;

Gets your jokes;

Is dishonest about your poetry;

Is honest about your nose;

Is married to the woman you love

KEY

■ Reserved for Keith and Mick	▨ Friend
■ Best Friend	▨ Know
▨ Close Friend	□ Who?

ORIGINAL CHART DESIGNED BY NIGEL HOLMES FOR SPY MAGAZINE

How to use the Punch Friendship Index

WHO'S A CLOSE FRIEND? Who's an acquaintance? Which person should you hang up on when a second call comes in? We've invented a simple, user-friendly Friendship Index to help ease the worry of deciding who's who.

Here's how it works: Choose the level of Desirability (left axis) that best describes what attracts you to your 'friend'. Then select the level of Actual Intimacy (right axis) that accurately reflects how well you really know this 'friend'. Plot the point on the graph above. The location will tell you whether you should refer to your 'friend' as your best friend, a friend and so on.

A test drive: a college chum of yours is seeing a hypothetical sister of Jeremy Irons; on a weekend in the country you talked with Irons. He has a Desirability factor of 3.6. The Actual Intimacy factor of your relationship is 1. Plotting these two co-ordinates, we see that Mr Irons, whom you barely know, is nevertheless your friend. A different case: your best school friend has always kept in touch. She is coming to live in the city you moved to in order to escape the stifling hometown of childhood. She plans to open a pet store. Her Desirability is 0; the Actual Intimacy is 3.3. The graph reveals she is someone you know.

Best friend to the music business, **Sun** pop columnist Piers Morgan, tenderly shares his private scrapbook of spontaneous moments

and guarantees a fun time and free lunches at book launches all over town.

And for wordmongers, one's wife is truly one's best friend. A couple of years ago, for example, the poet and critic Hugo Williams was asked for his book of the year in one of the annual fiestas of mutual appreciation that are as inevitable a part of Christmas as crackers and *The Great Escape*. Hugo's choice was *The Tightrope Walker*, a novel by Hermine Demoriane. He neglected to inform the casual reader that Miss Demoriane was also...Mrs Hugo Williams.

On a more serious note, when Salman Rushdie was sentenced to death after the Ayatollah's fatwah, he said that he soon found out who his friends were. He certainly did. London's literati fell over themselves to write their 'Me and Salman' pieces, including Martin Amis, Melvyn Bragg, Harold Pinter, Peter Preston, Fay Weldon, Derek Jarman and Antonia Fraser. The *New Statesman* had a special Rushdie issue packed with interested parties. It did little to help Salman, but it did wonders for his pals.

The Pinters are of course dab hands at presiding over friendly occasions at which leading lights of global politics and the arts discover subjects of shared interest. The Nicaraguan leader Daniel Ortega was the guest of honour at a party *chez* Harold and Lady Antonia. There he was able to network with British admirers like Melvyn Bragg, whose *South Bank Show* obligingly produced a typical PR puff on the poetic spirit of Nicaragua's revolutionary leaders. Sadly, however, the Nicaraguan people were unable to see Melvyn's meisterwerk, or they would surely not have voted Ortega out of office some months later.

Another Pinter pal is Vaclav Havel, Czech president and litterateur. When the Rolling Stones played Prague in the course of their last worldwide cash-fest, Havel turned out to greet the band at a special reception. He traded his mammoth credibility as a playwright-turned-political-prisoner-turned-national-liberator, for the Stones' fading

glory as rock's great rebels. It was a lousy deal for Havel, but then so is the Eastern Bloc's rate of exchange.

More evenly balanced is the friendship of those mid-life maestros Eric Clapton and Phil Collins. They have a lot in common after all. Both are nice lower-middle-class boys who are millionaires and like a local pub. But there had been some differences in the early Eighties. Eric was a musical legend (ie he had a hit in the Sixties), but Phil was the critical lightweight selling millions of records. The mutual benefits were obvious. Phil produced Eric's two comeback albums and played drums on his tour. Eric took Phil to Versace's and told him which suits to buy. Phil's squeaky-clean image was helped by proximity to former junkie and alcoholic Eric, and vice versa. They were *friends*.

Rock stars, who have innate laddishness, often strike up friendships with sportsmen, who have explicit laddishness. Ian Botham at the height of his cricketing success settled quickly into a round of charity matches with Phil and Eric and Bill Wyman. Now that Botham's profile is reduced to *A Question Of Sport*, the rock stars don't seem to be around so much.

Friendship with the Royals is a sub-genre on its own, because it's a fine line from Royal patronage. Elton John, who warbles away at parties for Princes Edward and Andrew, is the court troubadour. Billy Connolly is the court jester to the Yorks. Jackie Stewart, a great chum of the Princess Royal, is the court chauffeur and so on. The symbiosis is obvious. The celebrities gain prestige; the Royals gain fashionability.

Shake your moneymaker: court jester Billy Connolly greets fellow mason Fergie. The guy in the middle is not a friend

Prince Charles is, of course, notably more serious. His relationship with Laurens van der Post was much more that of guru and pupil. But he does have friendships. He takes walks with gentlewomen who share his interest in old churches. And at the height of Band Aid he was good friends with Bob Geldof. Six years on, the Prince and the pop has-been don't run into each other quite so often.

So now you have an idea of the definition and modern versions of friendship. To sort out who are your close friends and who are people you just know, turn to our

The Dread Kennedys

With a Kennedy now awaiting trial for rape, ANTHONY LEE charts the curse of the dynasty that makes *Dallas* look like a soap opera

I t remains the family saga to end them all. Dynastic ambition, sibling success, patriarchal manipulation, lust, money, murder, madness, corruption, adultery, alcoholism, violence and death. But the Ewings of Dallas have finally been despatched, so it's back to the real thing – the Kennedys of Boston.

A current joke doing the rounds of American political circles has alleged rapist William Kennedy Smith saying to Patricia Bowman: 'Come to a party or I'll get my uncle to drive you home.' William's uncle is of course Edward Moore Kennedy, Senior Congressional Senator from Massachusetts, whose unorthodox prowess at the wheel of an automobile so engaged the legal world in July 1969 at Chappaquiddick. However it

was phrased, Ms Bowman accepted the invitation, not on Martha's Vineyard, summer home of America's PoWs (Prisoners of Wealth), but in balmy Palm Beach, the Kennedy's sunnier and richer winter retreat. She returned to what is reverentially called the Kennedy Compound, a six-bedroom house with swimming-pool and tunnel to the beach.

As a result of this chance encounter in an up-market burger bar, Mr Smith stands accused of rape. ('Stands' may prove to be over-optimistic. One Florida television news show referred to the accused's alleged difficulties in readying himself for the sexual act – a condition vulgarians attribute to brewery produce.) The fact that a trouser-free Uncle Teddy appeared to be

And the clan played on: those good-time Kennedys (from left) Young Patrick, his dad Teddy, Bobby, lover Marilyn, Jack, the accused William Kennedy Smith, attentive Palm Beach serving wench, and in front, the man who started it all, Joseph Patrick Snr

involved in the long evening's superfluity of pastimes promoted much media interest. Newspaper persons felt moved again to stir the slimy old cauldron containing the Curse of the Kennedys.

Like the Curse of Tutankhamen, the Curse of the Kennedys seems forever to be with us. It is revived every so often to frighten the credulous, whenever one of 'America's Royal Family' is waist high in doo-doo, to coin the verbiage of Kennebunkport as opposed to Hyannisport. The astonishing ascription of 'America's Royal Family' is, however, a totally undeserved condemnation. The Kennedys are not as ungainly or as boring as our own First Family. And while the Mellons of Pittsburgh and

the Du Ponts of Delaware are nearer in largesse to the Windsors, they (apart from the excitable Governor Peter Du Pont) shun the limelight. The Kennedys most certainly do not.

The Kennedy fortune (property, stocks, bootlegging and Hollywood) encompasses much of the American dream, while the fates of John and Robert elaborate its nightmare. That neither is yet exhausted says much for the clan's staying power, even if today the reputation of JFK the lover has long outstripped the reality of JFK the legislator.

As private individuals the Kennedys just happen to be sitting on a fortune in trust funds ($400m says one 1950 estimate). ☞

ILLUSTRATION: DAVID HENSLEY

🦢 Grope opera

Unkind observers might say that if the Kennedys are cursed, it is a self-inflicted blow. But this fails to comprehend the real curse.

Joseph Kennedy Snr, father to John, Bobby, Teddy et al, inspired his sons with no end of good examples, the most interesting being the kernel of the Curse. As a businessman, he conducted a thriving business in alcohol supplies – which continued after 1919, the only inconvenience being that Prohibition had by then made the trade illegal. Here is the unexamined origin of the real Kennedy curse: mere forgetfulness. Old Joe forgot that bootlegging was against the law. Years later when his sons fought for the rights of the poor, they were able to utilise their late father's expertise in poverty, forgetting only that it had come from turfing mortgage defaulters onto the streets. Equally inspiring was Old Joe's repeated forgetfulness that he was married. Screen siren Gloria Swanson was only one of a well-discussed stream of conquests. She compared Irish Joe's love-making with that of 'a roped horse, rough, arduous, racing to be free.'

The Las Vegas socialite Judith Campbell Exner revealed in her memoirs how JFK inherited his father's neglectful trait – and his carnal coltishness. Originally introduced to Ms Exner through Frank Sinatra, JFK seems to have drawn the line at sharing a mistress who had forgotten her own relationship with Mafia boss Sam Giancana. An understandable restraint on the part of the President, although he once forgot how many people in bed together constituted acceptable behaviour. Ms Exner drew a virginal line at a presidential *menage à trois*.

Younger brother Teddy's memory lapses began at Harvard, where he paid a friend to sit a Spanish exam in his place. Cruelly expelled for this (a situation the family forgot for ten years), Teddy suffered further amnesia. Re-entering Harvard in 1953

Teddy, the patriarch of party animalism, shyly demonstrates the Kennedy mystique

he mistook a rugby game for a boxing match and was expelled from the game.

At the University of Virginia Law School, Teddy's inventive abilities behind a steering-wheel were closely observed by the local constabulary. He tended to forget that red lights were for stopping at, headlights were a help at night and the suburban speed limit was not 90mph. These were understandable misdemeanours for somebody used to the fast lanes and back streets of Hyannisport and Palm Beach. Teddy's blonde ex-wife Joan has obviously acquired some of this freewheeling verve. She was recently arrested in Massachusetts on a drink-driving charge.

Most famously, in 1969 Teddy forgot to notify anyone officially of the accident for ten hours after driving his car into the drink. At one point Teddy actually suggested that it was Mary

America's Royal Family – on its best behaviour

● **Joseph Kennedy II**
'Once a Kennedy, always a Kennedy,' he wailed, bemoaning (!) how easy it was to get girls. His father once asked 'Who is Ho Chi Minh?' Joe said: 'The Emperor of China?' Thinks the British should leave Ireland and has his uncle's penchant for traffic violations.

● **David Kennedy**
Joe's younger brother was involved

with cocaine, morphine, heroin, and for a time actress Rachel Ward. Stephen Smith (father of William) told the press David suffered 'from an ailment similar to drug addiction.' Very similar: he died, Palm Beach, 1984.

● **Chris Lawford**
The son of Patricia Kennedy was expelled from school for drug abuse. Indulged with dad, actor Peter.

Became a heroin addict and entered a clinic for the emotionally disturbed.

● **Robert Kennedy Jnr**
Pleaded guilty to possessing heroin, having been taken unconscious from a plane at South Dakota.

● **Ludovic Kennedy**
Did You See? presenter. Happily married, sober. Not a real Kennedy.

Jo and not he who was driving. That the dead girl's parents were prepared to support the political career of their late daughter's chauffeur only serves to show how sentimental an electorate can be.

Not that Teddy needed their help in his candidacy for the Amnesiac Party. In 1979 he was asked by CBS TV's Roger Mudd: 'What would you do different from (President) Carter?' Teddy promptly gave his most authoritative statement yet on the platform: 'Well, it's a-on-on what-on-you know, you have to come to grips with the – the different issues that we're – we're facing.'

On a more social note, the senior senator from Massachusetts was lunching with a female companion at Washington's fashionable brasserie. When the two were reportedly discovered in a pants down/dress up situation, people professed to be shocked. Ignorant people, no doubt, because the lady happened to be a Congressional lobbyist and, God knows, it's hard to get the ear of a politician at the best of times.

In 1989 voters were undoubtedly reassured when Teddy helped vote against a senior appointment for Texan, John Tower. The unofficial grounds included allegations of drinking and womanising – on the part of the nominee, of course.

In Palm Beach, a few weeks ago, according to witness Michele Cassone, Teddy appeared before her during early morning cocktails without what Americans call pants. If true, this state of undress shows that his amnesia is now positively Alzheimerian.

Gore Vidal, himself a lapsed Kennedy confidante, once told me that when the Kennedys were up to something crooked, 'which was most of the time', if they were caught at it, the other person was guilty of bad taste.

Consider Maria Kennedy Shriver, an on-screen eminence at NBC News. She eschewed the bad taste of a political dynastic marriage for the good taste of a wedding with the distinguished thespian Mr Arnold Schwarzenegger. He escaped the fate of being renamed Kennedy, so Maria Shriver Schwarzenegger (not a name to be tried after a night on a bar-stool in Palm Beach) found herself instead with Conan the Republican. This must make for interesting political cross-talk at the Hyannisport pool.

Apart from Maria's good example, other Kennedy children have let the side down and picked politics over entertainment. Jackie O's son, John-John, is an assistant district attorney in Manhattan, despite twice failing his bar exams. And Patrick became a member of the Rhode Island State legislature while still at college.

For Uncle Teddy though, the political lights may have finally dimmed. Ironically, his removal from presidential potential has proved to be an effective ameliorator of what's left of liberalism in the United States. His senior position in the Senate gives him a platform and a modicum of power. Of course, he has little prospect of effecting major social reforms, and so he can stridently and safely give voice to them.

Meanwhile Palm Beach has occluded the horizons for one dynasty just as the disappearance of *Dallas* has done for another. But wait – even as we speak, PBS in the US is preparing the definitive TV documentary series on the Kennedys. For JR read JFK. Say 'bye, bye' Jock and 'hello' Joseph. They're even better than the real thing.

Anthony Lee is a producer on BBC's The Late Show.

ERIC STRATTON observes the eerie coincidences between the fun-loving Kennedys of Camelot and another enlightened ruling family

Borgias	Kennedys
1. A powerful Catholic dynasty who came from Spain to Italy.	**1.** A powerful Catholic dynasty who came from Ireland to America.
2. They reached the top of the political greasy pole. Alfonso became Pope Calixtus III. Rodrigo became Alexander VI. Cesare was captain-general.	**2.** They reached the top of the political greasy pole. Joe was ambassador to Britain. Jack became President. Bobby was attorney-general.
3. Lucrezia inherited the duchy of Ferrara.	**3.** Teddy inherited the seat of Massachusetts.
4. Fondness for wife-swapping orgies and 'debauched partying' with other relatives.	**4.** Fond of debauched partying as a family (Palm Beach). Jack romped in a pool with Angie Dickinson.
5. Favoured the use of spies to maintain power.	**5.** Bobby bugged Martin Luther King's telephone.
6. Rodrigo had famous mistresses. He kept a portrait of one, dressed as the Madonna, over his bedchamber door.	**6.** Jack and Bobby had the same famous mistress, Marilyn Monroe. They kept her, dressed like Madonna, in California.
7. Lucrezia married aged 13, and twice more in her teens.	**7.** JFK Jnr romped aged 12 with Daryl Hannah and later dated her.
8. When Julius II became Pope he pursued a vendetta against the Borgias.	**8.** J Edgar Hoover, when head of the FBI, tried to discredit the Kennedys.
9. Rodrigo was poisoned. Cesare was killed on military service in Navarre.	**9.** Jack and Bobby were shot, their brother Joseph was killed in World War II.
10. 1981: BBC screened a series called *The Borgias*.	**10.** 1983: ITV mini-series called *Kennedy*.

DREDGE
Villain station

'You have the right to make one phone call, son!'

'Just tap the shoulder of the man who has made your life hell, madam!'

182

IDENTITY PARADE

'He was mugged in the gents at the Dog and Ferret'

'Sorry I'm early – some bastard switched off my life-support machine!'

'Would yer like to see a photo of your wife 'n' kids, chief?'

'Now tell me, Mr Wingrove – how long have you believed yourself to be Dr Anthony Clare?'

Hello! I think I love you

Having put his problems behind him, warm-hearted bachelor MIKE CONWAY invites us into the nicest of all possible magazines

When the actor Richard Harris met Lynn Barber, the *Independent on Sunday*'s merciless profile-writer, she devoted her column to a devastating account of his skill as a sportsman – the sport in question being pocket billiards. When Kevin Costner came to England to film *Prince Of Thieves*, he found the tabloid press ready and waiting with tales of his alleged extra-marital nightlife. What else could one expect from the ogres of the British press?

But now, stars like Richard and Kevin have an alternative means of reaching their fans. At last there's a publication in which the sporting contests going on in Mr Harris's trousers remain unreported by journalists as the actor 'introduces us to his first grandchild'. And Mr Costner can finally reveal 'why he'll always put family love above stardom,' while asserting: 'I'm very much in love with my wife.' And that's just on the cover.

The magazine in question is *Hello!*, the runaway success story of contemporary publishing, with sales standing at a ☞

Take one be-syruped croonster, a portly chatelaine, a 'loveable' child and a pile of magazines and...bingo! It's a Hello! *feature*

ILLUSTRATION: CHRIS CHAISTY

Those Heart-Warming Hello! Couples

- Lysette Anthony and her 'dashing Dutchman' Luc Leestemaker
- Sicilian 'businessman' Guiseppe Paterno Castello Marchese di San Giuliano and wife Fiamma
- Racing driver Alessandro Nannini and wife Paola
- Linda Evans, 45, and the handsome Greek in her life, Yanni, 33
- Tony Peck, 32, son of Gregory, and wife Cheryl Tiegs, daughter of Mr and Mrs Tiegs, 43
- Sir Francis Dashwood and wife, former model Marla Landi
- Julio Iglesias and Tahitian beauty Vaitiare (no surname)
- Princess Stephanie and her former fiancé Jean-Yves Lefur
- Edward Heath with the plate that belonged to Benjamin Disraeli

Bereft of her other half, Princess Caroline, Hello!*'s crying cover-girl*

mighty 346,540 every week. Launched in May 1988, this British younger sister of the Spanish title *¡Hola!* features a non-stop parade of pouting personalities.

As the threat of the P45-O-Gram stalks the land, and that nice man from the building society suddenly turns nasty, *Hello!*'s unthreatening universe is the perfect escape. Ailing troupers, ageing starlets, glitzy new money, glamorous old royalty – all in a photo-led magazine at an economic price.

'When the stars talk, they talk to *Hello!*' claims the magazine's publicity – and it's right. Anyone will talk to *Hello!* Because *Hello!* never, ever says anything nasty about anyone. The magazine's reporters ask questions designed to flatter and reassure their subjects: 'What does winning this award mean to you?' or 'Tell me about the special man in your life.' Then, just like the brown-nosing Boswells they are, they write down the answers without comment or criticism.

Reality takes a long time to gatecrash *Hello!*'s party. Jane Seymour's marriage was portrayed as a fairytale dream in issue after issue, even though tabloid newspapers were simultaneously exposing her husband's drinking, drug-taking and philandering. Now, of course, the former love birds sing their hearts out to *Hello!* giving their side of the story – in separate interviews.

Love, with all its associated joys and pains, is central to the winning formula. Equally vital is redemption, or, as the old-fashioned women's magazines used to call it, TOT – triumph over tragedy.

In almost every issue you will find a piece of prime-time American beefcake talking about how 'his woman' has changed his life. Then there is the alcoholic actor or former cocaine-addict singer, with salvation again coming in female form. For Fifties' crooner Eddie Fisher, formerly married to Debbie Reynolds and Elizabeth Taylor, the drug problem was solved with the help of a Rubenesque Chinese property developer. Here, again, the magazine's niceness means that blame lies with others. Fisher's unspecified addiction, says *Hello!*, began 35 years ago when a 'rogue doctor opened his black medicine bag and filled a hypodermic with a "magic elixir"...'

Faced with such sentimental drivel, conventional journalists are appalled. But readers love it. Readers, after all, are busy: they don't have time for anything that requires extensive brainwork. And what *Hello!* gives its punters is a nose poked into famous lives, without some snooty writer getting in the way. In any case, the words are irrelevant. The real information comes in the pictures. And *Hello!*'s blissfully naïve style of photography (which regularly features interviewees pretending to read a copy of the magazine) reveals more about its subjects than any grilling by Torquemada.

The shots come in two distinct styles. One has a touch of the airbrush about it; the celebrities are snapped with a vaseline-covered lens in ultra-soft focus. These look disturbingly like a Timotei advertisement.

The other style is brutally candid. The less fortunate subjects (or those without a protective agent) pose awkwardly in a domestic *mise-en-scène*; their surgical nip 'n' tucks exposed for the nation's coffee-time scrutiny. Old men smile at the camera, horribly unaware that their toupee is all-too obvious. Ancient *chatelaines* lie on the beach in cruelly revealing swimwear.

Sometimes the two styles combine for a moment of perfect kitsch bliss. For example, *Hello!* has long been obsessed by Mandy Smith. When the precocious poppet married the near-pensionable Bill Wyman, the magazine devoted more than 20 pages to their nuptual celebrations. And in one of the many luscious colour pictures the happy bride could be seen smiling prettily at the cameras...with a discarded fag-end lying crushed beneath one of her dainty shoes.

Every week the readers can peer at the decorative or sartorial follies of the undeservedly rich. Ivana Trump showed off her

Harris's ultimatum: Give me the cover or I eat the kid!

Those Heart-Warming Hello! Introductions

- Lady Sarah Armstrong-Jones, the young royal whose first exhibition has marked her as a talented artist 'not to be sniffed at'
- Meeting Miss World, proving that brains, not just looks, win today's contest
- Adnan Khashoggi putting his jet-set life behind him to return to his roots in Saudi Arabia
- Bringing a smile once again to her mother's lips, the Duchess of York and Susan Barrantes spend precious time together in St Moritz
- Photographed for *Hello!* in her Hollywood home, Dyan Cannon shedding her 'dumb blonde' image to become director-writer – and contented woman

- 'John Hurt at home in the country with wife Jo and daughter Sasha.' Actually it's son Sacha, short for Alexander – *17 November 1990*
- Elizabeth Quinn's husband is referred to as 'British classical actor Richard O'Sullivan', instead of O'Callaghan – *26 January 1991*
- Crown Prince Willem Alexander of the Netherlands, born 1967 is described as an 'ancestor of William of Orange', who died in 1702 – *6 August 1988*
- Sir Richard Attenborough is described as late golfing croonster Dickie Henderson – *2 February 1991*

An error of taste? Celebrity sick-person Mandy Smith tells all

gold-flecked yacht and matching 'little sailor boy' *haute couture* dress. Adnan Khashoggi stood in front of a wall of elephant tusks in one issue, and dressed up like Lawrence of Arabia in another, apparently to prove his Saudi Arabian roots. Paddy Ashdown, in his living-room, meekly held a copy of parliamentary report *Hansard*, no doubt to prove that he was a real MP.

Princesses Stephanie and Caroline of Monaco are adored by *Hello!* The sisters are the perfect combination – royal, rich, jet-set and Eurotrash all in a bikini-clad bundle of grieving widow/caring mother/fun-loving heiress. If Stephanie is recording a video, rest assured that *Hello!* will be with her on location. If Caroline is in tears at her husband's funeral they will show that too, along with a wreath floating where his boat crashed, and many months of post-bereavement zoom-lensed coverage.

The mawkishness with which *Hello!* has hovered over Caroline's personal tragedy makes one wonder whether the magazine is really quite as kind as it seems. It is sometimes difficult to tell whether the fawning style is a super-subtle joke or just witless insensitivity.

Commenting on Muhammad Ali's Parkinsonism the magazine said: 'The lowness and slowness of his voice and the odd tremor in his hand are clues to his illness, but his eyes still sparkle with fun as he deliberately misinterprets a question.'

This ambiguity can occur in photos too. After her wedding, Mandy Smith moved from blushing bride to sickly skeleton as she spent 18 months 'battling with a mystery wasting disease'. *Hello!* ran page after page depicting the recovering Miss Smith on her hospital bed. Her make-up, nightie and pout could be interpreted in several ways, not all sympathetic. Was the brave Mandy battling against her weight loss? Or was this an ill-timed comeback attempt with ghoulish erotic undertones? *Hello!* continued the Mandy saga by interviewing her mother and sister. The climax was a tearful reunion with her estranged father.

When the *Sun* attempted similar saturation coverage of the anorexic adolescent, it was condemned for its needless intrusiveness. *Hello!* did nothing without the Smith family's consent, but

is the end result any more savoury? Or is *Hello!* merely a means by which the public can satisfy its curiosity while retaining a comforting sense of moral superiority?

After all, we all enjoy a good bit of tittle-tattle. The tastelessness of cavorting rich-raff in Gstaad, self-pitying has-beens, or hideous newly-bought furnishings – all are certainly gossip-worthy. *Hello!* acts like a local newspaper for the whole country, never being overtly offensive and always making sure a picture of everyone is printed at least once a year.

For the social diarists, all this ego-massaging is anathema. The idea that former belly-dancer Patricia Kluge, who made a good marriage to America's richest man – and then an even better divorce – should be treated with the same gushing reverence as the Princess of Wales is just not on, old boy.

They continue to despise the magazine. 'It's a lapdog,' reveals Ross Benson, the *Daily Express* diarist, 'but I've seen it at the best addresses.' And in a barb that recalls all those rumours about the £250,000 alleged to have been paid to the Duchess of York for her 48-page photo-spread, he adds, 'People who swore they'd never "invite" *Hello!* into their house, invited it in when they saw *Hello!*'s chequebook.'

The magazine's phenomenal success is affecting a Fleet Street already concerned about its unsavoury reputation. Last year the *Daily Mail* (briefly) organised a tie-in with *Hello! Mail* editor Sir David English has supposedly spoken about 'the new journalism' and staffers take this to be the *Hello!* style.

Will this mean a diary in which Nigel Dempster has nothing but good news about the starlets and aristobrats that fill his pages? Will Paul Johnson be reduced to rhapsodising about the wonders of Cybill Shepherd – 'even more radiant at 40'? And will Lynda Lee-Potter finally decide that if you can't say something nice about someone you shouldn't say anything at all.

One can only hope not. Niceness is all very well. But one can have too much of a good thing. Even if it is loving, caring, brave, warm-hearted and charming as well. 🐾

- Kind-hearted royal	in pink designer togs	emergency ward	bring cheer to the young
- Dubious Euro-royal	in Ruritanian military outfit	new East German haus	plead his authenticity
- Cinema stalwart	in tweeds and red socks	wedding anniversary party	declare its 'gloriousness'
- Ex-mini-series star **poses**	barefoot with pregnant wife **at**	nouveau farm house **to**	say he 'awaits' the right part
- Heavily made-up grande dame	beside ludicrous bouquets with attentive nurse	under-attended royal jelly publicity stunt	proclaim the return of true romance (in her new book)
- Superstar's distant relation	in cheap cowboy boots, tights and leather jacket	kitchen sink of northern council house	announce her cameo role in a regional soap opera

HUSBAND
Hornography

'When I first came to this country I tried
all sorts of jobs – plumbing, mechanics, computers you name it...'

'I told you the bouncers
were big bastards'

'Damn it, Karen, are you marking the drinks again?'

'She's starting up a
chat-line'

'You've just missed him – he's gone racing his pigeons'

'I've decided I'm going as Long John Silver'

'He says he feels the cold'

'That's the neighbours – they're very nosey'

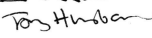

'Fetch, boy...Oops'

Hello John need a new voter?

Could John Major ever be exciting? STEVE SMETHURST asked the experts to give the Prime Minister a new, winning image

The Tories have got a problem. They got rid of one of the planet's most famous women; a leader known and respected all over the world; the winner of three consecutive general elections. And they replaced her with a man who made Steve Davis look, well, interesting.

Why did they do this? Because they were way behind in the polls. And after seven months of caring, compromising, consultative Mr Major, how are they doing? They're way behind in the polls. To a very considerable degree. Oh yes.

So now, as panic begins to grip the upper reaches of the Conservative Party (not to mention the lower reaches, and the bits in-between), the time has come to try something new.

They're calling it the Summer Offensive. A dog-day dinner of political manoeuvres designed to persuade the public that they should ignore the siren call of Messrs Kinnock and Smith, in favour of the wonders of Majorism.

But what is Majorism? Well, it's dryish on economic issues but distinctly damp on social ones. It says that the free market can be quite a nice place once you get to know it. It's the *Independent* made flesh. And it's just as boring.

The problem, when all is said and done, is Mr Major himself. He's quite simply the least inspirational leader on the face of the globe. Of course, he's fearfully bright and hard working and so forth. But he's duller than a Sunday night in Stoke-on-Trent. He's got as much chance of inspiring an electorate as Nigel Mansell has of finding a car that actually works. Basically, he's boring.

So, in the hope of livening up what might be the most tedious election campaign in history, we began a two-pronged summer offensive of our own.

FIRST we commissioned a team of top artists to remake Major in the style of the most interesting, exciting, crowd-pulling men in the modern world.

THEN we asked a gaggle of gurus, 'What would you do to Mr Major to give him a new image?'

THIS is what they came up with...

Loyd Grossman
Writer, restaurateur (ret'd) and 'Through the Keyhole' snoop

I see John Major as the rest of the world does. He's so grey he's imageless. He's like a photostat of himself. Because of that, he needs to be defined. I would ☞

Give Major a mask. Have him cook the Cabinet (just chop up Mr Hurd, add oil, garlic and plenty of salt and pepper – voilà! The next Sainsbury's ad). It worked wonders for Anthony Hopkins's career. It could do the same for Mr M.

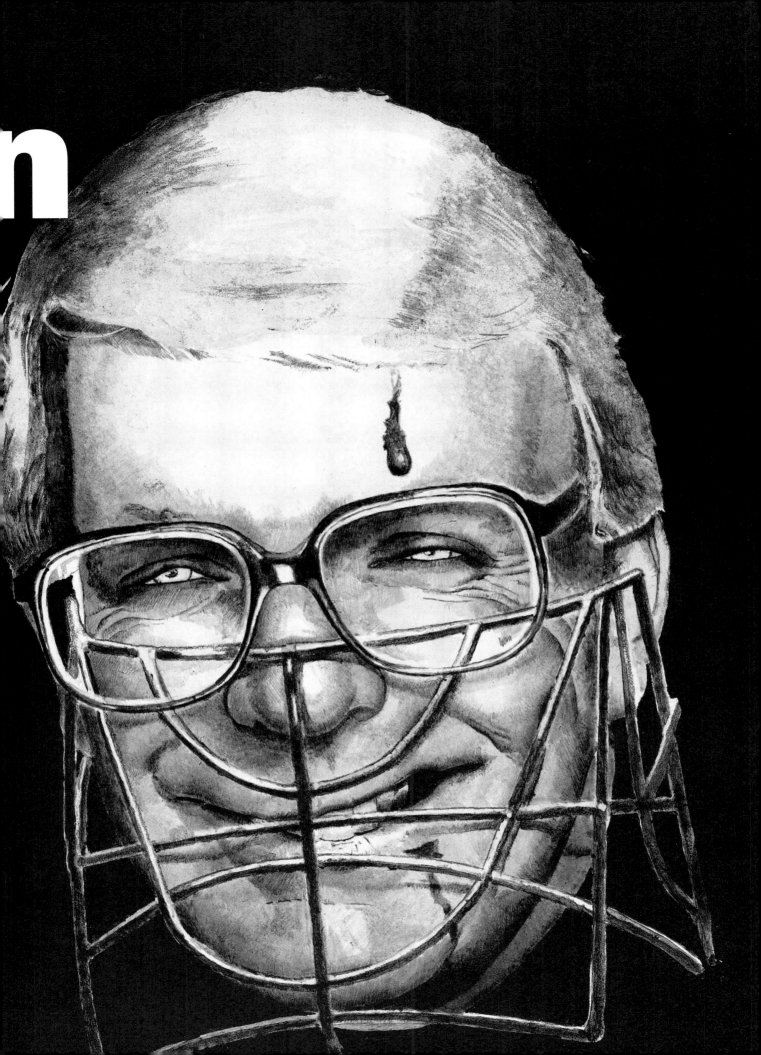

Artist's Image No. 2
John Botham, by Mark Draisey

He's the beefy all-rounder the whole country takes to its heart.

LABOUR

P.M'S QUESTION OF SPORT TIME

get him away from grey suits and put him in dark blue. I'd also suggest that he could make a profitable investment in a few smart ties. He could go for Hermes – their jovial, jocular nature would appeal to people if they didn't know how expensive they were. But if you do know, it's quite a good code he can send to the plutocratic core of Toryism – a code flashing, 'One of us...one of us.'

He shouldn't have his voice fixed – it's the only branding he's got. But they should do something about his prose. It's all so heavily qualified. He has adopted to an extraordinary degree the protective colouring of the administrative classes. But I think he's probably more interesting and intelligent than he dares to be in public.

I kind of like Norma. I think she's got a good image for a politician's wife. When she tells *YOU Magazine* that she has discovered non-iron tea-towels I believe her.

FOREIGN AFFAIRS DUDE

P.M. MAN!

Artist's Image No. 3
Bart Major (and friends), by Phil Elliott

Even exile on satellite television cannot diminish the love that the nation's young feel for those multi-coloured, two-dimensional funsters, *The Simpsons*. Think ten-year old, Mr Major, and get a new catch-phrase: 'Eat my shorts, Delors!'

Artist's Image No. 4
The Darling Buds of Major,
by David Hensley

If the polls are anything to go by, more people like the Larkins than the Tories. So for maximum voter appeal, here comes Pop Major.

Her eye is on the ball domestically. But there's a bit of highbrow thrown in with all those books about opera.

Peter York
Market researcher, style guru and Sloan Ranger author

He looks fine. It's the way he speaks...the way that sounds hit the back of his throat. It's a very bank-managerly way of talking and you immediately want to copy it.

He sounds as though he's got the sort of shirts in whose pockets many, many pens can be found.

I'd like to believe in John Major and he does seem to be a nice man. But somehow his niceness seems to be alienated from the effective part of him. The truthful, if unfunny thing is that here is a nice and competent man who has never – as the Americans would say – got in touch with his inner self. He needs to be reminded of what he really cares about.

You remember how Mrs Thatcher used to have those electric baths. That's what Major needs – stimulation induced while he's in the bath, so that he can get in touch with himself.

Colin Hammick
Managing director of Huntsman, Savile Row tailors

I'm sorry, that's not something I feel I could comment on.

Wally Olins
Corporate identity guru of Woolf Olins: BT image-maker

We don't do chaps, we only do companies, but like companies people are what they are. A naff company with a dull image can only become a naff company with a racy image. It doesn't change the nature of the ☛

product. There have been a whole series of prime ministers in the flamboyant tradition, like Thatcher and Churchill, and to make Major appear like this would be a grave mistake. Of course, it would be very funny if they did.

Sometimes beneath a grey exterior, there is a grey interior but there is another tradition of prime ministers, who appear as rabbits but have a ratty personality. Attlee was a great example of this; he was a tough fellow with a dull image.

Image makers must examine their product and promote its strengths. People are what they are and to pretend otherwise is fatal.

As for the cost, for a large company it costs a lot, for a small hairdresser's it would cost a lot less.

Meryl Thomas
TV-am's 'After Nine' fashion stylist

John Major definitely should not use Grecian 2000 or anything like that. We have found on *After Nine* that a touch of pink often helps and perhaps some jazzier ties too. The best thing he could do would be to take a leaf out of Norma's book, as she is very stylish.

Peter Mandelson
Former image adviser to the Labour Party

I'm afraid I never comment on John Major's image, although I'm incessantly being asked. It's because he hasn't got one.

Nesta Wyn Ellis
Author of 'John Major', and one-time 'Punch' contributor

John Major's problem is that everyone thinks he's boring, and yet he was a very forceful Chancellor. Everyone is fascinated by his clothes but they do not reveal the real person. His main qualities are that he is enormously determined and tough. He knows exactly what he wants but often keeps it secret for too long.

This habit was formed on the streets of south London in his youth. One of his techniques is to wait until his plans are so advanced that they cannot be altered, before revealing them. He has always kept his policy close to his chest but this is not an aspect I feel the Conservatives should stress.

He is very resistant to change as he is afraid of criticism saying that he is not his own man and is bowing to media pressure. Friends say he is very moody and each time I have met him his mood has been slightly different, more relaxed as we got to know each other better.

On the fashion front I've told him, and

Norma's told him, he must wear tailored suits. And he should have a handkerchief from Savile Row for his top pocket.

The first time I met him I thought 'What a smasher. He was a lovely guy, very charming, gracious and considerate.' He has knocked out everyone in his constituency as he is very beguiling. Unfortunately, this does not come across on the television.

He needs to take lessons from a media expert but 'he is what he is' and is reluctant to become a creation of other people. But I expect in time he will adjust his style as he is a great learner.

McLachlan
cartoonist

Dylan Jones
Editor of the style monthly 'Arena'

Major needs a complete overhaul, which is almost impossible. This is because it needs to be so subtle in getting rid of his awful clothes, hair, manner and glasses without it being noticed. Mrs Thatcher managed to change her image without it being noticed until years later. President Bush has done the same, he appears much more statesmanlike now, using very surreptitious changes. Major needs to be taken seriously and he won't be if they try to turn him into a young trendy-looking MP. He needs to wear tailored suits but to suddenly get a

Artist's Image No. 5
MP Hammer,
by Steve Bliss

Yo, voters, it's Major time!
It may be a bit of a radical leap
from grey Crombie suits to
sequinned scarlet harem pants
but what has John got to lose?
Apart from the
election, that is...

whole new image with contact lenses would be the worst thing they could do, or leave him as he is of course.'

John Hegarty
Bartle, Bogle and Hegarty

He needs better promotion. He should start by changing his name to John Colonel.

Neil Kinnock MP

The Labour leader's spokesperson was asked if Mr Kinnock had any comment on John Major's image: 'Absolutely not,' was the reply.

Nigel Dempster
'Daily Mail' diarist

No comment. I am totally apolitical.

Peter Snow,
'Newsnight' presenter

If I get any ideas I'll give you a ring.

Charles Kennedy MP

If they are going to remodel John Major, what he is crying out for is a blonde wig, handbag, high voice and a nice blue outfit. Then all he would need is a few Europeans to start hitting.

On a serious note, the best thing they could do is to let him get tough with the malcontents in his party. But to make him into a macho-man just will not work.

Katharine Hamnett

John should study Winston Churchill's style, minus the cigar and go for a classic English Savile Row suit from Anderson & Shepherd, avoiding grey at all costs. John wants and needs to look like a statesman so he should adopt this look.

On the other hand maybe he should just wear a T-shirt that says 'SHUT UP THATCHER'. 🐀

CHRIS WARD and DUNCAN TERRACE get snappy with the loitering lensmen outside celebrity watering holes

Flash bang wallop

How To Get In The Papers, Lesson One: The Mini-Skirt. Painfully shy Denice Lewis flashes some fetlock

You want to be famous, you want to be in the papers. But how do you set about it? Who are the people who can put you in the tabloids? The *paparazzi*, that's who.

They took their name from Signor Paparazzo, the little sleazeball in Fellini's *La Dolce Vita* who drove around Rome on his Vespa taking snaps of the rich and adulterous on the Via Veneto. Not many people know that, you know. And talking of Michael Caine, there's a story – apocryphal, of course – that he once walked out of his own restaurant, Langan's, to find the *paparazzi* incessantly snapping away at some gorgeous young actress. Beside himself with fury, he stormed back inside and didn't emerge again until the cameramen had quite finished with her. And were ready for him.

Any male star trying to pull the same trick today would find himself ignored by the leering lensmen. They know that the tabloid papers aren't interested in a picture unless it contains a woman, preferably one who is, by any normal standards, semi-naked. The reason that Rod Stewart, for example, makes such regular appearances in the press is that he always ensures that he is accompanied by his young wife Rachel, whose frocks are notable, above all, for their brevity.

Celebrities who refuse to play the game risk the wrath of the snappers. For example, explains Dave Bennett, who works for the *Star* and the *Evening Standard*, 'Gazza is a real pain. There's a certain way of acting in nightclubs, and he doesn't understand that if you go to a party given by a famous person then you're not there because you're a nice guy but because you're a celebrity, and you shouldn't shun the publicity. He can't control himself, it's quite natural to him to react aggressively.

'George Michael is always ducking and diving to avoid having his picture taken, unless he's got a particular reason for wanting publicity. Andrew Ridgeley is the same. So photographers are always trying to get their photos, even though there's little interest in them from the papers.'

The *paparazzi*'s prey are often less-than complimentary. Madonna's press agent called them 'scheming little animals'. But

As her minders sort out professional Peeping Tom Richard Young, the gap-toothed Seventies supermodel Lauren Hutton begins training for the latest Pro-Celebrity Biathlon: a five-mile sprint followed by 20 minutes of ju-jitsu

then, that's the same press agent who ensures that Ms Ciccone gets her face in all the papers. Stars are apt to thump *paparazzi* when they're disturbed by them. But they're apt to thump publicists when they're not.

So how do you make sure the *paparazzi* know you're worth photographing? And how do you know where to find them? And what do you have to do to get them to put you in their frame? We asked them. They invited us into their beautiful lives and opened their hearts EXCLUSIVELY to *Punch* readers.

Alan Davidson, Richard Young, Alan Grisbrook, Nikos, Dave Bennett: these are the guys who've been standing on pavements for years. Fleet Street picture editors will pay them anything from £80 to £400 a snap. They all earn around a hundred grand a year. And, for that, all they have to put up with is cold nights, enormous lab bills and the occasional left cross.

As they're the A team, party hosts know that they are much more likely to get a picture in the papers than the new lads out on the pavement. Some of them even invite them to their weddings. Better the *paparazzi* you know...

'If they got a really embarrassing picture of someone,' said a very knowledgeable but understandably anonymous source, 'they wouldn't know what to do with it. They'd have a serious career decision to make.'

But then the poor devils freezing to death on the pavement will say that those inside aren't real *paparazzi* anymore, that they've simply become part of the establishment and have sold out. Young *et al* really don't care – they're getting the pictures and they're staying warm. And they're also angry that any pimply youth with an Instamatic now thinks being a *paparazzo* is a quick way to fame and fortune.

So if you want to be on the inside too, keep this handy *Punch* guide to the *paparazzi* about your person, and you'll never have to worry about there being no flashbulbs going off in your face. Oh, and if your name's George Michael, don't bother – they all hate you.

The Paparazzi

Alan Davidson

Hairy all over and covered in cameras; tends to walk too close to people and cars – who then bounce off him.

Favourite haunts: 'Anywhere Richard Young isn't sitting on his Harley Davidson.'

Least favourite haunts: 'Anywhere Richard Young turns up when I'm doing an exclusive. Mind you, I do it to him too.'

Favourite personality: 'Richard Young. He's always there, even if he's not too handsome. He reminds me of a character in the book *Creed*, a horror story about a *paparazzo* who stumbles onto ghostly goings on. Young's named in it and so is Bennett, and everyone says the photographer in it is me except my solicitor, so I can't sue. Anyway, Young reminds me of the ghoul in it.' Which leads us to ...

Least favourite personality: 'Richard Young, for all the above reasons.'

Biggest scoop/favourite picture: 'One of Richard Young being beaten up by Bob Williamson who was with Lauren Hutton outside Langan's.'

Modus operandi: 'I have a contract with the *Daily Mail*. So I do what they ask me to. I don't do the hanging around outside Langan's, but I go along if I know there's someone there. The actual picture situation's not as good as it used to be. The headliners-type pages have ruined the business. The wrong sort of pictures with embarrassing captions appear now, so you don't get invited back to things. The true *paparazzo* has had his day in England.'

Transport: 'I've just sold the Jag for a Mercedes, but I'm buying a new XJS next year. Image is terribly important.'

Income: 'Enough.'

Thumped by: Ryan O'Neal, McCartney's minder.

Fergie's diet has been so effective, she now blows over in a high wind. Or is she just looking for that last bit of Ryvita?

Richard Young

Self-appointed doyen of *paparazzi*. Hairy. 'Bit intimidating.' Good friend of Joan Collins – 'although they'd both deny it.' Enemy of Alan Davidson.

Favourite haunts: 'Private homes and parties. If you get in on your own you can get some good pix, especially if you're discreet.'

Least favourite haunts: 'Nightclubs, I've never been a nightclub sort of person anyway and I don't like the bridge-and-tunnel sort of crowd that frequent them.'

Favourite personality: 'Anyone who is nice and polite. Liz Taylor is both.'

Least favourite personality: 'Any rude aristocrats who turn their noses up. They don't realise we're richer than them.'

Biggest scoop/favourite picture: 'Being invited by Paul Getty to do an at home with him and his girlfriend and the Richard Burton birthday party before he died.'

Modus operandi: 'Doing lots of paperwork in the mornings – replying to invitations like this great one that arrived this morning to go to Longleat to celebrate Viscountess Linka's 21st birthday. That should be great because the theme is Erotica. I think I'll go as a dickhead – then no one will recognise me.'

Transport: Black BMW 325i, black Harley Davidson motorbike.

Income: 'The taxman knows more than I do.'

Thumped by: Robert Redford
Roman Polanski – after Polanski had been charged with statutory rape, Young asked him to pose in a pair of handcuffs.

Alan Grisbrook

Young; looks like a salesman in a hardware store. Has sewn-up pockets; never known to have bought a drink.

Favourite haunts: 'I don't really have any favourite places and I wouldn't say if I did because you'll all just go there. I just cruise around, read the papers and go on my instinct.'

Least favourite haunts: 'I don't get chucked out of many places now, and I don't like it when there's all these new kinds of photographers hounding people all night – they push and shove all the other guests and it turns into a bun fight.'

Favourite personality: 'I like taking pictures of women, and the more (or, rather less) miniskirt, the better. Elton and Boy George are nice and flamboyant but also stand still. I like Diana, she's got a lot going for her, and Fergie. They're usually OK although you can get pushed down the road a bit if they're out privately.'

Least favourite personality: 'George Michael is a miserable geezer who keeps his head down and always comes off as being very moody. I'm not 100 per cent on pop people, there's a lot of pretentiousness and hypocrisy: like that Sinead O'Connor deliberately leaving a party through a door where she knows there's a lot of photographers and then kicking up a fuss.'

Messrs Young, Davidson and Grisbrook proclaim their innocence. Intrude on someone's privacy? Us?

Photo ergo sum

Little Elizabeth Jagger demonstrates the good manners and fine breeding for which her family is justly renowned

Nikos

Grinning and moustachioed; brings a touch of continental colour to the *paparazzi* brigade.

Favourite haunts: 'Places don't matter, just as long as they've got famous people there.'

Least favourite haunts: 'Langan's is not very good now because a lot of people go there to take pictures. It's best to be on your own.'

Favourite personality: 'I take pictures of anybody who's famous, as long as they sell. Pix always sell of women with legs, the more leg the better to sell in the tabloids. Dustin Hoffman is the very best person – he says "Thank You" when you take his picture.'

Least favourite personality: 'George Michael is a horrible person and I don't like Yasmin Le Bon, although models are usually the best because they're used to having their pictures taken.'

Biggest scoop/favourite picture: 'Two years ago the first really good picture I did was of Mick Jagger and his daughter, who stuck her tongue out at me. That was in four or five papers in one day and helped me get started. Last year my favourite was Ivana Trump, and then this year I got Bob Dylan - that picture went into six papers.'

Modus operandi: 'I get up about ten or 11 and go to sleep at about two or three in the morning. I sell the pictures I take in the evenings when I get up. People think it's an easy job, but it's not. You have to be around 24 hours a day.'

Transport: 'A black BMW 325i.'

Income: 'Quite a good living. Can't say no more.'

Thumped by: Denice Lewis – for taking a picture up her skirt when she was temporarily bereft of underwear.

Biggest scoop/favourite picture: 'The Duchess of York falling down outside Harry's Bar. I knew she was in there, but the police had pushed me over the road and weren't being co-operative. I was just about to say "Sod you" and go home when she came out. While the copper was pushing me away I leaned round him and done a picture and got away quick. Apparently they were trying to track me down after to get the pix.'

Modus operandi: 'I don't lie in bed all day. I get up about 10, 10.30, read the papers, process my film then go round the clubs of a night. I don't stay up that late.'

Transport: 'The one I got now I don't want to advertise because it's really faulty. I'm going to buy a Golf, a black convertible.'

Income: 'Not enough.'

Thumped by: John Hurt
A friend of Greta Scaachi in a Soho alley.

What a picture editor looks for in a *paparazzi* pic

The A List		The Z List
The people no picture editor can refuse	**1. People with appalling dress sense** – Su Pollard, for example	The people every picture editor refuses
Madonna (unless she's jogging in the park) **Kim Basinger Rosanna Arquette Princess Di Other Royals** (maybe)	**2. Bare breasts:** says one top tabloid picture editor, 'The ones where it's really deliberate are boring. The clever girls know how to do it deliberately but make it look like an accident. Professional models are best at it. Or when they're wearing something which, when the flash hits them, goes diaphanous and you can see the nipples. They don't intend it but it makes a super picture.' In other words: 'Phwooarh!' Alternatively...	**Wayne Sleep Kenny Everett Lionel Blair Bob Monkhouse Andrew Ridgeley** (unless with girlfriend) **Andrew Neil** (ditto)
	3. Unzipped flies – an Ollie Reed special	

HAEFELI
Frenzied relations

'I don't believe you stood there and let them laugh at you.
You're supposed to be my straight man'

'I'm going to keep my coat on, thanks. It's an integral part of my outfit'

'I'm not afraid of commitment. I'm afraid of you'

'Think about it. **This** is the man you're going to ask for advice about health food?'

'I love your hair!'

'I'll have the Dieter's Delite and he'll have the Hi-Fat Platter'

'Excuse me. We couldn't help but notice the two of you over here eating sushi like it's going out of style. Is it?'

Dear Sir, I wish to protest...

How responsive are corporations when the public starts to fuss and whinge? JOHN HIND and STEVEN MOSCO wrote moaning letters of complaint to find out

Just how far can you push somebody before they forget that the customer is always right? Using a series of assumed names, we sent a string of ridiculous complaints to see who really cared about their public. Then, whatever happened, we complained again! Here are the results of the survey, and if anyone's got any complaints, they can just shove it, OK?

Terry Wogan's tie makes me sick!

Using the name George Peartree we wrote to the BBC to complain that one of Terry Wogan's ties was too loud. 'It made both me and my wife Audrey feel funny for a good hour afterwards, so please can you assure me that Terry won't wear it again?'

There was no response, so George wrote to complain to the *Wogan* producer. 'My wife Audrey was most upset and had to take an extra couple of Rennies afterwards,' he claimed.

Beverley Thompson, from BBC Viewer & Listener Correspondence, did not seem sympathetic. 'Thank you for your letter,' she wrote, 'the contents of which have been noted.'

George was incensed. How could she be so sluggish, he wrote back, in the face of 'a subject of such vital importance as Terry's tie? Will Terry be wearing the tie again or won't he?' Two weeks later, Beverley was still stumped for a reply, so George phoned the *Wogan* studio 15 minutes before broadcast to demand a personal apology. Fiona, a stage assistant, said Terry was 'really frantic right now.' When 'George' called back the next day, he was promised a reply 'within the next two months, three at the most'. Nothing yet.

What's up with Ronald McDonald's lettuce?

'I can't help feeling that the amount of lettuce in a Big Mac has been reduced,' wrote 'Kevin Simpson' to McDonald's. 'This is a shame, as I find the lettuce acts as a nicely crisp counterpoint to the chewiness of your other ingredients.'

Kevin A Haag, McDonald's executive vice president & chief operations officer, replied that market manager Mr Michael Gomes was investigating, and 12 days later Mr Gomes himself reported: 'At McDonald's we pride ourselves on the consistency of our products wherever bought...The relevant operations personnel will be checking the procedures and the staff will be retrained as necessary.' Kevin then wrote to moan about the lack of empty seating on busy Saturdays, adding as an afterthought: 'Where do you obtain your lettuce from? It's so lovely and crisp I'd like to get some for myself?' No reply.

Get a shave, Branson!

Seraphina Langworthy's letter to Richard Branson praised him as 'an attractive figure, a man from the Sixties still firing on all cylinders, as it were'. But that beard! Seraphina was shocked at Branson's 'seeming refusal to tidy up (his) face...and thus gain full respect as Britain's most forward-thinking businessman, and Britain's most desirable pin-up for thinking girls!'

There was no reply from Virgin, so 'Seraphina' got tough: 'WHAT IN 747'S NAME IS GOING ON OVER THERE AT VIRGIN ATLANTIC!? You still have the beard, and I still have no reply.'

Twelve days later Branson responded cheerfully, but disappointingly: 'Dear Seraphina, Thanks for your concern, but I like my beard and for the moment anyway it's in no danger! – R'

Battle of the Small Brown Sliced

'Derek Tomlinson' complained to his local Sainsbury superstore about lack of bread late on Saturday afternoons. Branch manager Mr M May replied: 'You will appreciate we keep a tight control. I will, however, look at the bread order with a view to extending the range.'

'Derek' was not impressed and wrote again. 'I was not reassured by your generalised, non-specific intention to "have a look at the bread order."' He also complained about 'impersonal muzak, checkout girls, and strategically-placed displays of sweets by the till to catch the kiddies' attention when mummy's paying.' Derek recalled the good old days of the corner shop, and asked: 'Would it really be asking too much for you to reserve a bag of pretzels and a small brown sliced for me each Saturday?'

BUCKINGHAM PALACE

26th September, 1990.

Dear Mr. Sedgewick,

I am commanded by The Queen to thank you for your letter concerning the type of schooling proposed by The Prince and Princess of Wales for Prince William and to inform you that Her Majesty has noted your comments on this matter.

Yours sincerely,

Robin Janvrin

(ROBIN JANVRIN)

I. Sedgewick Esq.

Isn't constitutional monarchy wonderful

🐀 Whines of the year

Nine days later Mr May's deputy, Mr McGrath, suggested that he and Derek should meet to discuss 'a suitable arrangement for the reservation'. Delighted Derek wrote, 'Well done sir! Excellent, excellent, excellent! You've truly restored my faith in Sainsbury's as the supermarket of the common man...But couldn't anything be done about the pattern of the store's floor-tiles? They make me giddy.'

There was no reply, so Derek got on the phone to Mr McGrath, who told him: 'I can tell you that the store is now down for what we call an Enhancement next year, sir. I don't know if that includes tiles...But shall we say, they're in the pencilling-in situation?'

Tottenham's teas taste terrible!

'Jack Percival' had no satisfactory reply from THREE letters to Spurs' catering manager Peter Nicholls moaning about the quality of the tea served at half-time, simply a note stating that the complaint was being 'serviced'. When reached by phone, Nicholls confessed that he hadn't received any of the letters, but asked that they be faxed. Pushed for a spoken apology, he said: 'We've put these water-boiling machines in, so I'm wondering if there's a problem with the water.' When asked what kind of tea he used Nicholls replied, 'It's like tea in the cup, mate. When you're trying to keep up with thousands of cups of tea, you've got to look at volume and speed, yeah? So it tends to be what they call "an in-cup drink"...Listen, I'll definitely speak to Stanley Lew, our Controller of Public Areas, and get back to you.'

Nothing since from White Hart Lane.

What's happened to the Page Three Sauce Pots?

'Bobby Hewlett' felt let down by the quality of the *Sun*'s Page Three girls. As he told the editor, 'I'd like to know whether you're running out of horn-bags or whether you're trying not to be so saucy.'

Editorial executive Eddie Johnson replied promptly: 'We are sorry that you think we are running out of hot girls. This could be associated with the long dry summer! Now that we're printing in colour we hope that they will appear a little warmer for you throughout the forthcoming winter...Best wishes.'

'Bobby' wrote straight back with a thundering complaint. 'There was a Page Three girl the other week whose nipples were a colour I've never seen nipples before.' Johnson replied equally quickly, enclosing a *Sun* report about the Army's refusal to allow the *Sun* to fly a bevy of busty beauties to 'Our Boys'. 'Imagine being in the desert with just yashmaks and orange juice,' proposed Johnson. 'How one would welcome Page Three even with flesh-tones all askew!'

Incensed, 'Bobby' wrote to complain about the *Sun* being sent to The Gulf at all. 'Imagine if Mad Saddam was invading Saudi Arabia,' he contemplated, 'and Our Boys had their gas-masks off and rifles unloaded while admiring a ration of Page Three. The less they're allowed the better. The sex will well up in them and they'll fight like mad stallions. Surely a few months without Corrine's curves won't do them any harm?!' That was enough for Johnson. He did not reply.

Your Majesty, it's about your grandson

'Ian Sedgewick' complained to Her Majesty about the decision to send Prince William to boarding-school ('...I would not want

Felix Bennett

him to repeat my tawdry experiences there'). Two weeks later came a reply from Robin Janvrin: 'I am commanded by The Queen to thank you for your letter...and to inform you that Her Majesty has noted your comments on this matter.'

'Sedgewick' wrote back post-haste to register his disappointment with this reply, complaining for good measure about 'Prince Philip wearing what can only be described as an anorak...a casual item of clothing which is completely unsuitable for the maintenance of royal dignity.' He received no reply and so telephoned Janvrin at Buckingham Palace. 'I'm afraid I didn't receive your letter,' Janvrin said. 'It might have got diverted to Balmoral by accident.'

Dear Mary Whitehouse, it's disgusting!

'Duncan E Fothermere' was furious that Mary Whitehouse had let Channel 4's *Sex Talk* slip through her net, and wrote to tell her so. Mary took only three days to reply, sharing his concern about *Sex Talk* but admitting she had no power over the programme makers. She also suggested that Fothermere should join the National Viewers & Listeners Association and enclosed an issue of their newsletter.

'Fothermere' was furious. He wrote to the NVLA to complain about a reference in the magazine to '...a naked man, with his face in the crutch of a prostitute hanging on a cross, shouting "Hail Mary full of grace!"' Fothermere said that his daughter

Dear Emma Freud, about your Great Grandad

'Morecai Esnik' wrote to TV personality Emma Freud THREE TIMES to complain about her great grand-father Sigmund Freud's crude theories on sexuality. Freud's assistant Tony Moulsdale responded more than six weeks later with the message that 'Ms Fraud has no knowledge' of his first two letters. 'Regarding the apology you seek, it may be due to you from the Post Office.' 'Esnik' immediately complained to the manager of Post Office HQ in Grosvenor Place about Sigmund Freud's theories ('at the recommendation of Ms Freud's assistant'). He also wrote a note to Moulsdale about his blaring Freudian slip (Ms Fraud indeed!). Both remain unanswered.

Dear Archbishop, it's an outrage!

'Dudley Warmington' wrote to George Carey, the Archbishop of Canterbury-in-waiting, expressing concern at the 'inexorable slide into acceptance of women in high-office of our church.'

A Lambeth Palace research officer, Andrea Mulkeen, replied advising Dudley to read a pamphlet, published by The House Of Bishops. Dudley wrote back moodily, complaining about a) not having a reply from the Archbishop, b) the fact that the research officer was a woman, and c) that a lady is not one to whom 'a gentleman' should pass his anti-ordination mail.

E G Peacock, Secretary to the Archbishop, swiftly replied that 'The Archbishop receives a very great number of letters on the ordination of women, expressing several viewpoints often forcefully and in strong language'; and noting that those who reply – regardless of gender – are used to it all.

'How do I know that E G Peacock is not a woman?' demanded Dudley, repeating his complaint that the Archbishop hadn't replied 'man-to-man'. Peacock remained gentle-tempered when, only two days later, he responded: 'I am glad to assure you that I am male...The Archbishop's post-bag is so great it would be a physical impossibility for him to reply personally to each correspondent, let alone allowing him any time to carry out the other duties biblically enjoined upon him as a Bishop.'

He nevertheless enclosed a transcript of a speech by the Archbishop on Women's ordination. He was additionally Christian enough to apologise for the 'illegibility' of his previous (gender-confusing) signature, and sent God's Wishes.

Also ran

Marks & Spencer replied swiftly to the complaint that there was no lightly sparkled peach crush on the shelves of a branch, but the cry that no prawn, lettuce and mayonnaise sandwiches were available went unheeded.

British Rail, which should be used to dealing with complaints, made us wait two months for a typed response to three complaints about putting a foot in a box on 'litter-strewn' King's Cross station. (A post-card of acknowledgement had arrived after nine days.) The actual reply was from M J Storey, InterCity area retail manager. His reference for 'Keith' was K3/15439/90-LD1/MM1210A/SCG/3/. He said: 'I have taken this opportunity to remind our staff of their responsibilities and I trust you will not have cause to complain in the future.'

BP, though, was courtesy itself when we wrote to complain of being overcharged for some chewing gum. 'I would be interested to hear how you can justify this blatant act of profiteering,' we had asked. Marketing co-ordinator Jackie Howard replied, asking for details of which petrol station the gum came from. Even after learning that a Shell station was to blame, BP sent a free box of gum – just for all the trouble of writing. And very nice it was too.

had come across the disgusting newsletter and he was upset by her subsequent questions about the meaning of 'prostitute' and 'crutch'. He also enclosed the relevant membership fee.

John C Beyer, NVLA General Secretary, replied: 'We are most distressed to know that your ten-year-old daughter read the unsavoury material in our summer issue and we will bear this in mind. However, we do have to inform members of our activities and sometimes there is no alternative to publishing material of this kind in order to give an accurate picture.' He welcomed Fothermere on board.

Fothermere wrote back with four complaints, about:

* NVLA's lack of self-censorship
* The 'unresounding campaign' against *Sex Talk*
* Lack of membership cards
* 'The fact that my daughter now calls you The Crutch People'

He enclosed £1.75 for 100 NVLA 'programme complaint cards' (to keep by the television). John C Beyer replied, a full week later, declaring 'I simply cannot guarantee that we will never again publish anything in *The Viewer & Listener* that will be tawdry.' He proposed that '...you have no alternative but to explain to your daughter, and your son, that there is a right way to live and a wrong way.' He enclosed 97 complaints cards. Ferocious Fothermere immediately telephoned to complain, and promptly received an extra six cards post-haste.

BARGEPOLE

Hello? Hello? Yes, Ted, I can pokka-pokka-pokka wheeeee CRUMP! Hear you just fine, can you Booooooom! Thud! hear me? Uh, yes, well the situation here is very confused here in, er, here in, well in kerrrrPOW my flat, actually.

Blam! Thwock!

Yes, Yes, I think I can say that I'm here in, uh, my flat. Obviously I can't give you more precise information than that without jeopardising the operation, except that I can tell you that all of us here will be doing our best to keep you informed in this, frankly, critical period. Bang.

It's not going to be easy, obviously, and...hello? Hello, Ted? Ah, there you are. Seemed to me we were maybe cut off there for a second, which is something, of course, we have been expecting. I can't tell how much longer communications will hold out, although we do have an emergency backup system...if communications go down completely I may have to go out onto the streets here with a cheque and, uh, pay the, uh, bill at what they're already referring to here as the 'Post Office'. It has become clear that it's pretty dangerous out there on the streets at this moment. Blammmmmmm! I don't know whether you caught that, Ted? Blammmmmmm! See?

Uh, yes. I'm actually underneath my desk at the moment, Ted, but if I crawl across to the window – bear with me for a moment – uh, yes, the streets are fairly deserted at the present time although we have had definite warnings of a second wave coming in. However, the precise direction of that attack is uncertain, although I will be keeping you up-to-date. All I can say right now is that I am following procedure and wearing my protective NSM kit at all times, although it's...sorry, Ted? Oh, right, yeah, NSM that stands for 'Nose, specs and moustache', it's a kind of rubber protective, uh, apparatus, you wear it on your head. The idea is that it confuses and hopefully, er, jams enemy identification systems, though thankfully we haven't yet had to put it to the test.

As I said, we aren't yet sure of the direction of an attack, although it has been confirmed that we are a target. What we do know is that there are considerable forces downrange, and I can confirm that American Express, the Inland Revenue and a number of other forces, including, of course, the crack Customs and Excise suicide squads, are now on a high state of alert and we are expecting incoming OHMS missives any minute. And...

kkkkrkrkkkkrkkksksskkrkkk...

Uh, sorry about that, Ted, bit of static there for a moment, but I did hear what any, er, combat veteran will recognise as the sound of incoming mail, it's a sound hard to describe...the nearest I can get is, well, you hear this terrible sort of whistling sound – that's the delivery system, – and then there's a clang as the material penetrates the building's defences, followed by a flup, and if you're wise, you eat rug the moment you hear that clang because by the time you get to the flup it's too late; as we old sweats say, 'the post's hit the mat,' which just says it all.

And I'm getting up now, Ted, and I can tell you that the room is spinning round and round and...hey! this is amazing! the whole sky is a mass of colours, red and blue and violet and indigo and colours you never even thought of, all spiralling around each other in an endless whirl of crystal fire...oh, this is incredible, Ted these gargantuan wings beating, beating, tilling the entire sky. I can also confirm that the carpet has gone all kind of spongy, like some primeval swamp...yes, the carpet is definitely spongy and swampy and saturated with blood, except it's green blood, Ted, probably the green blood of the creature whose gargantuan wings you may recall I mentioned a moment ago. And at the same time my feet have turned into claws. Yes, looking down, my feet have turned into huge bronze claws which is a good thing because otherwise how could I get a grip on this spongy carpet sodden in green blood, Ted? Of course, this could be something to do with prophylactic drugs, Ted. Uh, no, I can't say for sure what the drugs actually are, but we've all been taking them for some time now, myself and Sneezy and Dopey and Bashful and...uh, yeah, Ted, they were provided to us by a man in sunglasses and a BMW who met us on the main drag here, known locally as Balham Hill. Yeah, I guess he was some kind of official, yeah.

Yeah, Ted, the mood of the people here is pretty good right now, there's a guy in uniform – some kind of suit – staring up at the window as I look out, but the rest of us are fine, Sneezy and Sleepy and, er, Dave Dee, Dozy, Beaky, Mick and Titch, is it? And the naked woman handcuffed to the wardrobe, well, I say 'naked' but she's wearing black stockings and a latex bustier, that's the hell of war, huh, Ted? If the worst comes to the worst I guess we might be able to trade her for our freedom, Ted, and I want to reassure all the viewers there that if things get rough I will make sure the dwarves get out safely. We will keep filing until the last reporter is safely back home in the pub sporting his camouflage jacket and spinning bullshit about danger and nerve-gas and getting laid by lousy women.

Sorry, Ted, uh...Ted? Ted? Oh, hi, boss. What? Losing what grip? Well, hell, whaddya mean...? Insane with jealousy because nobody sent me to the Gulf? Hey, come on; you think I'm insecure? You think I've got something to prove? Well, why don't you just...

kkkkskskskkkkkkkkrsssssssssssssssssssss...

contributors

Punch 1991 was brought to you by...

EDITOR	DAVID THOMAS
Deputy Editor	Roland White
Features Editor	Sean Macaulay
Chief sub-editor	Caroline Proud
Sub Editors	Roger Perkins
	Paula Rodney
	Nigel Farndale
Art Editor	Fiona Hayes
Cartoon Editor	Steve Way
Designers	David Peregrine Haydn-Taylor
	Matthew Le Maistre Smith
	Lisa Goldsworthy
	Gary Phillips
Political Correspondent	Julia Langdon
Financial Correspondent	Simon Rose
Sports Correspondents	Patrick Collins
	Marcus Berkmann
	Brian Glanville
Columnists	Dillie Keane
	Simon Fanshawe
	Peter Tinniswood
	Bargepole
Critics	Dilys Powell *(Film)*
	Rhoda Koenig *(Theatre)*
	Richard Cook *(Music)*
	Sean Macaulay *(TV)*
	Big Ears *(Radio)*
	Hugh Fearnley-Whittingstall *(Food)*
	Jim Ainsworth *(Wine)*
ADVERTISING MANAGER	BARBARA PATTERSON
Deputy Advertising Manager	Mark Toben
Sales Executives	Max Greenall
	Sara Jubb
	Michelle Bladon
Telesales Executive	Craig Wilkie
Production Manager	Emma Shortt
Punch Secretary	Alex Cross
Library Manager	Amanda-Jane Doran
Library Assistant	Miranda Taylor